The Real Gaze

SUNY series in Psychoanalysis and Culture
Henry Sussman, editor

The Real Gaze

Film Theory after Lacan

Todd McGowan

State University of New York Press

Published by
State University of New York Press, Albany

© 2007 State University of New York

For information, address State University of New York Press,
194 Washington Avenue, Suite 305, Albany, NY 12210-2384

Production by Marilyn P. Semerad
Marketing by Michael Campochiaro

Library of Congress Cataloging-in Publication Data

McGowan, Todd.
 The real gaze : film theory after Lacan / Todd McGowan.
   p. cm. — (SUNY series in psychoanalysis and culture)
 Includes bibliographical references and index.
 ISBN-13: 978-0-7914-7039-8 (hardcover : alk. paper)
 ISBN-13: 978-0-7914-7040-4 (pbk. : alk. paper)
 1. Film criticism.   2. Motion pictures—Philosophy.   I. Title.   II. Series.

PN1995.M3795 2007
791.4301—dc22
                            2006013426

                  10 9 8 7 6 5 4 3 2 1

For Hilary Neroni,
who embodies nothing for me

Contents

Preface

FILM THEORY TODAY is almost nonexistent. The universalizing claims about the cinematic experience made by figures such as Sergei Eisenstein, André Bazin, Christian Metz, and Laura Mulvey have disappeared. Contemporary film scholars are increasingly content to make local, particular claims about film. This focus on particularity—that is, the analysis of isolated phenomena—completely dominates the field of film studies. Amid this contemporary landscape, proffering a universal and totalizing theory of the filmic experience seems outdated and naïve.

The turn away from film theory coincides with a turn away from film itself. Those working in film studies tend to understand film by contextualizing both the filmic text and the experience of spectatorship. Janet Staiger gives expression to this prevailing view when she claims, "I believe that contextual factors, more than textual ones, account for the experiences that spectators have watching films and television and for the uses to which those experiences are put in navigating our everyday lives. These contextual factors are social formations and constructed identities of the self in relation to historical conditions."[1] By focusing so intently on the context of film production and reception, we lose the possibility of being able to see the way in which an aesthetic object like a film might not fit within the context where it appears. Though every film emerges from within a context, not every film completely obeys the restrictions that the context places on it. Films can, in short, challenge their context through their individual mode of aestheticizing it. Or, to put it in Eric Santner's words, miracles do happen.[2] And even those films that end up recapitulating their context cannot be immediately reduced to it. A layer of mediation exists even in these cases: a completely conformist film must first alienate itself from its context in order to find the form to uphold it.

In what follows, I elaborate a psychoanalytic theory of film that takes film itself as the point of departure. I avoid discussing either the historical context of the films' production or their reception, and when I talk about spectatorship, I am talking about the spectator that the filmic text itself demands, not an empirical spectator. Of course, no film ignores its historical context or those who will watch it, but the context and the spectator do not exist in an external relationship to the filmic text. Each film carries its context with it through its aesthetic development, and each film structures its spectator through its specific mode of address. The wager of this book is that though one cannot ignore the context of a film's production and reception, one must find them inhering within the film itself, not outside of it.

If we locate the production and reception of a film within the film, then film theory once again becomes a possibility. It was the impulse toward contextualization that eliminated the space wherein one might theorize about film. The proper response is not a reactionary assertion of the text against the context, but a grasp of the interweaving of the two, the immanence of the context within the text. Every filmic text bears internally the manifestations of its historical situation, just as it anticipates the conditions of its reception. We find history and the spectator through filmic interpretation, not through archival research and audience surveys.

Acknowledgments

THE ESSAY THAT was the basis for this book, entitled "Looking for the Gaze: Lacanian Film Theory and Its Vicissitudes," appeared in *Cinema Journal* 42, no. 3 (Spring 2003): 27–47. Copyright © 2003 by the University of Texas Press, all rights reserved. An early version of a section in chapter 13, entitled "Resisting the Lure of Ultimate Enjoyment: Claire Denis' *J'ai pas sommeil*," appeared in *Kinoeye* 3, no. 7 (June 9, 2003). Thanks to these journals for permission to publish this material.

Cover concept by Hilary Neroni. Design by Hilary Neroni and Mike Hosier.

I would like to thank my senior and graduate seminars at the University of Vermont for their willingness to explore psychoanalytic theory and for their many ideas that spurred my thinking.

This book would not have been possible without the conscientious work of Marilyn Semerad and James Peltz at SUNY Press. James has done as much as anyone for the propagation of psychoanalytic theory in America, where it often receives a tepid response. Everyone invested in psychoanalytic theory owes him a tremendous debt.

Anna Kornbluh, Jennifer Friedlander, Jeff Rice, Jonathan Mulrooney, Dave Jenemann, and Sarah Nilsen provided insights that have shaped my thinking about film theory.

Henry Krips provided the best reading of a manuscript that one could ask for. I hope that I have answered some of his incisive comments without simply giving into them at every point, as I was tempted to do.

Thanks to Jill Delaney-Shal for alerting me to several oversights and for reminding me that sometimes absence truly is absence.

Sheila Kunkle has been a valuable partner in the attempt to work through psychoanalytic concepts in relation to the cinema.

I would also like to thank Phil Foster for always demanding that I pare things down to the minimal level necessary.

Thanks to Jean Wyatt for suggestions that anticipated the direction I wanted to go when I couldn't see it.

Thanks to Quentin Martin for an exacting reading that brought the project back to the ground at the last minute and for continuing to be a theorist in the guise of a historian.

Finally, thanks to Walter Davis, Paul Eisenstein, and Hilary Neroni for providing insight into what I've missed and for making up my fourfold.

Introduction:
From the Imaginary Look
to the Real Gaze

The Emergence of Lacanian Film Theory

When film theorists in the 1970s first looked to Jacques Lacan's thought to further their understanding of cinema, their focus was narrow. Since Lacan himself never theorized about film, film theorists looked to an area of his thought that seemed most easily transferable to the cinematic experience. They relied almost exclusively on an essay entitled "The Mirror Stage as Formative of the *I* function, as Revealed in Psychoanalytic Experience." Commonly referred to as the "mirror-stage essay," this brief text from Lacan's early career—Lacan delivered the paper as a talk in 1949, two years prior to the beginning of the seminars where he developed the thought that we now identify with him—offered a way for film theorists to think through the ideological problems inherent in the act of film spectatorship.[1] In this essay Lacan argues that infants acquire their first sense of self-identity (the formation of an ego) through the experience looking in a mirror and relating to their bodies. For Lacan, this experience metaphorically captures a stage in the child's development when the child anticipates a mastery of the body that she/he lacks in reality. The child's fragmented body becomes, thanks to the way that the mirror image is read, a whole. The ideal of the body as a unity over which the child has mastery emerges as the illusion produced through the mirroring experience. Though the mirror simply returns an image of what the child actually does, the mirroring experience deceives insofar as it presents the body through a coherent image. The wholeness of the body is seen in a way that it is not experienced.

By transposing this understanding onto cinematic spectatorship, film theorists were able to link the illusory qualities of film to the process through which subjects enter into ideology and become subjected to the constraints of the social order. This process, which Louis Althusser calls the ideological interpellation of the subject, involves concrete individuals misrecognizing themselves as subjects by taking up a socially given identity and seeing themselves in this identity. For early Lacanian film theorists, Althusser was a crucial bridge between Lacan's theory of the mirror stage and the cinematic experience because Althusser emphasized the social dimension of the kind of misrecognitions that followed from that of the mirror stage.[2] In other words, Althusser politicized Lacan's theory and offered film theorists an avenue for developing a critical understanding of the cinematic experience that was informed by psychoanalytic thinking.

The initial theoretical impetus in this direction was largely the work of French theorists such as Christian Metz, Jean-Louis Baudry, and Jean-Louis Comolli, as well as British theorists associated with the journal *Screen* such as Laura Mulvey, Peter Wollen, Colin MacCabe, and Stephen Heath.[3] These were the first theorists to bring psychoanalytic concepts to bear on the study of cinema in a systematic form. Though their specific approaches varied, they shared a belief in the connection between the psychic effects of the cinema and the workings of ideology, and this is why Lacan's analysis of the mirror stage, politicized by Althusser, proved so valuable.[4]

In the mirror-stage essay, Lacan stresses the illusory nature of the mastery that the child experiences while looking in the mirror, a mastery over her/his own body that the child does not yet have in reality.[5] According to the early Lacanian film theorists, the spectator inhabits the position of the child looking in the mirror. Like this child, the spectator derives a sense of mastery based on the position that the spectator occupies relative to the events on the screen. As Christian Metz puts it in his landmark work *The Imaginary Signifier*, "The spectator is absent from the screen *as perceived*, but also (the two things inevitably go together) present there and even 'all-present' as *perceiver*. At every moment I am in the film by my look's caress."[6] Being absent as perceived and present as perceiver allows the spectator to escape the sense of real absence that characterizes life outside the cinema. For Metz, the cinematic experience allows spectators to overcome temporarily the sense of lack that we endure simply by existing as subjects in the world. This experience provides a wholly imaginary pleasure, repeating that of the mirror stage. Jean-Louis Baudry makes this connection explicit, pointing out that "the arrangement of the different elements—projector, darkened hall, screen—in addition to reproducing in a striking way the *mise-en-scène* of Plato's cave . . . reconstructs the situation necessary to the release of the 'mirror stage' discovered by Lacan."[7] By perpetuating this reconstruction, the cinema leads spectators into self-deception. At its most basic level, this theoretical position understands the cinema as a machine for the perpetuation of ideology.

According to early Lacanian film theorists such as Metz and Baudry, cinema, like the mirror stage, is imaginary in Lacan's specific sense of the term. As Lacan conceives it, the imaginary provides an illusion of completeness in both ourselves and in what we perceive. In order to accomplish this, it dupes us into not seeing what is missing in ourselves and our world. For instance, looking out my window, I see a rustic farmhouse on a snowy morning and imagine a tranquil domestic scene inside. When I look in this way and view the farmhouse just on the imaginary level, what I miss is not only the violent quarrel taking place around the breakfast table, but also the violent exclusion that the very structure of a private home effectuates. We design homes, even rustic farmhouses, to shelter ourselves as much from others as from the weather, but this socioeconomic dimension of the farmhouse remains out of sight when one sees it on the imaginary level. Lacan's use of the term "imaginary" thus plays on both meanings we associate with it: it is at once visual and illusory. The imaginary most often works to conceal the functioning of Lacan's other categories that constitute our experience, the symbolic and the real.

Whereas the imaginary is the order of what we see, the symbolic order is the structure supporting and regulating the visible world. As the realm of language, it structures our experience, providing not only the words we use to describe ourselves and our world, but also the very identities we take up as our own. The symbolic identities of American, university professor, parent, and so on provide a way for me to have a sense of who I am without simply creating it for myself. They come ready-made, and as I become a subject, I see myself realized in these identities. Though no symbolic identity fits me perfectly—I never feel, for example, like I completely embody what it means to be a professor—my imaginary sense of a self, an ego, covers over this gap. The imaginary hides both the power of the symbolic order in shaping my identity and its inability to do so completely. That is to say, the imaginary also hides the real, Lacan's third category of experience.

The Lacanian real is the indication of the incompleteness of the symbolic order. It is the point at which signification breaks down, a gap in the social structure. By stressing the importance of the real, Lacan doesn't proclaim an ability to escape language and identify what is really actual; instead, he affirms the limitations of language—language's inability to say it all or speak the whole truth. To affirm the real is to affirm that the work of ideology never comes off without a hitch. Every ideology includes a point within its structure that it can't account for or represent. This is the point, the real, at which ideology opens up to the outside. The real thus allows ideology to include new phenomena, and at the same time, it marks ideology's vulnerability. When we call ideology into question, we do so from this real point within it. But unfortunately the real never appears in the psychoanalytic film theory developed in the 1970s.

For someone like Baudry, the cinematic image acts as an imaginary deception, a lure blinding us to an underlying symbolic structure and to the material cinematic apparatus. While watching a film, we remain unaware of the act of production that created the images for us, and in this way the cinematic experience dupes us. When we buy into the illusion, we have a sense of control over what we see on the screen. This theoretical approach conceives of the gaze (what would become the pivotal concept in Lacanian film theory) as a function of the imaginary, the key to the imaginary deception that takes place in the cinema. Early Lacanian film theory identifies the gaze with the misguided look of the spectator, even though such a conception has no significant roots in Lacan's thought (beyond the mirror-stage essay). Beginning with this idea, the task of the film theorist becomes one of combating the illusory mastery of the gaze with the elucidation of the underlying symbolic network that this gaze elides. Metz clearly articulates this as the goal of psychoanalytic film theory (though he doesn't employ the term "gaze"): "Reduced to its most fundamental procedures, any psychoanalytic reflection on the cinema might be defined in Lacanian terms as an attempt to disengage the cinema-object from the imaginary and to win it for the symbolic, in the hope of extending the latter by a new province."[8] This idea seems to follow from the original premises of psychoanalysis—specifically, its attempt to symbolize traumatic images through the "talking cure."

As psychoanalytic film theory developed, it began to examine the particular dynamics of the imaginary gaze in an effort to make clear its symbolic underpinnings. In "Visual Pleasure and Narrative Cinema," undoubtedly the most widely anthologized essay in film theory, Laura Mulvey associates this gaze with male spectatorship and with the ideological operations of patriarchal society.[9] According to Mulvey, classical Hollywood cinema allows the male spectator to identify with the gaze of the camera and the male protagonist, and female characters function solely as objects to be looked at. Thus, the spectator is inevitably gendered male and linked to the experience of imaginary mastery. But the further that Lacanian film theory moved in the direction of specifying spectators in their particularity, the more that it paved the path leading to its own demise.

In the 1980s and 1990s, waves of criticism confronted Lacanian film theory, especially Mulvey's essay.[10] This criticism most often took as its point of departure the theory's failure to account for differences among spectators.[11] Finally, in 1996 a collection of essays appeared that pronounced the death of Lacanian-centered psychoanalytic film theory (which, because of its hegemony over the field of film studies, editors David Bordwell and Noël Carroll simply label "the Theory"). As Bordwell and Carroll put it at the time in their introduction to *Post-Theory*, "Film studies is at a historical juncture which might be described as the waning of Theory."[12] In their view, this "waning of Theory" occurred largely in response to the universalizing pretensions of the film theory associated with psychoanalysis and Jacques Lacan.

The primary problem with "the Theory" was its proclivity to apply psychoanalytic concepts to the cinema without regard for empirical evidence that didn't conform to the theory. Carroll claims that "the Theory has been effectively insulated from sustained logical and empirical analysis by a cloak of political correctness,"[13] and Stephen Prince argues that "film theorists . . . have constructed spectators who exist in theory; they have taken almost no look at real viewers. We are now in the unenviable position of having constructed theories of spectatorship from which spectators are missing."[14] For these opponents of Lacanian film theory, the theory's great error lies in its attempt to account for everything on the level of theory alone without empirical verification. In short, traditional Lacanian film theory goes too far in its claims, extrapolates too much from its theoretical presuppositions. This is undoubtedly what led to its demise: film theory as such lost its influence because of its conceptual arrogance.

Rather than opening up cinematic experience, the Lacanian presuppositions have, so the *Post-Theory* critique goes, played a determinative role, producing the very cinematic experience that psychoanalytic film theory then explicates. For instance, the Lacanian film theorist begins with the idea that the spectator identifies with the male hero who drives the filmic narrative, and then the theorist posits this type of identification in the analysis of a specific film. The theory never encounters the particularity of the film itself or envisions how this particularity might challenge the theoretical edifice itself. In this analysis, what makes Lacanian film criticism vulnerable to critique is the very breadth of its claims—its theoretical universality. It is my contention, however, that traditional Lacanian film theory became a target for these attacks not because of its overreliance on purely psychoanalytic concepts, but because of its deviation from these concepts, and that, therefore, the proper response to the demise of Lacanian film theory is not a defense of its previous claims but rather a return to Lacanian concepts themselves in the analysis of the cinema—and with this a renewal of the endeavor to theorize the filmic experience.[15] We should greet the news of the death of Lacanian film theory as the opportunity for its genuine birth.

The Gaze as Object

Developing psychoanalytic film theory today demands a reassessment of the idea of the gaze. By locating the gaze in the spectator and analyzing cinema in terms of this gaze, early Lacanian film theory invited questions about the particularity of the spectator that perhaps would not have arisen had the theory conceived of the gaze as Lacan himself did. Lacan's conception of the gaze has been almost completely absent from the world of film theory and film studies. In the mirror-stage essay, Lacan never uses the term (*le régard*) that he would later use for the gaze. In the years after the essay on the mirror stage, Lacan comes to conceive of the gaze as something that the subject (or spectator) encounters in the object (or the film itself); it becomes an objective, rather than a subjective, gaze. Lacan's use of the term reverses our usual way of thinking about the gaze because we typically associate it with an active process.[16] But as an object, the gaze acts to trigger our desire visually, and as such it is what Lacan calls an *objet petit a* or object-cause of desire. As he puts it in *Seminar XI*, "*The objet a in the field of the visible is the gaze.*"[17] This special term *objet petit a* indicates that this object is not a positive entity but a lacuna in the visual field. It is not the look of the subject at the object, but the gap within the subject's seemingly omnipotent look. This gap within our look marks the point at which our desire manifests itself in what we see. What is irreducible to our visual field is the way that our desire distorts that field, and this distortion makes itself felt through the gaze as object. The gaze thus involves the spectator in the filmic image, disrupting the spectator's ability to remain what Metz calls "all-perceiving" and "absent as perceived."

Though the gaze is an object, it is not just an ordinary object. There is, according to Lacan, a form of the objet petit a that corresponds to each of our drives. The gaze is the objet petit a of the scopic drive (the drive that motivates us to look), functioning in a way parallel to the breast in the oral drive, the feces in the anal drive, and the voice in what Lacan calls the "invocatory" drive.[18] The objet petit a is in each case a lost object, an object that the subject separates itself from in order to constitute itself as a desiring subject. It is the loss of the object that inaugurates the process of desiring, and the subject desires on the basis of this loss. The subject is incomplete or lacking because it doesn't have this object, though the object only exists insofar as it is missing. As such, it acts as a trigger for the subject's desire, as the object-cause of this desire, not as the desired object. Though the subject may obtain some object of desire, the objet petit a lacks any substantial status and thus remains unobtainable.

Lacan invents the term "objet petit a" (and insists that it not be translated) in order to suggest this object's irreducibility to the field of the big Other (*l'Autre*) or signification. In contrast to the social domain of the big Other that houses our symbolic identities, it is a specific type of small other (*petit autre*) that is lost in the process of signification and ideological interpellation. The objet petit a doesn't fit within the world of language or the field of representation. It is what the subject of language gives up in order to enter into language, though it does not exist prior to being lost.

As the objet petit a in the visual field, the gaze is the point around which this field organizes itself. If a particular visual field attracts a subject's desire, the gaze must be present there as a point of an absence of sense. The gaze compels our look because it appears to offer access to the unseen, to the reverse side of the visible. It promises the subject the secret of the Other, but this secret exists only insofar as it remains hidden. The subject cannot uncover the secret of the gaze, and yet it marks the point at which the visual field takes the subject's desire into account. The only satisfaction available to the subject consists in following the path (which psychoanalysis calls the drive) through which it encircles this privileged object.

Early Lacanian film theory missed the gaze because it conceived of the cinematic experience predominantly in terms of the imaginary and the symbolic order, not in terms of the real.[19] This omission was crucial because the real provides the key for understanding the radical role that the gaze plays within filmic experience.[20] As a manifestation of the real rather than of the imaginary, the gaze marks a disturbance in the functioning of ideology rather than its expression.

In *Seminar XI*, Lacan's example of the gaze is Hans Holbein's *The Ambassadors* (1533). This painting depicts two world travelers and the riches they have accumulated from their travels. But at the bottom of the painting, a distorted, seemingly unrecognizable figure disrupts the portrait. The figure is anamorphic: looking directly at it, one sees nothing discernible, but looking at the figure downward and from the left, one sees a skull. Not only does the skull indicate the hidden, spectral presence of death haunting the two wealthy ambassadors—a *memento mori*—but, even more importantly for Lacan, it also marks the site of the gaze.

The skull is a blank spot in the image, the point at which spectators lose their distance from the picture and becomes involved in what they see, because its very form changes on the basis of the spectator's position. One cannot simply look straight at the picture and see this object: one must move one's body and turn one's head. The gaze exists in the way that the spectator's perspective distorts the field of the visible, thereby indicating the spectator's involvement in a scene from which the spectator seems excluded. It makes clear the effect of subjective activity on what the subject sees in the picture, revealing that the picture is not simply there to be seen and that seeing is not a neutral activity. The skull says to the spectator, "You think that you are looking at the painting from a safe distance, but the painting sees you—takes into account your presence as a spectator." Hence, the existence of the gaze as a disruption (or a stain) in the picture—an objective gaze—means that spectators never look on from a safe distance; they are in the picture in the form of this stain, implicated in the text itself.

The Ambassadors is a privileged example for Lacan because the form that the gaze takes in this painting—a skull—renders explicit the relationship between the gaze and the subject's complete loss of mastery.[21] The skull indicates the presence of death amid the wealth of the men pictured, but it also reminds viewers of their own death. Death is, as Hegel claims, the absolute master: it deprives the subject of any sense of mastery, and this constitutes much of the horror with which we respond to it. Even when a manifestation of the gaze does not make death evident directly like this, it nonetheless carries the association insofar as the gaze itself marks the point in the image at which the subject is completely subjected to it. The gaze is the point at which the subject loses its subjective privilege and becomes wholly embodied in the object.

By following Lacan and conceiving of the gaze as an objet petit a in the visual field, we can better avoid the trap of differences in spectatorship that snared traditional Lacanian film theory. Understood in Lacan's own terms, the gaze is not the spectator's external view of the filmic image, but the mode *of the text*

in which the spectator is accounted for within the film itself. Through their manipulation of the gaze, films produce the space in which spectators can insert themselves. Of course, not every spectator does so. There is, as the contributors to *Post-Theory* rightly point out, an unlimited number of different possible positions of empirical spectatorship. These empirical spectators have the ability to avoid the place that a film carves out for them, and we might even imagine a film that no actual person watches from the proper position. But this failure does not change the structure of the film itself, nor does it change how the film constitutes spectatorship through its deployment of the gaze. The gaze is a blank point—a point that disrupts the flow and the sense of the experience—within the aesthetic structure of the film, and it is the point at which the spectator is obliquely included in the film. This conception of the gaze entails a different conception of desire than the one that has predominated in early Lacanian film theory. As the indication of the spectator's dissolution, the gaze cannot offer the spectator anything resembling mastery.

Desiring Elsewhere

Though Lacan does claim that imaginary identification produces the illusion of mastery in his essay on the mirror stage, even at this early point in his thought he does not see desire as such as a desire for mastery. Early Lacanian film theory's conception of desire actually has more in common with Nietzsche and Foucault than it does with Lacan, which is one reason why Joan Copjec claims that "film theory operated a kind of 'Foucauldinization' of Lacanian theory."[22] For both Nietzsche and Foucault, power wholly informs our desire. Nietzsche insists again and again that our fundamental desire isn't the desire to survive but to attain mastery—what he calls the "will to power."[23] Rather than being something enigmatic or uncertain, the goal of our desire is clear: we want mastery over the other or the object; we want to possess the alien object and make it a part of ourselves. And as Foucault points out in *Discipline and Punish*, the gaze, as it is traditionally understood, serves as the perfect vehicle for this mastery—especially a gaze, as in the cinema, in which the subject remains obscured in the dark while the object appears completely exposed on the screen.[24]

This conception of desire as the desire for mastery sees desire as an active rather than a passive process: the desiring subject actively takes possession of the passive object. In this sense, desire is ipso facto male desire—and thus demands the conclusions drawn by Laura Mulvey. As Mulvey points out, "In a world ordered by sexual imbalance, pleasure in looking has been split between active/male and passive/female. The determining male gaze projects its phantasy onto the female figure, which is styled accordingly. In their traditional exhibitionist role women are simultaneously looked at and displayed, with their appearance coded for strong visual and erotic impact so that they can be said to connote *to-be-looked-at-ness*."[25] The cinema, according to this conception of desire, establishes sexual difference through the way that it caters to male desire: male subjects go to the cinema—they desire to see films—because the cinema provides for them an active experience, a way of mastering passive objects. To take perhaps the most obvious example, spectators desire to see a film like Charles Vidor's *Gilda* (1946) because it allows them, through the gaze, to achieve mastery over the female object on the screen (Rita Hayworth). From the safe distance of their seats in the darkened theater, spectators see Rita Hayworth's performance of "Put the Blame of Mame" and take possession of her image in their fantasies. The desire to attain control of this image of the female object informs spectatorship not just in *Gilda* but in the majority of classical Hollywood narratives, according to Mulvey. The filmic experience is an experience of power over the object, and when we desire in the cinema, we desire to dominate.

One of the best-known attacks on early Lacanian film theory responds directly to this conflation of desire and power. In "Masochism and the Perverse Pleasures of the Cinema," Gaylyn Studlar points out that the desire for mastery is not the most primordial or fundamental human desire. A masochistic, preoedipal desire precedes the oedipal desire for mastery. For Studlar, to conflate desire and mastery, to see desire as only an active process, is to miss a much more radical kind of desire—the desire to submit to the Other. Because the filmic experience involves submitting oneself to images of the Other, Studlar insists that a masochistic, passive conception of desire comes closer to approximating our experience of the cinema than does a mastering, active conception.

This leads Studlar to turn away from psychoanalysis and toward the thought of Gilles Deleuze as a way of understanding the filmic experience.[26] While Studlar claims that she finds Lacanian psychoanalytic theory ill equipped to explain the desire that operates in cinematic experience, what she is actually objecting to is not Lacanian theory itself but the deformation it undergoes as it becomes traditional Lacanian film theory. Studlar rejects the idea that the spectator's desire is a desire for mastery, which is exactly what Lacan rejects as well.

Studlar's conception of desire as fundamentally masochistic bears a resemblance to Lacan's own formulations. In *Seminar V*, Lacan even goes so far as to claim that "what we find at the foundation of the analytic exploration of desire is masochism."[27] Desire has this masochistic quality because its goal is not finding its object but perpetuating itself. As a result, subjects have the ability to derive enjoyment from the process of desire itself. Though an object triggers desire, the subject actually enjoys not attaining its object rather than attaining it. Desire perpetuates itself not through success (attaining or incorporating the object) but through failure (submitting itself to the object). Here, masochism is not, as Studlar would have it, a feature of preoedipal desire but of desire as such.

Object petit a
what is in the Other
more than the other

Desire involves the desiring subject allowing the object to control it, and through this submission to the object, the subject sustains itself as desiring.

Desire is motivated by the mysterious object that it posits in the Other—what Lacan calls the objet petit a—but it relates to this object in a way that sustains the object's mystery. Hence, the objet petit a is an impossible object: to exist, it would have to be simultaneously known and unknown. The subject posits the objet petit a as the point of the Other's secret enjoyment, but it cannot be reduced to anything definitively identifiable in the Other. It is, to paraphrase Lacan, in the Other more than the Other. The enjoyment embodied in this object remains out of reach for the subject because the object exists only insofar as it is out of reach. Lacan describes this process at work in the scopic drive: "What is the subject trying to see? What he is trying to see, make no mistake, is the object as absence. . . . What he is looking for is not, as one says, the phallus—but precisely its absence."[28] Rather than seeking power or mastery (the phallus), our desire is drawn to the opposite—the point at which power is entirely lacking, the point of traumatic enjoyment. This enjoyment is traumatic insofar as it deprives us of power but nonetheless compels us.[29] This appeal that enjoyment has for us explains why power fails to provide satisfaction and why a psychoanalytic conception of desire must be absolutely distinguished from the Nietzschean or Foucaultian conception.

No matter how much power one acquires, one always feels oneself missing something—and this something is the objet petit a. Even those who are bent on world conquest nonetheless feel the allure of the hidden enjoyment of the Other, and they locate this enjoyment at the point where power seems most absent. This explains the master's secret envy of the slave. Through the act of mastery, the master hopes to appropriate the slave's enjoyment, but this appropriation always comes up short. In an experience of absolute mastery, the master imagines that the slave has access to an enjoyment that power cannot provide. Or the upper-class subject imagines unrestrained enjoyment hidden in the activities of the lower-class subject. It is the Other's seeming enjoyment that acts as an engine for desire, not mastery. The image of an active desire mastering and possessing a passive object obfuscates a much more disturbing alternative: the object drawing the subject toward a traumatic enjoyment—the enjoyment of total submission to an unattainable object.

When the subject enjoys the gaze, it enjoys its submission to this object. Enjoyment or *jouissance*, in Lacan's sense of the term, is thus far removed from mere pleasure.[30] It marks a disturbance in the ordinary symbolic functioning of the subject, and the subject inevitably suffers its enjoyment. One cannot simply integrate one's enjoyment into the other aspects of one's daily life because it always results from the injection of a foreign element—the real—into this life. As Alenka Zupančič notes, "It is not simply the mode of enjoyment of the neighbour, of the other, that is strange to me. The heart of the problem is that I experience my own enjoyment (which emerges along with the enjoyment of the other, and is even indissociable from it) as strange and hostile."[31] The subject cannot simply have its enjoyment; it is more correct to say that this enjoyment has the subject.

The enjoyment associated with the gaze acts as a cause for the subject's desire, but enjoyment is not reducible to desire. Desire thrives on the experience of absence, on what it lacks, whereas enjoyment lacks nothing. The desiring subject pursues what the enjoying subject already experiences.[32] The gaze triggers the subject's desire because it appears to hold the key not to the subject's achievement of self-completion or wholeness but to the disappearance of self in the experience of enjoyment.

This is not to say that subjects never act out of—nor go to the cinema because of—a desire for mastery. However, this desire for mastery is not fundamental for the subject; it represents an attempt to short-circuit the path of desire in order to derive satisfaction from the objet petit a without experiencing the trauma that accompanies that satisfaction. Mastery aims at regulating enjoyment rather than being overcome by it, but it nonetheless posits the experience of the objet petit a as its ultimate end. That is to say, when the subject appears to seek mastery, it is actually trying to find another, less traumatic way of relating to its object. Freud notices this dynamic in his exploration of male fantasizing about mastery. Though some male subjects fantasize about mastery, their desire remains thoroughly erotic. Freud points out that "investigation of a man's day-dream generally shows that all his heroic exploits are carried out and all his successes achieved only in order to please a woman and to be preferred by her to other men."[33] In short, the man who dreams of conquering the world wants to do so in order to access his erotic object. Here, the desire for mastery is nothing but the disguised articulation of another desire—the desire occasioned by the impossible object. The desire for mastery is itself never primary but always the displacement of another desire. If we think of desire in terms of mastery, we submit ourselves to the subject's own self-deception.

In Lacan's conception of desire, the gaze is not the vehicle through which the subject masters the object but a point in the Other that resists the mastery of vision. It is a blank spot in the subject's look, a blank spot that threatens the subject's sense of mastery in looking because the subject cannot see it directly or successfully integrate it into the rest of its visual field. This is because, as Lacan points out, the gaze is "what is lacking, is non-specular, is not graspable in the image."[34] Even when the subject sees a complete image, something remains obscure: the subject cannot see how its own desire distorts what it sees. The gaze of the object includes the subject in what the subject sees, but this gaze is not present in the field of the visible.

Despite the resistance of the gaze (and the real as such) to specularization, the cinema offers an arena in which the subject can relate to the gaze in ways that are impossible outside the cinema. Early Lacanian film theory was, in a sense, correct: the attraction of the gaze draws us into the cinema. But as we have seen, this is not the attraction of mastery but rather that of enjoyment.

Film holds out the promise of enjoyment through the way that it deploys the gaze as objet petit a. This object, which cannot be integrated into the visual field (or, consequently, into the filmic image), is the cinematic object par excellence, the object filmic spectators are hoping to glimpse—or take up some kind of relation to—on every trip to the cinema. Thus, though the gaze itself is the antithesis of power, the enjoyment that the gaze as objet petit a promises does have a certain power—the power to excite spectators and bring them into the cinema. It is in the direction of this power that a psychoanalytic analysis of film must turn in order to understand the nature of film's relationship to the gaze that it deploys.

Privileging the Unconscious

No medium places the subject in a position as close to its position in the dream as does cinema.[35] Like the dream, film lures the subject into accepting the illusion that it offers. In the dream state, our faculties of critical thought disengage, and we accept the experience as it presents itself. Because we experience rather than think critically in the dream, we lack the sense of mastery in the dream that we have during our waking experiences. In *Seminar XI*, Lacan claims, "In the final resort, our position in the dream is profoundly that of someone who does not see. The subject does not see where it is leading, he follows."[36] Our inability to see is crucial because when we see things going in the direction of trauma, we necessarily turn away. Consequently, we cannot consciously will ourselves toward an encounter with the real, which is why the filmic spectator's absence of mastery is significant.

As in the dream, while watching a film the subject follows rather than leads—and thus doesn't have the opportunity to turn away from the traumatic encounter. In dreams, the subject does not direct the narrative movement but follows where the narrative leads. This lack of conscious agency does not imply that the subject has no role in directing the dream narrative. But the agent of the dream is not consciousness; it is the subject of the unconscious. Films also relate to the unconscious, but in a way that we can recall and can access more readily than the dream.

Notwithstanding this unleashing of the unconscious, dreams would seem to offer, at least for some dreamers, more of an opportunity for conscious agency at the point when the dreamer becomes aware that she or he is dreaming. This awareness appears to allow consciousness to wrest control of the dream from the unconscious: aware that I am dreaming, I can decide actively on the course my dream should take. But Freud quickly deflects this possibility, pointing out that such moments of awareness are ultimately deceptive. He says, "When the thought 'this is only a dream' occurs during a dream, . . . it is aimed at reducing the importance of what has just been experienced and at making it possible to tolerate what is to follow. It serves to lull a particular agency to sleep which would have every reason at that moment to bestir itself and forbid the continuance of the dream."[37] Even at the points in the dream when we become aware that we are dreaming, conscious control continues to elude us. Conscious control is itself nothing but an illusion that the subject of the unconscious uses to bypass the psyche's internal censorship. No experience marginalizes consciousness like the experience of the dream—or film spectatorship.

While this doesn't present a problem in dreams because, in a sense, we are both the director of the dream and the spectator, in the cinematic situation things become more politically charged. The spectator's lack of conscious control renders the spectator extremely vulnerable to ideological manipulation while at the cinema. The pseudo-dreamworld of the cinematic spectator represents the key political problem of the cinema; rather than serving as a tool for making spectators aware of the functioning of ideology, the very form of film itself seems to operate in the opposite political direction—as a crucial ingredient in the propagation of an uncritical subjectivity. Cinema appears to produce uncritical subjects who fail to realize that they are uncritical. The pseudo-dreamworld allows ideology to enact an unconscious process of interpellation.

For years, psychoanalytic film theory documented this ideological effect of mainstream cinema. The fascination of spectators was *the* political problem. This becomes apparent most profoundly in the case of Laura Mulvey. According to Mulvey's conception of cinematic politics, the fundamental political problem of the cinema is the extent to which the spectator submits to the fantasmatic dimension of the cinema. Nearly every early Lacanian film theorist shares this position, this belief that a politically progressive cinema is one that destroys rather than produces spectator fascination.

What this position misses is an understanding of the relationship between consciousness and ideology. One does not resist ideology through the act of becoming conscious; instead, consciousness is itself a mode of inserting oneself into ideology and avoiding one's unconscious desire. Ideology operates not only in unconscious ways, but also through the illusions of consciousness itself—namely, the assumption of mastery implicit in consciousness. It is our association of consciousness with vision that allows us not to see the role of the gaze in structuring our vision. Instead, consciousness provides the subject with an image that obscures the distortion of the gaze, that allows no room for what is missing in the field of vision. The very structure of consciousness cannot admit absence because the operations of consciousness are inevitably totalizing. This is where film stands out from our quotidian experience: we can potentially experience the gaze when we submit to the process of fascination and cease to hold ourselves at a distance from what we see, which is what often occurs in the cinema. We can meet the gaze when we follow the logic of the cinematic or dream image and in doing so deprive consciousness of its priority. Rather than advocating suspicion about the cinematic experience (and thereby taking the side of consciousness), psychoanalytic film theory should pave the way to a more intense submission to the dictates of this experience in order to facilitate an encounter with the gaze.

The cinematic experience can lead us to the encounter with the gaze if it takes up the psychoanalytic session as something of a model for film viewing.[38] The analytic process of free association works only when we as subjects avoid reflection—to the extent that this is possible—and invest ourselves in the dynamic of the session itself, associating without regard for the apparatus (the form of the analytic session) that produces the associations. During the process of associating, the analyst interrupts the subject with an interpretation which, if correct (and correctly timed), hits the subject with the weight of the real. It is only after this encounter with the real that subjects can begin to interpret their relationship to this real.

To return to the ground of the cinema, we can see how the filmic gaze can function in the same way as the analyst's interpretation, provided that we as spectators fully invest ourselves in the filmic experience. While invested in the film, the subject (like the analysand free associating) is able to encounter the gaze as a disruption within spectatorship. We can—and must—interpret our relationship to this gaze after the fact, after the traumatic experience of it. But we must first have the experience, and this requires that we follow the logic of the film we are watching.

This is what differentiates the film theory I am advocating here from the practice of early Lacanian film theory. For the latter, we must gain critical distance from the scene of cinematic manipulation and view the cinematic experience with an attitude of suspicion from the beginning. For a truly psychoanalytic film theory, on the other hand, critical distance is but another way of avoiding the real of the gaze. No matter how the critic goes down the path of radical doubt, no matter how much one draws attention to the ideological manipulation occurring in the cinema, it never goes far enough as long the subject consciously controls the direction of thought. Consciousness itself is a barrier to the real. This is the problem with the cinematic politics of figures such as Jean-Louis Comolli (working in the tradition of Metz and Baudry). He argues, "What modern cinema needs is lighted theatres which, unlike the darkness, neither absorb nor annihilate the clarity which comes from the screen, but on the contrary diffuse it, which bring both the film character and the spectator out of the shadows and set them face to face on an equal footing."[39] A well-lit cinema appeals to Comolli because it offers the spectator respite from the darkened dream world and some degree of control over the cinematic experience. In this sense, Comolli attacks psychoanalysis proper along with the darkened cinema.

Comolli's revolt against the darkened cinema exposes the ultimate allegiance of early Lacanian film theory as a whole. For the thinkers in this tradition, psychoanalysis is a tool to be used for political ends rather than a theory that might generate political ends of its own. Psychoanalysis allows them to expose the illusions that inform the typical cinematic experience; they can then advocate an alternative that owes no debt to psychoanalytic thought. The alternative follows from the politics of Bertolt Brecht and privileges the idea of the alienation effect: it would be a cinema that draws attention to its own artifice and shocks the spectator with constant self-awareness, like Laura Mulvey and Peter Wollen's own film, *Riddles of the Sphinx* (1977). But this is a political alternative that leaves spectators secure within their conscious reflection. It alienates them into increased self-consciousness and critical distance, but not into an abandonment of conscious control.

Our ability to contest an ideological structure depends on our ability to recognize the real point at which it breaks down, not on our ability to distance ourselves from that structure through the process of conscious reflection. When cinema lulls the subject into its dreamy, fantasmatic netherworld, it may insert the subject into ideology, but it also may open up the possibility of an encounter with the traumatic real that disrupts the power of ideology. The answer to the political problem of cinematic fascination thus lies in the opposite direction of the one taken by early Lacanian film theory: the problem is not that spectators have submitted themselves completely to this fascination, but that they sustained some distance from this fascination. Rather than importing the attitude of everyday life (that of conscious reflection) into the cinema in order to disrupt its fascinating spell, we should export our attitude in the cinema (our openness to the gaze) to our everyday life. This is the project that psychoanalytic film theory calls us to take up.

A genuine psychoanalytic film theory advocates fully immersing oneself in cinematic fascination and focusing on the points of rupture where the gaze emerges. These are the points where film disturbs the spectator, but at the same time they are the points where the spectator enjoys. To be a psychoanalytically informed spectator is to allow oneself to enjoy and to pay attention to the moments of one's enjoyment. It also implies not simply confining this enjoyment to the cinema.

The Radicality of the Cinema

The most radical aspect of the cinematic experience lies in the ability of the gaze to show itself there. In our waking lives, we avoid the gaze; we avoid recognizing that the objet petit a shows itself to us. We experience the world as if it were there ready-made for us to approach. We think of ourselves as the agent directing our interaction with this ready-made world, and this understanding is the fundamental deception of waking life. As Lacan puts it, "In the so-called waking state there is an elision of the gaze, and an elision of the fact that not only does it look, *it* also *shows*. In the field of the dream, on the other hand, what characterizes the images is that *it shows*."[40] In dreams, we do not approach things, but things show themselves to us. This showing is what allows us to experience the gaze in the dream: when we encounter the gaze, we encounter an object that shows itself to us but which does not fit within our visual field. The form of the dream, like the form of the cinematic experience, makes this encounter possible. In both, the fact that things show themselves to us holds the key to the encounter with the gaze qua objet petit a. This is what the cinema offers us that we cannot find anywhere else outside our dreams.

When we consider the usual fate of the gaze, we can begin to recognize the unique value of the cinematic experience. Our look—the scopic drive—obscures the objet petit a more than any other of the drives because of the extent to which we seem in control of the visual field. Vision gives us an implicit sense of mastery over what we see insofar as we direct where and how we look. It is, for example, much easier to hear the objet petit a in the form of the voice than to see it in the form of the gaze because we are more often confronted with sounds that we would rather not hear than sights that we would rather not see. We can close our eyes but not our ears, with the result that the gaze is much more difficult to discern in the visual field than the voice in the aural field. This difficulty causes the gaze to play the most intense role in the structuring of our fantasies. We fantasize about the form of the objet petit a—the gaze—that we can access least.

In the cinema, as in the dream, this form of the objet petit a shows itself. This eroticizes the cinema, and at the same time, it constitutes the cinema as a site where the structure of ideology finds itself most imperiled. The relationship to the gaze is central to the political and existential dimension of film. Ideology constantly works to obscure the traumatic real of the gaze because this real threatens the stability of the social order that ideology protects. This stability depends on the illusion of wholeness and the power to account symbolically for everything. The real marks a point of failure, not just of the subject's look but also of ideology's explanatory power. That is to say, the real traumatizes not just the subject that encounters it but also the big Other as well. The hold that symbolic authority has over subjects depends on the avoidance of the traumatic real that exposes the imposture of all authority. When the subject experiences the traumatic real, it recognizes symbolic authority's failure to account for everything. This is the key to the political power of the gaze. Though the encounter with the gaze traumatizes the subject, it also provides the basis for the subject's freedom—freedom from the constraints of the big Other.[41]

The encounter reveals to the subject the nonexistence of the big Other, its inability to provide support for the subject's own symbolic identity. The big Other sustains its hold over the subject through the creation of a world of meaning: when one accepts the meaningfulness of this world, one subjects oneself to the big Other and its authority. This process of subjection allows the subject to exist in a world where things make sense. But retaining this world of sense depends on the continued capitulation of the subject to the big Other. The subject pays the price for meaning with its freedom. The encounter with the traumatic real, which is an encounter with a point of non-sense within the big Other (what the big Other cannot render meaningful), frees the subject from its subjection. In the moment of the traumatic encounter, the subject experiences the groundlessness—and ultimately the nonexistence—of the big Other and the symbolic world that the big Other sustains. The traumatic encounter reveals the nonsensical status of our master signifier. As Paul Eisenstein puts it, "It exposes the ridiculousness or stupidity of the principle that enables us to make sense of the world. It reveals the Law as something we institute, but whose ultimate ground cannot be found within the domain of reason."[42] Our dependence on the master signifier for meaning necessarily evaporates as we witness its failure to provide any.

As a result of the traumatic encounter with the real, freedom opens up for the subject. The point at which the symbolic order fails—and our relation to this point—becomes foundational for us as subjects. One finds the basis of one's being in the failure of ideology's master signifier rather than in its success. This transforms the ideological subject into a politicized and free subject. Our ability to contest an ideological structure depends on our ability to recognize the real point at which it breaks down, the point at which the void that ideology conceals manifests itself. Every authentic political act has its origins in an encounter with the real. This is not to say that the encounter with the traumatic real is magical. It simply opens up the possibility of freedom for the subject, which the subject must constantly work to sustain.

Film's ability to facilitate an encounter with the real represents a threat to the power of ideology. However, the history of the film, perhaps more than the history of any other art form, is also a record of capitulation to ideological demands. Classical Hollywood cinema and its contemporary descendants consistently provide a fantasmatic support for the ideology of capitalist society. As Theodor Adorno describes it in *Minima Moralia*, "The film has succeeded in transforming subjects so indistinguishably into social functions, that those wholly encompassed, no longer aware of any conflict, enjoy their own dehumanization as something human, as the joy of warmth."[43] At the same time that it promises an encounter with the traumatic real, film works to domesticate every trauma by producing docile subjects.

The coexistence of these countercurrents suggests that the ideological valence of film remains up for grabs—to be decided on a case-by-case basis. And we can look to a Lacanian film theory to provide a way of embarking on this kind of analysis. When we look at and analyze a particular film, the question concerns the relationship to the gaze—and, in general, to the trauma of the real—that the film takes up. Does a particular film obscure the gaze throughout? Does it sustain the gaze as an unapproachable absence? Does it domesticate the trauma of the gaze through a fantasmatic scenario? Does it take this fantasmatic scenario so far as to undermine it from within? And perhaps most importantly, does it allow us to encounter the gaze in its full traumatic import?

In answering these questions, the point is not to assemble a set of categories that will allow us to praise or condemn films but to establish a way of understanding the psychic and political power that particular films have.

Deployments of the Gaze

The four parts that follow will explore the various relations that film can take up to the gaze, looking at films that make the gaze present through fantasy, films that sustain the gaze as a fundamental absence, films that obfuscate the gaze through a turn to fantasy, and films that enact a traumatic encounter with the gaze. The way in which a film deploys the gaze is, I would argue, the fundamental political and existential act of the cinema. If it is true that no film can entirely eliminate the gaze, the politics of cinema comes down to film's struggle with the trauma and the enjoyment of the gaze as objet petit a. Thus, in the process of looking at the different ways that film can deploy the gaze, the political valence of different kinds of films will come into relief.[44]

By privileging cinema's relationship to the gaze and looking at different films (and filmmakers) in this light, a new way of thinking about the history of film emerges. Instead of grouping films by genre, nation, historical epoch, or some other category, we can group films in terms of how they approach the gaze. What results defies chronological history: all the possible deployments of the gaze have been present since the invention of the medium. We can thus see similarities between filmmakers from different times and different parts of the world because of a related approach to the gaze in their films. Thinking about films in this way also allows us to see what unites the films of a certain filmmaker or a particular film movement.

Given the centrality of the gaze in the filmic experience, one could find countless other examples besides the ones that I've chosen for each approach to the gaze. I've included filmmakers and film movements for two seemingly contradictory reasons—their extremity and their familiarity. I highlight films that deploy the gaze in definitive and unmistakable ways because such films offer insight into all other films in which the deployment of the gaze is less clear. I also focus on films that film students and scholars (and even film buffs outside the field) will be aware of. My aim is not to privilege the canonical but to show how the potential radicality of the cinema manifests itself even there. One could easily imagine extending this book to cover the many lacunae, but the restrictions of space demand that the examples be suggestive rather than exhaustive.

Each of four approaches to the gaze that I detail manifests itself in various ways. After explaining the different approaches theoretically, the four sections of the book trace these manifestations, moving from the more fundamental to the more nuanced. That is, each section begins with the filmmaker or film movement that exemplifies the particular deployment of the gaze most straightforwardly. Subsequent examples complicate and qualify this relationship to the gaze. But again, this is not a chronology or a progression. Oftentimes, the more nuanced developments of an approach to the gaze precede the more direct chronologically. The sections thus attempt to establish a logical development, not a historical one. This logic does not imply that the more straightforward approach to a deployment of the gaze (which I present first) is inferior to the more complicated. The logic of the development is dialectical: for every gain in nuance, there is a loss in directness and power.

Part 1 explores films that depict the gaze through its fantasmatic distortion in the overpresence of the cinematic image. In these films, the normally invisible fantasmatic dimension of our social reality becomes visible. Fantasy provides private support for public ideology, covering the ground the ideology cannot. Thus, it necessarily involves the dirty secrets, the hidden obscenity that cannot safely appear in public. A film such as *Dr. Strangelove, Or How I Learned to Stop Worrying and Love the Bomb* (1964) makes public the fantasmatic underside of military authority and thereby undermines its public authority. Even though this kind of film offers a fantasy that obscures the gaze, it immerses itself so completely in the fantasy that it destroys the fantasy's power from within. The spectator of such a film is not politicized through dissatisfaction but is instead politicized through being forced to grapple with the public display of the social order's underside. This represents an order of politicization that works to dissolve the spectator's libidinal ties to the public ideology. It is only through analyzing the gaze that one can understand how this politicization arises and functions.

Part 2 will look at films that sustain the gaze as an absence that haunts the cinematic image. Such films refuse to provide the spectator with any relief from the desire they engender through their emphasis on absence. Here, the desire of the Other, embodied in the absent gaze, remains just out of sight (and thus out of reach)—and irreducible to the filmic image itself. In this way, these films expose the traumatic real through its absence rather than through its presence, and they facilitate desiring spectators who leave the cinema with questions rather than fantasmatic answers. This represents a different order of cinema than the cinema of fantasy, but one no less politically and existentially engaged. The paradigmatic instance of this type of film is *Citizen Kane* (1941), which refuses to fantasize a resolution of the spectator's desire. This refusal politicizes spectators as it supports their sense of dissatisfaction and their desire, even if they remain unaware of this process.

It is difficult, however, for a film to sustain fidelity to the logic of desire. Films that do so most often meet with popular indifference or even hostility. As a result, the most common tack for a film lies in providing a fantasmatic resolution for the constitutive dissatisfaction of desire. Part 3 looks at the films that incite desire only to resolve it into a fantasy scenario that provides a screen through which the spectator can experience the gaze without its attendant trauma. This describes most films, as they blend desire and fantasy in order to produce first a sense of lack—the gaze as absence—and then a sense of the absence filled in. These films deploy the gaze only in order to domesticate it, and, in the same process, they aim to domesticate spectators as well. Here the example of *Schindler's List* (1991) reveals how film can fantasize a scenario that domesticates even the most horrifying trauma. The fantasmatic resolution of the traumatic gaze represents the chief ideological operation of Hollywood film—and it is the temptation that all film flirts with because of the exigencies of the medium itself.

Up to this point, the gaze remains an object either constitutively out of reach or brought into reach through a process of distortion. But there are films that allow for an experience of the gaze without the fantasmatic screen. Part 4 looks at the films that push the cinema in this direction. By strictly separating the world of desire (the absence of the gaze) and the world of fantasy (the illusory presence of the gaze), film has the ability to stage a traumatic encounter with the gaze and with the real as such. The strict separation allows the spectator to experience the real as the piece that does not fit, the element from one world that obtrudes into the other. This process reaches its apotheosis in the films of David Lynch. The example of *Lost Highway* (1997) reveals the traumatic power attained through separating the worlds of desire and fantasy. It lures the spectator into a traumatic encounter with the real of the gaze, an encounter that completely relocates spectators in relation to their symbolic identity. The political value of the traumatic encounter with the real lies in this reconfiguration: it allows spectators to look at themselves—and the prevailing symbolic structure—from the perspective of a void. In this sense, the traumatic encounter represents the possibility of freedom, as it releases the spectator from all symbolic constraints. It is at once horrifying and liberating.

The potentially radical dimension of the filmic experience—even in the case of Hollywood film—is what Lacanian film theory has historically elided. And it is what I hope to accentuate in the pages that follow. But because film can take up multiple positions toward the gaze, it is impossible to discover the political valence of a film a priori. Certainly, film can often work to disseminate ideology and even to provide a fantasmatic support for ideology, but it also has the power to do the opposite. To find out what a film is doing, one must always look and see.

PART 1

The Cinema of Fantasy
Exposing the Excess

1

Fantasy and Showing Too Much

THE SUBJECT CANNOT directly apprehend the gaze. It is a lost object that the subject never had, which means that there is nothing for the subject to recover. Because the loss of this object is at once the moment of its emergence, desire can never achieve satisfaction by obtaining this lost object. When one obtains any object that appears to promise the satisfaction of desire, one inevitably discovers that "that's not it." Or, to put it in other terms, the moment when the subject would see the gaze directly would be the moment when the gaze would cease to be the gaze. Consequently, the subject can take up a stable relationship to the world of objects but not to the gaze qua objet petit a. It doesn't exist within the represented world through which the subject finds its bearings. Fantasy, however, offers the subject a way out of this dilemma.

We often think of fantasy as a particular artistic genre that includes literary works such as J. R. R. Tolkein's *Lord of the Rings* or films such as Peter Jackson's adaptation of Tolkein's trilogy. What defines fantasy in this sense of the term is the depiction of a magical world in which the limitations of our physical universe no longer hold. The psychoanalytic conception of fantasy bears some resemblance to this generic definition, though it is significantly broader.[1] For psychoanalysis, fantasy is an imaginary scenario that fills in the gaps within ideology. In other words, it serves as a way for the individual subject to imagine a path out of the dissatisfaction produced by the demands of social existence. The act of fantasizing takes myriad forms: from a simple daydream to works of art to entire belief systems. By distorting social reality through an imaginative act, fantasy creates an opening to the impossible object and thereby allows the subject to glimpse an otherwise inaccessible enjoyment. Works of art translate private fantasies into public ones, which provide an imaginary response to shared forms of dissatisfaction and thus have an appeal beyond the individuals who generate them. If we understand fantasy like this, every film is a fantasy insofar as it distorts the social reality from which it emerges and translates a private imagining into a public spectacle. Even the realist film has a fantasmatic dimension: the very representation of reality mediates that reality and moves it into another form. This formal gesture is the key to fantasy's importance.

Through its form, fantasy allows the subject to relate to the lost object as an object that is simply out of reach. In fantasy, a spatial or temporal barrier, rather than an ontological one, intervenes between the subject and the lost object. Though the subject still may not obtain the object in the fantasy, the subject can imagine obtaining it as a possibility, even if not for the subject itself. Fantasy is above all the creation of possibility out of impossibility.

Fantasy works for the subject just as Giorgio Agamben sees the state of exception functioning for the juridical order. According to Agamben, the state of exception suspends the normal working of the juridical order and allows sovereign power to exercise itself directly on subjects without the mediation of law.[2] We can see this at work, for instance, in the status of the Guatanamo Bay detainees. They are neither criminals nor prisoners of war; they occupy an exceptional position where the rule of law does not apply. In order to place them in this position, sovereign power (specifically George W. Bush) had to declare a state of exception to the law. This state of exception carves out a position beyond the rule of law in the way that fantasy carves out a position beyond the constraints of ideology. Both the law and ideology rely on this exception to their functioning (the state of exception and fantasy) in order to function. In this beyond, one imagines the achievement of the impossible: direct justice in the case of the state of exception, or accessing the impossible object in the case of fantasy.

Like the state of exception in relation to the juridical order, fantasy is not secondary in relation to desire. Fantasy establishes the scenario and the coordinates through which the subject experiences itself as a desiring subject. Without fantasy, there would be no initial impetus for desire, and yet, paradoxically, fantasy compromises the subject's desire, providing a justification or a rationalization for the impossibility that it presents. In other words, despite its supplementary position in the psychic economy of the subject, fantasy has a phenomenological priority. This is evident nowhere as clearly as in the cinema. Even the film that tries most steadfastly to strip away the dimension of fantasy sustains it at a minimal level. In this sense, a cinema of fantasy is a mode of cinema that merely accentuates a direction that inheres in the medium as such.

The fantasmatic dimension of the cinema allows it to stage the impossible objet petit a in the form of the gaze. In the everyday experience of social reality, we do not see the way in which the gaze shapes (through distortion) the structure of that reality. Instead, we see a world constituted by a symbolic structure that renders it meaningful and seemingly complete. Despite this symbolic structure, the gaze nonetheless appears continually in our experience. The gaze is the basis of visibility as such, which is why we take it (and its distortion of the visual field) for granted. We see, instead, a reality in which everything seems to fit.[3]

But the gaze is an object that does not fit, an object that cannot be reduced to the level of other objects. It protrudes as an excessive piece of reality that we cannot find anywhere within the reality. The gaze is a disturbance in the normal functioning of reality because it indicates that our social reality is not simply there as a neutral field. Instead, reality exists as something seen, something that we ourselves constitute through the act of seeing; in consequence, our seeing itself is included within our reality as the gaze. In this sense, the gaze as objet petit a is nothing but the way in which subjectivity necessarily stains the objective structure of social reality. There is no visibility at all except through our subjectivity, which distorts the field of the visible in the act of constituting it. We don't see, for instance, how our parents act like parents in relation to us as children rather than because their identity is defined by being parents. Or we don't see how the president has authority because we invest the position with authority, not because of any personal qualities. This stain that eludes our everyday experience becomes visible through film's ability to stage fantasy publicly.

The chapters that follow in part 1 will examine the attempt to create a cinema that renders the gaze visible through fantasy, a cinema that foregrounds the cinematic distortion of the field of the visible. Of course, no film can completely eliminate spectator desire as it constructs a fantasy, but the films I examine here evince little concern for producing desire. They focus on disturbing spectators with moments of too much satisfaction rather than reminding spectators of their dissatisfaction. We can see this effort commence even among early filmmakers such as Sergei Eisenstein and Charlie Chaplin. However, the main focus will be on the distinct turns that various movements within the history of film give to the fantasmatic depiction of the gaze. This analysis begins with Stanley Kubrick, moves to Spike Lee, to Michael Mann, and finally ends with Federico Fellini. The aim of this trajectory is to see how the development of a cinema of fantasy has the potential to transform spectators through what it allows them to see and experience. By rendering the excess of the gaze visible through fantasy, cinema makes us aware of the hidden enjoyment that silently informs our social reality. In doing so, it confronts spectators with the sources of their own enjoyment and deprives them of the illusion of a neutral social reality. This gives the cinema of fantasy its political, ethical, and existential power.

With Kubrick, filmic fantasy exposes in an extreme way the hidden enjoyment of symbolic authority itself—its libidinal underside, the fact that authority figures get off on the exercise of their power. Spectators see the absence of neutrality in the authority but not in themselves. Thus, though these films have a revelatory power, they tend to leave the spectator unscathed. The turn to Lee's cinema shows how this hidden enjoyment is present not just in authority figures but in all subjects. It stains every social relation. But Mann adds another twist to our experience of excessive enjoyment depicted through fantasy: his films reveal that we must avoid the temptation to believe we can eliminate this excess. Excessive enjoyment is not just the source of oppression: it is also the foundation of our ethical being. By concluding with a look at Fellini's films, the limits of this way of relating to the gaze become apparent. By taking fantasy to its extreme, Fellini shows its stifling nature. The trajectory from Kubrick to Lee to Mann to Fellini traces the fantasmatic presentation of the gaze as it becomes increasingly complicated.

One of the fundamental impulses driving cinema is that of visibility—rendering the previously invisible (or unseen) visible, allowing spectators to see what they ordinarily do not see. Many theorists of film have identified this aspect of film as its salient feature. For instance, Joel Black contends that "one of film's key effects has been to provide viewers with a kind of enhanced, X-ray vision that allows them to feel that they can penetrate the veil of superficial appearances and see the hidden structure of reality itself."[4] For Black, this sense of enhanced visibility represents the chief danger of the cinema and its link to our contemporary culture of immediacy and total exposure. Cinema threatens to render everything visible to a public (and publicizing) look. Black is certainly correct to stress that film creates a sense of enhanced vision, but he misplaces the accent of this enhancement (and thus overestimates the dangers of the cinematic experience). Contra Black, it is not that spectators feel that they can see "the hidden structure of reality itself," but that they can see what is in reality more than reality—the excess of the gaze as objet petit a that accompanies our experience of reality but remains hidden in that experience. The promise of an encounter with the distortion that this excess produces is one of the main reasons that spectators go to the cinema, and it is the fantasmatic dimension of cinema that renders excess visible.

In the 1970s and 1980s, film theorists began to pay attention to the role of excess in cinema—all the ways that films go beyond what is necessary for producing meaning. Specifically, Roland Barthes, Stephen Heath, and Kristin Thompson emphasized the importance of acknowledging and theorizing excess, though none linked it directly to the gaze. Barthes labels filmic excess the "obtuse meaning," a meaning that transcends both denotation and connotation. It is a meaning that resists meaning, a signifier without a signified.[5] Obtuse meaning does not add to the narrative or to what the narrative communicates, but instead exceeds the narrative structure of a film. For these theoreticians of filmic excess, the excess is excessive in relation to the exigencies of narrative structure, and thus it limits our ability to read and interpret the filmic text. It indicates what our interpretation cannot include.[6]

It is at this point that the theoreticians of excess encounter a stumbling block: if excess remains irreducible to and blocks any effort at interpretation, if "excess innately tends to elude analysis," then the critical task becomes one of "pointing out" this excess rather than including it in an interpretation, as Thompson recognizes.[7] This represents a danger for the interpreter of film who privileges excess. According to Thompson, "To discuss [excess] may be to invite the partial disintegration of a coherent reading."[8] This aspect of excess—its status as antithetical to interpretation—may be why the theoretical focus on excess never addressed its precise function in the cinema. Though theorists pointed out instances of excess in film, this critical act did not lead to a fully developed theory of filmic excess. Instead, theorists of excess used the concept primarily to discuss the limitations of narrative and of interpretation. Which is to say, excess has had almost exclusively a negative value in the history of film theory.

Despite the differences in their positions relative to excess, Barthes, Heath, and Thompson share the view that excess reveals narrative's inability to become total, that it indicates the necessity of some element that will always escape narrative structure. In this sense, the act of pointing out excess is an act of subverting the dominance and unity of narrative. Here, the political dimension of excessive cinema (and of the critical act of noticing excess) stems from the relationship between narrative and ideology: to subvert narrative is to subvert the way in which the social order creates ideological justifications. However, the problem is that this vision of excess wrongly sees it as external to the narrative structure of film rather than internal to this structure.

Excess exceeds the filmic narrative from within; it is not an external barrier. It is nonsensical, but it is a point of nonsense (or non-sense) that exists within a structure of sense. Because they posit excess as the subversion of narrative, Barthes, Heath, and Thompson imply that excess occupies a transcendent position beyond filmic narrative. But if it were actually beyond the narrative, we would have no way of understanding excess at all: we would lack even the ability to point it out. The only properly conceivable excess is the point at which filmic narrative exceeds itself. This excess is the product of sense, not its external limit or subversion. To put it in Barthes's language, the obtuse meaning is not a barrier to signification but the signification of a barrier. Even as the excess resists signification, it does so within a world of signification—or else we would not even be able to register it.[9] This means that we can actually do much more with filmic excess than simply point it out.

If we understand excess as an internal excess, this does not mean that we render it meaningful (and thus deprive it of its excessive dimension).[10] Excess remains the nonsensical point embodying enjoyment. But this does allow us to see how excess functions. We can observe how a film reveals excess to the spectator and where a film situates this excess. Excess becomes, according to this line of thought, a piece of nonsense that a film can deploy sensibly in order to reveal how excessive enjoyment itself functions for the subject and for society as a whole. Significance arises from the way in which cinema depicts excess, the use to which cinema puts it.

Cinema can depict this excess in many different ways, but it can never depict it directly, which is why Joel Black's fears about the link between the cinema and a culture of total exposure are unfounded. Total direct exposure is impossible, and one argues against it only to create the illusion that it is possible. If a film attempts to render the excess directly, the film completely misses it. The example of pornography illustrates this dilemma and reveals that despite the link made by numerous critics, pornography is not the ultimate truth of the cinema. As Linda Williams famously notes, pornography is a filmic genre of excess, specifically bodily excess.[11] And yet, because the porn film attempts to show the objet petit a directly, this object rarely becomes visible. Porn's directness—its direct approach to the object—hides the inaccessible dimension of the object, what is in the object more than the object, the source of its attractiveness. In this sense, porn is not excessive enough: it never shows enough precisely because it attempts to show everything.

The porn film aims at rendering visible the secrets and fantasies—the obscene enjoyment—that one never sees in everyday experience of social reality but that nonetheless lie hidden within that reality. But unlike the fantasmatic film, pornography assumes that the objet petit a (in the form of the gaze) is an actual object that one can see rather than a distortion in the fabric of the social reality that one must see in the process of distortion itself. Thus, this direct rendering of the objet petit a fails because there is no actual object that one might pin down and display. In fact, the oft-noted tedium of the porn film stems from its obfuscation of the objet petit a in the effort to expose it. Pornography fails because the gaze, the objet petit a in the field of the visible, is irreducible to the field of the visible itself. The films that actually enable us to recognize the gaze do so by making it visible as a distortion in this field.

Film depicts rather than eludes the excess of the gaze by producing it as a disturbance in our looking. We see the gaze in the filmic fantasy when a film makes evident an excess that haunts what it shows on the screen. This excess of the gaze can occur either on the level of content or form. In *Spectacular Passions*, Brett Farmer points out, "Moments of excess appear as a deviation from or a going beyond the motivations of dominant narrative demands either at the level of narrative content, such as certain scenes, shots, characters, or actions that have no apparent narrative function and bear little if any relation to dominant diegetic foci, or at the level of textual form, such as unconventional camera work, obtrusive editing styles, extravagant mise-en-scène, and the like."[12] The obtrusive aspects of the cinema reveal that the field of the visible is not a neutral field and that the gaze stains the seeming neutrality of this field.

Much of the appeal of cinema derives from its ability to depict the objet petit a in the form of the gaze. Many film lovers discover a way of relating to the gaze in the cinema that they cannot find anywhere else. According to Farmer, cinephilia—and he deals specifically with gay male cinephilia—

stems directly from cinema's fantasmatic rendering of this excess. The cinephile enjoys the fantasmatic dimension of the cinema. Farmer claims that the long history of gay cinephilia is not merely the result of gay men desiring male screen icons, but of gay men being drawn to the cinematic depiction of what exceeds the symbolically structured social reality.[13] Cinema constantly shows us that there is something more in our social reality than we ordinarily experience, and in this sense, it offers, for the gay subject, the promise that there is something beyond normative heterosexuality, even within the social order as it is presently constituted. Cinephilia derives not from a thirst for a window into reality that the cinema offers, but from its window into what exceeds reality. It has its basis in the cinematic rendering of the gaze, an object that does not appear outside the filmic fantasy.

Cinephilia is an extreme response to the lure of filmic fantasies, but it nonetheless reveals something fundamental in the art of the cinema. Much of the political and existential importance of the cinema stems from its depiction of the gaze through a public staging of fantasy. Film has the ability to stage the gaze fantasmatically not because of its ability to penetrate into the essence of reality, but because of its very failure to do so—its capacity for distortion. By allowing the spectator to see and embrace this fantasmatic distortion, film can use fantasy to expose an enjoyment hidden by the power of ideology, and this is precisely what some of the earliest theorists of film celebrated in the discovery of this new artistic medium.

2

Theoretical Fantasizing

THE FIRST PROMINENT theorists of the cinema share a belief that the essence of film art stems from film's resistance to realism and to a photographic representation of the external world. For thinkers as disparate as Sergei Eisenstein, Hugo Münsterberg, and Rudolf Arnheim, film offers unique insights—insights that no competing art form offers—that have nothing at all to do with its ability to depict the external world with verisimilitude. Instead, these three early theorists of cinema draw attention to how film art captures and mirrors the logic of an internal world. Even though film cannot depict thoughts (unlike, say, the novel), it nonetheless has a structure that links it to the operations of the psyche or psychic reality rather than to the external world. Like the psyche, film has the ability to create—or make manifest—connections between related ideas or images that the exigencies of time and space render impossible in our everyday experience of external reality.

Münsterberg was the first to stress film's power to reproduce the associative patterns of the psyche. In *The Photoplay: A Psychological Study*, he contends that film "can act as our imagination acts. It has the mobility of our ideas which are not controlled by the physical necessity of outer events but by the psychological laws for the association of ideas. In our mind past and future become intertwined with the present. The photoplay [i.e., film] obeys the laws of the mind rather than those of the outer world."[1] For Münsterberg, film marks an artistic innovation because it does not simply represent the content of the psyche but actually reflects its very structural logic. Eisenstein refines this line of thought even further, linking film not just to the psyche as such but to its most fundamental thought processes. He says that "at the basis of the creation of form lie sensual and imagist thought processes. Inner speech is precisely at the stage of image-sensual structure, not yet having attained that logical formulation with which speech clothes itself before stepping out into the open."[2] Here, the worth of this insight—and thus the worth of film for these early film theorists—begins to become clear: film reveals the psychic processes that everyday experience and ordinary ways of thinking obscure. In this sense, film has the unique ability to render visible what would otherwise remain invisible or hidden.

Münsterberg and Eisenstein's insight into the structure of cinematic logic is, at bottom, a psychoanalytic insight. Though they would not put it this way, they understand that film follows the dictates of the primary process— that is, the logic of unconscious fantasy—and eschews the reality testing of the secondary process. Just as fantasy allows subjects to bypass the exigencies of time and space insofar as they act as barriers to enjoyment, so too does the cinema eliminate such barriers. In the cinema, everything obeys the logic of fantasy to such an extent that the very distinction between fantasy and reality no longer holds. The fantasmatic dimension of cinema permits spectators to recognize and experience public fantasies that remain otherwise beyond their awareness.

Understood in this way, cinema is valuable not for its ability to make visible the hidden contours of our reality, but for its ability to reveal what reality itself obscures—the dimension of fantasy. This is why, to a person, the first great theorists of film decried the introduction of sound and other technical innovations (such as color) that pushed film in the direction of realism. Since cinema was an entirely fantasmatic art, these innovations were completely unnecessary. And what's worse, they could do nothing but turn filmmakers and audiences away from the fantasmatic dimension of cinema, potentially transforming film into a mere delivery device for representations of reality. As long as the irrealism of the silent black and white film predominated, one could not take filmic fantasies for representations of reality. But sound and color threatened to create just such an illusion, thereby destroying the very essence of film art. As Arnheim puts it, "The creative power of the artist can only come into play where reality and the medium of representation do not coincide."[3] The task of the filmmaker, for Arnheim and for the other early film theorists, consists in constructing a fantasy for the audience.

Film constructs a fantasy for spectators in order to allow them to see openly and publicly the hidden enjoyment that governs subjective experience. Through film, we see not our reality itself, but the fantasy structures that shape that reality. In this sense, the early film theorists implicitly grasp the psychoanalytic insight that understanding fantasy is the key to understanding reality. They see that film's exploration of fantasy offers us a unique insight into the foundations of reality, which is far more important than the depiction of reality itself.

Unlike the fantasies of individual subjects, filmic fantasies are always public and visible. They can entrance us just like private fantasies, but we can also explore and inhabit them more thoroughly than private ones. The fantasy that we find in a film brings into public view aspects of our social reality that remain invisible in our everyday experience. This is what constitutes the political possibility for filmic fantasy. Going further than either Münsterberg or Arnheim, Eisenstein insists on the political utility of film's fantasmatic disposition. By taking up filmic fantasy, we might, according to Eisenstein, work to break the hold that ideology has over us as subjects by shattering our usual conception of social reality.

3

The Politics of Cinematic Fantasy

IN ORDER TO grasp the political possibilities and consequences of film's tendency toward the depiction of fantasy, we must first examine the politics of fantasy itself. Fantasy functions most conspicuously in a conservative way, as a vehicle for depoliticization and acceptance of the ruling ideology. It provides an imaginary enjoyment that often persuades subjects to accept their actual immiseration. We can see the most dramatic instance of this in the case of lotteries, which sell the fantasy of being a millionaire to impoverished subjects in order to render their poverty bearable. As long as I can purchase a lottery ticket (and its attendant fantasy), I endure the drudgery of my situation rather than revolt against it. In this way, fantasy functions as the direct and necessary supplement to ideology. The social law demands the obedience of subjects, and ideology serves to justify this obedience, to provide a rationale for it.

But subjection to ideology nonetheless leaves subjects in a state of dissatisfaction, even if ideology does in fact justify this dissatisfaction (through recourse to original sin, human nature, the exigencies of the free market, and so on). The ideologically interpellated subject accepts this fundamental dissatisfaction, and yet a high degree of dissatisfaction among subjects imperils the functioning and stability of the social order. This places the social order in a contradictory position vis-à-vis the dissatisfied subject: on the one hand, it depends on the dissatisfaction of subjects in order to function, and on the other hand, dissatisfied subjects represent a barrier to social stability. Dissatisfied subjects are always incipiently revolutionary subjects, which is why it is precisely at this point that fantasy supplements ideology in stabilizing the social edifice. Fantasy deflects the revolutionary impulse that the dissatisfactions of living under the social law tend to produce.

Ideology also needs fantasy to compensate for its constitutive incompleteness. No ideology can ever provide all the answers for the subject, and fantasy fills in the blank spaces in an ideological edifice. For instance, official Christian ideology holds out the idea of heaven as a reward for accepting Christ. Heaven (or eternal bliss) provides the incentive for the fledgling believer to abandon the seemingly more enticing life of sin. But Christian ideology never describes this eternal bliss in any detail, not because it refuses to reveal this information, but because it can't. The description of heaven represents a lacuna in Christian ideology insofar as it represents the promise of an enjoyment that we cannot signify. Christians must fantasize about heaven in order to compensate for this lacuna, and Christian ideology depends on this moment of fantasy in order to function at all. One can't even imagine the Christian who has never once indulged in a fantasy of heaven.

Ideology is always limited because it functions on the level of the signifier. The signifier gives ideology its power to constitute identity, to provide the totality of identities that the subject can possibly adopt, but it also limits the ability of ideology to create a social reality complete unto itself. Every system of signification—and thus every ideology—is beset by lack, lacking what exists beyond the signifier. We can think of the incompleteness of the signifier—and thus of ideology—in the same terms that Kant thinks of the limits of human reason. According to Kant, reason goes astray because it attempts to extend the concepts of our understanding beyond experience. In so doing, in attempting to conceive what Kant calls cosmological ideas, reason necessarily involves itself in antinomies, speculations in which both opposing arguments are true or both opposing arguments are false. These antinomies—concerning the origin of the world, for instance—indicate the failure of reason and its constitutive incompleteness. No amount of reasoning can fill in this gap and solve the impossible problem represented by the antinomies. As Kant argues in his discussion of the first antinomy, if we try to reason about the origin of the world, we will inevitably fall into contradiction, proving that an origin cannot exist and, at the same time, that there must be an origin. Thus, both the origin and an infinite time without origin are unthinkable for us (because the world as a whole is not an object of possible experience, indicating that reason here oversteps its bounds). Fantasy, however, allows us to realize this cosmological idea of an origin, to stage the origin that we cannot conceive on the level of the signifier. We can fantasize a cosmological primal scene. In trying to think the origin with signifiers, we involve ourselves in an infinite regress in which we can always posit something prior, but fantasy provides the illusion of an absolute origin that we cannot go beyond.[1]

Ideology fails along with the signifier because the origin of every ideological system, even that of capitalist democracy, is violent and unjustifiable within the ideology. No ideology can explain or justify its own genesis, the point at which ideology generates itself. We can see this in the way that contemporary apologists for capitalism emphasize its link to human nature rather than avowing its historical origins. Ideology must repress its own origin because this origin represents the senseless dimension of the law, the law simply proclaiming itself as law without any attempt at justification. At its origin, the law relies on a fundamentally extralegal, lawless moment in which legality itself begins.[2] The origin necessarily remains a blank space within ideology, which is why ideology needs fantasy to answer the questions that it must leave unanswered.[3]

If the subject attempts to use another signifier to fill in the illusory beyond of the signifier, this will simply create the illusion of another beyond. As long as one remains on the level of the signifier and on the level of ideology, one never escapes perpetual lack. As a result, the subject of ideology cannot but be a dissatisfied subject. But fantasy intervenes here to offer the subject a way of accessing this illusory realm beyond the signifier. Fantasy convinces the subject that it can have that which is constitutively denied—the satisfaction that comes from having the impossible object.

Fantasy is able to provide the subject a relation to the impossible object because of the form that fantasy takes, a form that makes it especially amenable to the cinema. Fantasy does not give the subject the object of desire. Instead, it furnishes a scene in which the subject can take up a relation to its impossible object. The fantasmatic scenario provides a setting in which desire can locate itself, thereby alleviating the constitutive indeterminateness of desire. Fantasy transforms the dissatisfied subject of desire into a subject satisfied with an imaginary enjoyment. Here, the political role of fantasy seems perfectly clear.

One of the chief critiques of classical Hollywood film centers on its investment in fantasy, an investment that serves to obscure the ideology that produces the fantasy. Though it provides the illusion of transcending the limits of the symbolic law and ideology, filmic fantasy remains, according to this critique, entirely within the confines of ideology. And yet, fantasy also takes the subject beyond the rules that govern possible experience and thereby envisions the impossible. On the one hand, this image of the beyond deceives the subject into thinking that it has access to an enjoyment that it doesn't in actuality have; but on the other hand, the fantasmatic scenario exposes the excessive enjoyment inherent—though invisible—in the functioning of the social order. It is for this reason that Slavoj Žižek claims, "A fantasy is simultaneously pacifying, disarming (providing an imaginary scenario which enables us to endure the abyss of the Other's desire) *and* shattering, disturbing, unassimilable into our reality."[4] When we immerse ourselves in fantasy, we experience a disturbing excess that sustains our everyday experience but that one never encounters there. The fantasy shows too much—namely, the obscene, repressed excess that inheres in the functioning of the ruling ideology.

Though the fantasmatic dimension of cinema often works in an ideological way, it also has the ability to undermine the functioning of ideology by exposing the traumatic excess that is central to the ideology and that ideology cannot publicly acknowledge. The political valence of fantasy in a film depends on how the film depicts excess: if it uses excess to fill in ideological gaps and pacify the spectator, then it functions as an ideological supplement; but if it allows excess to stand out and distort the spectator's look, then it functions as a challenge to ideology. This latter use of fantasy is what Eisenstein, in particular, found so valuable in the cinema. Ideology justifies the subject's sacrifice of enjoyment for the sake of the social law, and it does this by presenting itself as a neutral enjoyment-free zone. But despite this deceptive self-presentation, ideology relies on all sorts of enjoyment that it cannot avow. The very submission of subjects to an ideology depends on the surplus enjoyment that it provides for them. But the seeming neutrality of ideology is a necessary fiction. If it avowed its own investment in enjoyment, ideology would lose its pretension to neutrality, its status as the neutral ground through which subjects find meaning. Ideology can operate publicly and openly because it presents itself as a neutral structure created for the sake of the larger social good. But when fantasy becomes public—which is precisely what occurs in the cinema—this gives the lie to ideology's pretensions to neutrality and exposes the excessive enjoyment that stains this supposed neutrality.

4

Early Explorations of Fantasy

THE OVERTLY POLITICAL dimension of a cinema devoted to fantasy is evident in the films of two central figures of early cinema—Sergei Eisenstein and Charlie Chaplin. Film theorists and critics often think of Eisenstein and Chaplin as polar opposites, contrasting Eisenstein's rationalism with Chaplin's humanism. But both share a commitment to the revelatory power of the cinema of fantasy. What distinguishes the films of each is the way in which they deploy cinema's fantasmatic dimension in order to reveal the excessive enjoyment embodied in the gaze. Eisenstein depicts this primarily through his use of editing, whereas Chaplin tends to depict it through the mise-en-scène that he constructs. Both are filmmakers of fantasy, but they explore fantasy in two very different directions. In this sense, they establish the paths for filmic fantasy that have remained in place even until today.

Just a cursory look at the cinema of Eisenstein and Chaplin—even isolating the best-known moments from their films—reveals the central role that the fantasmatic depiction of excess plays for each. For instance, in the Odessa steps sequence from *Battleship Potemkin* (1925), Eisenstein depicts a group of Cossacks attacking the people of Odessa. During this bald exercise of oppressive military power, we see the Cossacks as they march down a long series of steps and as they fire on unarmed civilians. Eisenstein exposes the excess in this display of power not simply through the graphic images of its victims (the mother shot at point blank range while holding her dead child, the baby carriage holding an infant toppling down the steps, or the women shot directly through the lens of the glasses she is wearing), but primarily through the way he edits the scene together. Eisenstein uses montage in this sequence in order to overlap images, and as a result, we see the attacking Cossacks and fleeing citizens of Odessa traverse the same ground multiple times. According to David Bordwell, here Eisenstein is "accentuating an action by repeating it almost *in toto* in succeeding shots."[1] Though the event itself might take a couple of minutes, in filmic time it lasts more than twice this long because of Eisenstein's use of overlapped images. We see more of the attack than we could possibly see were we to actually witness the event in reality rather than on film.

Through cinematic invention, Eisenstein can show the excess that remains invisible to our ordinary experience and perception. This excess stains the image and reveals the violent dimension of social authority. The montage of images depicting the soldiers' relentless march forward toward the citizens of Odessa and the citizens' frantic flight shows that social authority exercises itself through unnecessary and unprovoked brutality. This brutality is an expression of authority's hidden enjoyment, and the stain of this enjoyment is what a realistic depiction of the attack would necessarily miss. The distortions of filmic fantasy bring this enjoyment to light, thereby allowing us to see and to contest the appeal that social authority has.

While Eisenstein exposes this excess through montage, Chaplin reveals a different form of excess through mise-en-scène. The revelation of excess is visible throughout Chaplin's work, but especially in *Modern Times* (1936). Here, it is not the manipulation of the image that exposes an excess but the figure of Chaplin himself that sticks out in the image. This becomes most conspicuous when the film shows Chaplin working on an assembly line in a factory. Here he sticks out through his inability to keep up with the speed of the line when the factory manager demands that it increase. Initially in this scene, we see him repeating his particular task on the assembly line, using a wrench in each hand to tighten nuts on parts as they pass in front of him on a conveyor belt. His exaggerated rendering of this movement offers the first sense of an excess. Chaplin performs the movement in an overly mechanical way, as if to indicate the way in which the monotony of the work has reified him as a worker. But eventually, as the speed of the line becomes unmanageable, Chaplin actually climbs onto the conveyor belt in an effort to keep up with the passing parts, which are moving too quickly for him to tighten the nuts on each part. The conveyor belt then sucks Chaplin into the central machinery of the factory. The film shows Chaplin's body as it winds its way through this machinery, following the path meant for the manufactured objects, not the human body.

While Chaplin's body moves through the machinery, we see it clearly as an excess in the process of industrial production. The very body of the laborer has no place within the productive apparatus; it thus sticks out and stains this apparatus, as the shot of Chaplin in the machinery allows us to see. This bodily excess remains visible even after the other workers rescue Chaplin from the machinery. Once free and off the assembly line, he continues the motion of twisting his wrenches even where there are no nuts to be tightened. The production process has such a hold over Chaplin's body that it continues to perform its task in the absence of an object. He goes so far as to "tighten" the body parts of people he encounters. Through Chaplin's performance throughout this scene, the film depicts an excess that exists in the process of capitalist production.

While Eisenstein's portrait of excess reveals the link between excess and social authority, Chaplin's depiction of it reveals an excess in the body of the working class that results from the imprint of the capitalist mode of production. Chaplin's body evinces too much reification in this scene, and this visibility of reification has the effect of calling it into question. Chaplin's body reveals the violence of the mechanization process and its success in fully incorporating the body. We are drawn to Chaplin here insofar as his body exposes the truth of the productive apparatus and thereby opposes it. This is what Béla Balázs uncovers about Chaplin. In his *Theory of Film*, Balázs notes,

> If Charlie Chaplin came to be the best-beloved darling of half the human race, then millions of men and women must have seen in his personality something that means much to them; Charlie Chaplin's personality must have expressed something that lived in all of them as a secret feeling, urge or desire, some unconscious thought, something that far transcends the limits of personal charm or artistic performance. The golden-hearted, shiftless, blundering, cunning little tramp, the victim of mechanization and capitalism, who hits back with grotesquely resourceful pinpricks—Charlie, with his melancholy optimism, expresses the opposition of all of us to an inhuman order of society.[2]

As Balázs sees, spectators embrace Chaplin as the excess produced by the capitalist order of production that nonetheless resists that order.

Ordinarily, we do not see the excess that Chaplin embodies in *Modern Times*. When we purchase a product, we don't see anything that exceeds or resists the process that produced it. But Chaplin's film exposes this excess through its depiction of the body of the worker in *Modern Times*. This gives the film—and Chaplin's work on the whole—an inherently political edge. It demands that we see what doesn't fit and that we address this excess. In a related way, Eisenstein's films also force us to see what doesn't fit within our social order and yet silently informs the functioning of that order. By avowing this excess as it manifests itself in the fantasmatic distortions of the gaze in cinema, we force ourselves—and perhaps even the social order as such—to come to terms with this excess rather than quietly exploiting it. In this way, the excessive enjoyment that often plays a central role in sustaining the unfreedom of subjects can play a part in their freedom.

Through its fantasmatic dimension, cinema has the ability not just to supplement the functioning of ideology, but also to interrupt this functioning by exposing the obscene jouissance at the heart of ideology. Ideology depends on an excessive enjoyment that it must constitutively disavow and hide, but the cinema of fantasy enacts a process of unmasking it. Filmic fantasy reveals this excess as it manifests in different ways: most fundamentally, as the obscene activity that accompanies the functioning of symbolic authority, the enjoyment that authority figures derive from the exercise of their authority; and, subsequently, as the unspoken enjoyment that stains our everyday social interactions. We can see an instance of the first in the tightly constructed worlds of Stanley Kubrick and the second in the explosions of enjoyment that populate the films of Spike Lee.

5

The Coldness of Kubrick

JUSTIFYING THE STATUS of Stanley Kubrick as a fantasmatic filmmaker seems almost impossible, given his reputation. For most critics and viewers of Kubrick's films, the chief characteristic of those films is their overwhelming coldness, the sense of distance that he creates between characters and between character and viewer. Often this coldness leaves us, as viewers, unable to identify with any character within the films. As Robert Kolker points out in a representative statement, "The Kubrick community is cold, as cold as Kubrick's own observation of it. There is rarely any feeling expressed, other than antagonism, and certainly no integration."[1] Kubrick's universe seems to be a universe of structure, where human beings scarcely have a place. Kolker adds that "Kubrick uses his imagination to show that subjectivity is forever destroyed by monolithic, unchanging, dehumanized structures."[2] Kubrick's films are dehumanized to such an extent that it has even become a commonplace to note that the HAL 9000 computer is, ironically, Kubrick's most human character. HAL displays more of the emotion that we associate with humanity than any of Kubrick's other characters—even Alex in *A Clockwork Orange* (1974), who performs the most outrageous acts of ultraviolence in a completely mechanical way, as if he had no emotional investment in or derived no emotional benefit from these acts. This coldness would lead us to believe that Kubrick is a filmmaker divorced from any exploration of fantasy, which we tend to associate with an emotional response. But the opposite is in fact true: Kubrick strikes us as cold precisely because his films so thoroughly immerse themselves in the realm of fantasy.

Fantasy proper has nothing to do with affect; it concerns, instead, our relationship to the ineffable and unapproachable maternal Thing that appears to embody the ultimate enjoyment, which is, as Lacan says, "something that is far beyond the domain of affectivity."[3] When we enter the

43

realm of fantasy, we enter a place beyond affect, beyond all emotional investment. Fantasy itself is a structure, a structure that operates with the same mechanical coldness that we see in Kubrick's films. Emotions serve only to provide a way of relating to fantasy, of making it palatable, but they have nothing to do with the fantasy structure itself. Affect merely serves as the outward and public manifestation of and response to an underlying fantasy. In this sense, affect indicates distance from fantasy. But Kubrick stages fantasy without a corresponding emotional response to it, which gives his films a coldness but also allows us to partake in the fantasy without the disguise within which it usually appears.

The radicality of Stanley Kubrick as a filmmaker consists in his ability to use film's fantasmatic quality to bring to light the hidden obscene dimension of symbolic authority. This is the most basic development of the cinema of fantasy because it is the most easily recognizable way of presenting the distorting power of the gaze. Kubrick himself claims that "the basic purpose of a film . . . is one of illumination, of showing the viewer something he can't see any other way."[4] This does not mean that film shows a hidden reality; instead, it illuminates the underside of power through its deployment of the gaze. In Kubrick's films, we see symbolic authority through the distortion of the gaze, a distortion that manifests itself in excess. Every time it appears in Kubrick's films, symbolic authority appears excessively, in a way that is seldom visible during our daily experience. In revealing this side of power, Kubrick illustrates the potential of the filmic medium not for direct attacks upon ideology, but undercutting ideology's fantasmatic underside. By exposing the underlying obscene enjoyment that stains symbolic authority's illusion of neutrality, Kubrick's films work to break the hold that symbolic power has over us, if we pay attention to them.

The fantasmatic dimension of Kubrick's work becomes most evident in his final film—*Eyes Wide Shut* (1999). From the title of the film to the final scene, *Eyes Wide Shut* suggests that the characters are, at almost every point, if not in the midst of a fantasmatic scenario, then at least having experiences that are informed by their own fantasies. Fantasy shapes how Bill (Tom Cruise) and Alice (Nicole Kidman) relate to each other and even determines what they see and experience. Both fantasize rather than act, and this fantasizing, as we see, is what sustains their marriage. Throughout the film, Kubrick allows the viewer to experience events not as they really occur, but through the lens of the characters' fantasies. This is especially true in the case of Bill, who fantasizes about an obscene enjoyment lurking beneath legitimate society and then, not so coincidentally, constantly encounters it (in Marion, the woman whose father has just died; in the passers-by on the street who challenge Bill's sexuality; and, most importantly, in the mansion on Long Island where a mysterious sexual ritual takes place). In *Eyes Wide Shut*, Kubrick uses film's unique ability to represent fantasy—not external reality—to reveal the key role that fantasy plays in our experiences.

Most importantly, however, through his exploration of fantasy, Bill accesses and exposes the obscene underside of power. This side of symbolic authority is most directly evident in the secret orgy that Bill attends at the Long Island mansion. Kubrick films this orgy in a way that emphasizes its ritualistic and perverse nature. As Bill enters the main room of the mansion, he sees a circle of seminaked women (wearing masks and g-strings) with the leader of the orgy (also masked, but fully clothed and sporting a red cape) in the middle of the circle spreading incense and holding a scepter. We hear a chant and organ music accompanying this scene, which gives it a historical feeling. It is as if the film transports us into an ancient time when power operated through ritual in the way that we see on the screen. The ritualistic aspect of this scene also creates a sense of danger that a simple orgy would have lacked. When, at the end of this orgy sequence, a woman offers to sacrifice herself in order that Bill might be allowed to leave unharmed (after he has been exposed as a trespasser), he—and we along with him—believe that she will be killed as a result. This belief itself attests to the extreme enjoyment that this scene conveys. Here, there is enjoyment because there seems to be so much at stake.

This sense of extreme enjoyment also follows from the depersonalization in this scene. The sense of ritual and the ubiquitous masks suggest that the individuals involved are replaceable. All that matters here is the enjoyment. No one is an individual; instead, everyone is a tool for enjoyment. By creating this type of mise-en-scène and associating it with the most powerful men in the country (as we learn later in the film), Kubrick shows us the kind of obscene enjoyment that always accompanies the exercise of power, even if every authority figure is not attending ritualistic orgies.[5] The film's revelation of the obscenity of symbolic authority deprives that authority of its guise of neutrality. We obey symbolic authorities because we don't see this underside, because they seem to be acting in the interest of the public good rather than for their own private enjoyment. Kubrick's film forces us to question this assumption and to see the obscene dimension that exists hidden from public view.

Kubrick further exposes the obscene dimension of power through the character of Victor Ziegler (Sydney Pollack). The film introduces Victor when Bill and Alice arrive at a Christmas party at his luxurious home. We first see Victor, dressed in an expensive tuxedo, greeting guests with his wife. But his next appearance in the film is altogether different. Victor is dressing himself while standing next to a naked woman who has overdosed on drugs and is sprawled out on a chair in his bathroom. It is clear that Victor has just had sex with this woman while the party was going on downstairs. What sticks out in this scene is the body of Mandy (Julienne Davis), the woman lying on the chair. The presence of her naked and drugged body attests to Victor's obscene enjoyment. Victor makes no effort to cover her naked body when he calls Bill to assist her, leaving her to stain the mise-en-scène. Victor's attitude toward her while Bill revives her indicates that even he is aware of what she reveals about him. He evinces absolutely none of the concern that we would expect someone in the situation to feel—or at least to feign. Pollack's performance of Victor's absence of sentiment exposes Victor's obscene enjoyment. He simply wants to dispose of Mandy as quickly as possible so that the stain she represents does not become publicly visible. Even though no one in the diegesis (other than Bill) sees this stain, the film does render it visible to the spectator. We see that wealth does not simply buy security and luxury; it buys an obscene enjoyment. In this way, the film demands that we acknowledge the link between wealth and obscenity, which is a link that capitalist ideology continually works to disavow.

At the conclusion of the film, Victor appears again when he summons Bill to his home to discuss Bill's presence at the orgy. In this lengthy scene, he informs Bill of his own knowledge of what Bill has seen and done. Victor adopts the position of the all-knowing and all-seeing father vis-à-vis Bill. Not only does he know everything about Bill's activities, but he also knows all the secrets of enjoyment (specifically, all the inside information concerning the orgy). Victor Ziegler is thus a typical figure of symbolic authority in a Kubrick film. As Michel Chion notes, "Ziegler unquestionably belongs to the family of provocative, shocking and libidinous father figures, at once both highly intelligent and extremely base, that are to be found throughout Kubrick's work."[6] Victor's exchange with Bill throughout this scene foregrounds Victor's obscene paternity.

Through his revelations (that he attended the orgy, that he had Bill followed) and through his behavior during this scene, Victor evinces libidinousness. As he talks with Bill, we see Victor roll billiard balls back and forth on his (red) pool table and twirl his pool cue. He also uses language ("She got her brains fucked out, period") that reveals his intimate familiarity with the kind of obscene enjoyment that took place at the mansion. The little tics in Pollack's performance (even the way he smacks his lips for emphasis) highlight and make evident the obscenity that inheres in Victor and in the father figure as such. It is when he adopts a fatherly pose with Bill in this climactic scene that the film lays bare this underlying obscenity. The obscenity of paternal authority is something that remains invisible throughout most of our everyday experience. This authority presents itself as neutral and even compassionate, and this guise prevents us from questioning the exercise of symbolic power. When we see paternal authority's obscene dimension, we begin to question its legitimacy. Through the depiction of Victor Ziegler in *Eyes Wide Shut*, Kubrick pushes us toward this questioning.

The obscenity of the father figure becomes even more pronounced, however, in the character of Milich (Rade Sherbedgia), the costume-shop owner whom Bill encounters as he searches for a costume for the orgy. Perhaps no character in all of Kubrick's films embodies Kubrick's attitude toward symbolic authority more than Milich. When Bill first meets Milich, we see Milich discover his daughter (Leelee Sobieski) furtively playing sexual games with two older men after hours in her father's costume shop. At this point, Milich acts as an outraged patriarchal figure, reproving his daughter for her "depravity." In this scene, Kubrick shows the public face of paternal authority—paternal authority as the agent of prohibition and the defender of feminine virtue. This is typically all that we see and acknowledge publicly concerning paternal authority. But Kubrick's film shows us more—its hidden excess—and this results in the destruction of its power over us. When Bill later returns the costume he has rented, Milich's attitude toward his daughter undergoes a radical shift. This time, rather than trying to rein in her sexuality, he becomes her pimp and offers her to Bill. Through this interaction, Kubrick again reveals the underside of the father figure. The point here is not that Milich has become corrupt, but that his character exposes the two sides of symbolic power—its official refusal of enjoyment and its hidden embrace of it. By showing Bill's two encounters with Milich in the order that he does, Kubrick first depicts our ordinary way of viewing symbolic authority, and then he allows us to see what our ordinary way of seeing misses. When we see this, we are able to challenge symbolic authority as such, if we respond to the opening that Kubrick's cinema of fantasy provides for us. But Milich is simply the endpoint of the logic that lies at the core of all Kubrick's films.

Throughout these films, we see the obscene underside of symbolic authority in the very way that authority figures enact their authority. Rather than simply inhabiting a position of authority, each character enjoys the position in a way that he is not supposed to, and Kubrick works to make this enjoyment visible. Whenever a character takes up a position of authority in one of Kubrick's films, he—always he—inevitably finds an obscene enjoyment in this role. This enjoyment is often exposed in the over-the-top performances of the actors in these roles, such as Michael Bates (the chief prison guard in *A Clockwork Orange*), Lee Ermey (Sergeant Hartman in *Full Metal Jacket*, 1987), Jack Nicholson (Jack Torrance in *The Shining*, 1978), George C. Scott (General Buck Turgidson in *Dr. Strangelove, Or How I Learned to Stop Worrying and Love the Bomb*, 1964). Rather than just exercising their authority evenhandedly, the performances in each case indicate that these characters overly enjoy their position for itself and for the domination that accompanies it. Bates, for instance, raises his voice to a scream when Alex (Malcom McDowell), his prisoner, steps over a white line painted arbitrarily on the prison floor in front of his desk. Bates's duty in no way requires this type of excessiveness; his enjoyment becomes visible beyond his duty, through the tone and volume of his voice. Even a computer, the HAL 9000, begins to act perversely when it occupies a position of authority in *2001: A Space Odyssey* (1968). Through each of these characters, Kubrick indicates that the stain of enjoyment resides in the structure of symbolic authority rather than in the particular subject that inhabits the position. Kubrick uses the fantasmatic dimension of cinema to expose this stain and allow us to see its disruption of the image and the narrative in his films. This is one reason why *2001* is such an important film in Kubrick's career: here, we see how the enjoyment associated with authority infects even the seemingly unflappable neutrality and rationality of a computer.[7]

In *Paths of Glory* (1957), Kubrick illustrates the obscene dimension of military authority not through performance (as is most common in his films) but through setting. An excess becomes apparent in the opening scene of the film, which depicts General Broulard (Adolphe Menjou) arriving at the headquarters of General Mireau (George Macready) in order to convince him to attack an impregnable enemy position known as the Ant Hill. After an opening shot of the outside of Mireau's headquarters (which is an opulent chateau), Kubrick cuts to a long shot inside the chateau, where we see Mireau striding across the large hall to greet Broulard. The long shot allows Kubrick to show the full luxuriousness of the chateau—its beautiful paintings, carpet, chandeliers, tables, and chairs. Everything in the chateau has the look of nobility, and in fact, Broulard's opening remarks focus solely on the décor—especially Mireau's taste in carpet. Mireau's understated response—"I try to create a pleasant environment in which to work"—only serves to highlight the fact that this is much more than just "a pleasant environment." Simply from the setting itself, *Paths of Glory* makes it clear that Mireau enjoys his role as a commanding officer too much, that he derives a surplus enjoyment from his symbolic position of power.

The spectator of *Paths of Glory*, like the spectator of *Dr. Strangelove*, should be unable to regard symbolic authority without at the same time recognizing its obscenity. The films compel the spectator to examine the motivations driving the exercise of this authority. Of course, not every spectator—and perhaps no spectator—reacts in this way, but this is the response that the logic of Kubrick's films demands. When we answer this demand and recognize the obscenity at work in this process, we free ourselves from our investment in this authority. In this sense, Kubrick's fantasmatic depictions of the obscenity of symbolic authority are in the service of the subject's freedom. Recognizing authority's obscenity is the path to freedom from it.

6

Spike Lee's Fantasmatic Explosions

IN SPIKE LEE'S films, the revelation of obscene enjoyment extends beyond authority figures to ordinary subjects as well. In this sense, Lee takes the fantasmatic capacity of the cinema in a related but more complicated direction than Kubrick. While watching Lee's films, spectators cannot exempt themselves from the implications of the gaze, as might be possible with Kubrick's films.

The most common complaint that critics level against the films of Spike Lee concerns their excess. According to such critics, Lee lacks the discipline to pare his films down to a single idea, resulting in overstuffed films lacking coherence. As Desson Howe puts it in a review of *25th Hour* (2002), "Spike Lee is always the best and worst thing about his movies. *25th Hour* is no exception. It's wildly pleasurable in some places, groan-inducing and heavy-handed in others. It's the usual undisciplined, overextended Spike symphony: more fun than it is any good."[1] Howe's lament here is a common one: Lee's films go too far, showing us too many of the filmmaker's own idiosyncrasies and violating the exigencies of the filmic content. Precisely because they include formal sequences that fail to mesh with the material they represent, Lee's films evince, for his detractors, a "hamfisted, over-the-top approach."[2] This approach consistently produces reservations and suspicions about even the best of Lee's work.

At the same time, however, Lee's excessive treatment of his material remains the salient feature of his aesthetic and the key to his importance as a filmmaker. Lee is fundamentally a filmmaker of fantasy; he deploys the gaze through the distortion of the images he presents. His films immerse spectators within an overly present world that engages them on the level of fantasy rather than enticing their desire with absence. As a result, Lee's films seldom rely on mystery or work to create suspense.[3] Instead, he uses

49

the fantasmatic dimension of film in order to reveal to us the excess that conditions our experience of social reality but nonetheless remains invisible outside of the fantasmatic structure. The very excesses of Lee's style indicate his effort to depict the excesses of enjoyment that define, but cannot be reduced to, our social reality.

In our everyday experience of social reality, we don't see the fantasies that inform and accompany every social interaction—the racist fantasies, the sexist fantasies, the paranoid fantasies, and so on. These fantasies determine how subjects relate to each on the social terrain, and yet they exist in an unspoken and hidden form. As a result, our typical experience of social life doesn't produce a direct awareness of these fantasies and their power over our social interactions. This lack of awareness is the very thing that allows social life to continue in a normal way. In order to continue to live comfortably within our social reality, we must experience it as a neutral territory. Even if we know intellectually that the neutrality is a fraud, we implicitly subscribe to its authenticity during our social interactions. There are, of course, times in which this facade of neutrality breaks down—occasions of public trauma (such as riots or terrorist attacks)—but these moments cannot, for structural reasons, last long. As a result, we can dismiss such moments as exceptions and continue to disavow the excess that accompanies our social reality. Lee's films, in contrast, have the ability to expose this excess in a way that forces us to experience it as normal rather than exceptional—as inherent in the very day-to-day activities of our social reality—and thereby break the hold that this facade of neutrality has over us.

When spectators or critics balk at the excessive dimension of a Spike Lee film, they are retreating from his rendering of the gaze. Their demand for more realism implicitly reflects a desire to continue to experience social reality without the stain that Lee makes evident and forces us to take up. On the other hand, spectators who enjoy Lee's films do so because of this stain. Much of the enjoyment that derives from a Spike Lee film involves our complete immersion in the excessive dimension of the fantasy structure. We experience fully and openly the enjoyment that we must ordinarily experience stealthily. In the act of allowing us to openly experience this excess, the Spike Lee film destroys its ability to act as an ideological supplement. This is what Lacan means when he says that "fantasms cannot bear the revelation of speech."[4] The enjoyment that fantasies provide for the subject stems from the secrecy that surrounds them, a secrecy which allows the subject to experience fantasies as transgressive. One can, of course, talk publicly about one's fantasies, but in doing so one always disguises the way that the fantasies produce enjoyment. The way that fantasies stain the subject must remain secret. The racist fantasy, for instance, functions effectively and retains its power only insofar as it remains hidden. To experience a fantasy openly is to wake up from the dream that is our everyday social reality.

This refrain—"Wake up!" (articulated first in the concluding scene of *School Daze*, 1988)—occurs on more than one occasion in Lee's films. At first glance, it seems straightforward enough, encouraging characters (and spectators) to see objective reality rather than their looking at reality through the dream lens of their racist fantasies. However, seen in light of Lee's overall aesthetic and its privileging of fantasy, the phrase takes on a radically different connotation. In this sense, it admonishes us not to wake up out of fantasy and into reality, but to wake up from the dream of reality itself. As long as we continue to fail to see the constitutive power of fantasy in our experience, we remain asleep and unaware. Lee's films attempt to make us aware by forcing us to identify ourselves with this fantasmatic excess.

For Lee, the exposing of a fantasmatic excess has an explicit political value. The point of a film like *Do the Right Thing* (1989) is not to present a positive image of political activity, but to expose the excessive enjoyment that informs social relations and thereby work to break the hold that this enjoyment has over us. Lee's films are political in that they force racist fantasies to the surface, but they are not political in the way that many critics would like. For instance, according to Douglas Kellner, "Lee presents racism in personal and individualist terms as hostility among members of different groups, thus failing to illuminate the causes and structures of racism. Moreover, the film denigrates political action, caricaturing collective action and the tactic of the economic boycott, which served the Civil Rights movement so well."[5] While it is undoubtedly true that *Do the Right Thing* does not present either a workable political program that one might follow or an explication of the historical causes of racism, it does illuminate the appeal of racism and the structural role of this appeal to the racist subject. It reveals the enjoyment that racism provides, an enjoyment that leads subjects to hold on to their racism even when they know better. In doing this, the film attacks the heart of racism in a way that no fully articulated political program ever could.

Lee constantly uses film form to indicate the presence of the racist excess that stains the social reality, as becomes apparent whenever the form of one of his films draws attention to itself through its break from the standard conventions of realism. The two most dramatic and revelatory moments of this effect occur in *Do the Right Thing* and *25th Hour*. In what is perhaps Lee's most celebrated sequence, *Do the Right Thing* depicts a series of characters articulating their hidden racist fantasies—fantasies that they do not articulate publicly in the rest of the film—directly into the camera. Through this montage sequence, Lee allows the characters to say what they fantasize about saying but never actually say. Though unsaid (and often unconscious), these fantasies inform all of their daily interactions and give a tint of racism to these interactions. And yet, they never (or rarely) come fully to light, which allows the subject to disavow its own enjoyment of this excess. Here, however, the enjoyment of both the character articulating the slurs and the spectator listening to them moves to the foreground. Even if spectators remain properly horrified by the words that the characters say, they must confront the enjoyment implicit in the film form itself. Lee shoots the characters in a montage sequence as they directly address the camera, which gives the sequence a poetic quality. The direct address forces us to experience these outbursts without the mediation of the narrative structure, and the demeanor of the characters evinces the great satisfaction that they feel with every slur.

A similar effect occurs in *25th Hour* when we see Monty Brogan (Edward Norton) launch a long diatribe against a number of ethnic groups and others. In this scene, Lee again makes clear the fantasmatic quality of Brogan's outburst through his filming of it. Rather than have Brogan actually pronounce the words, Lee has him look into a mirror, and the mirror image speaks while Brogan himself does not. This effect is, initially, disconcerting because it immediately removes us from the conventions of realism. We become aware of the film as a film and Lee as a director, which is precisely what critics have attacked about the film. But rather than blocking our investment in what Brogan says, this break from realism heightens our investment. Lee's formal trick here draws attention to the excess that structures Brogan's relationship to his reality. There is no way that Lee could depict Brogan's underlying fantasmatic structure in a realistic way; it requires an excessive cinematic style because the fantasy itself is excessive, just as the montage in *Do the Right Thing* indicates. By using cinematic excess to register an excess of enjoyment, Lee's films address racism in the form that it takes most prominently in contemporary subjects—a fantasmatic form.

This method reaches its apogee in *Bamboozled* (2000), which focuses directly on the power of racist fantasies in the contemporary world. As the film indicates, rather than having lessened with the Civil Rights movement and the waning of overt socio-symbolic racial barriers, racist fantasies have actually increased their hold over subjects. The point is not simply that racism has now become subtler, but that it increasingly occurs on the fantasmatic rather than the legal level. Racism has historically utilized both legal and fantasmatic levels, but as legalized racism declines, fantasmatic racism become more powerful. Without the direct support of legal institutions, it must become increasingly hidden. On the fantasmatic level, racism has a hold over subjects in the way that they derive their enjoyment, and this hold is extremely powerful. At the same time, fantasmatic racism allows subjects to experience themselves as profoundly nonracist, as colorblind, because racism here functions unconsciously and not as a part of the subject's conscious symbolic framework. Thus, subjects who partake in racist fantasies often have no awareness of their own racism, which makes it all the more difficult to extirpate and gives it all the more power over their activity.[6]

This becomes evident in *Bamboozled* at the writers' meeting that Pierre Delacroix (Damon Wayons) convenes in order to create his new television show entitled *The New Millennium Minstrel Show*. The specific way in which Lee shoots this meeting highlights how the stain of enjoyment, derived from racist fantasies, informs the actions of the white writers present here. This stain becomes visible in the way the writers respond to Pierre's lament about the absence of any black writers working on the show. In each of the white responses, Lee depicts something excessive—an inability to address Pierre's statement in a neutral way. For instance, one of the white writers agrees and says, "I think it would be good to have some . . . African American writers, but for whatever reason, they're not here." This writer's pause before he says "African American" indicates that this term represents a stumbling block for him, that it stands out from other words.

The role of racist fantasies in shaping the writers becomes more evident when they begin to talk about their initial encounters with blackness. Another writer stumbles much more than the first writer as he says, "My first experience of the black people . . . of Africa . . . is that . . . these shows like *The Jeffersons*." The many pauses in the delivery of this line and the nonsensical construction indicate that some excess has blocked the normal flow of signification. By emphasizing through the delivery of these lines the writer's inability to speak sensibly or clearly on race, Lee makes evident how racist fantasies stain all our race thinking. As other writers in this scene recount their favorite moments of black television, Lee intersperses clips from the actual television shows of the 1970s that they mention, and these clips all depict black characters embodying racist fantasies of blackness. Through these excesses added to this scene, we see the fantasies that inform all thinking on race, and we also see the great enjoyment that the white writers obtain from these fantasies. These interruptions and distortions of the film form represent Lee's method of mobilizing the gaze. We don't see it directly but indirectly, through our very way of seeing too much.

The shots that begin and end this scene also reveal the fantasmatic dimension of this interaction. Whereas the scene begins with a long shot of the conference table with the writers at the sides and Pierre centered at the end, it concludes with another shot of the table from the other direction. The concluding shot repeats the look of the opening shot almost exactly, but because it is from Pierre's point of view, we see an empty chair at the end of the table rather than Pierre. Pierre becomes an absence. In this sense, the concluding shot emphasizes the fantasmatic dimension of the writers' interaction with Pierre. They encounter Pierre just as they do all black subjects—through the lens of racist fantasy—and thus they don't encounter him at all.

The most obvious instance of the power of racist fantasies in the film is the very success of *The New Millennium Minstrel Show*. This program employs black characters in blackface who enact and repeat the most pernicious racist stereotypes. The main characters on the show, Manray/Mantan (Savion Glover) and Womack/Sleep'n Eat (Tommy Davidson), live in a watermelon patch on a plantation. On the show, they openly express their nostalgia for "a simpler time, when men was men, women was women, and niggas knew their place." When a studio audience first sees the show, members of the audience express shock and horror at its obvious racism. In the shots of the audience, we see a white man with his jaw dropped, and a white woman anxiously rubbing the back of her neck. Soon, however, individuals begin to laugh and quickly the whole audience openly expresses its enjoyment. Lee shows the laughter beginning with a few black audience members. As the scene unfolds, white spectators look to this laughter as a license for their own: when they see black spectators laughing, they feel as if they have an implicit permission to abandon any restraint and unleash their own enjoyment.

The very ability of the spectators to enjoy the self-abasement of the black characters in the show indicates the presence and the power of racist fantasies for the contemporary subject.[7] Even if subjects consciously believe in equality, these fantasies nonetheless dictate how they interact with the world. By bringing these fantasies to light, *Bamboozled*—and Lee's cinema as a whole—serves to break the power that such fantasies have. Exposed by the cinema of fantasy, the fantasies that inform our daily interactions lose the appeal that derives from their very hiddenness.

Summer of Sam (1999) moves this exploration from the terrain of racist fantasies to the related terrain of paranoid fantasies. The film contains two of the most important sequences in all of Lee's work. These are the montage sequences during which we hear songs from The Who ("Baba O'Reilly" and "Won't Get Fooled Again"). Through the use of montage and the correlation of image and music, Lee emphasizes the enjoyment that accompanies outbreaks of paranoid violence. Toward the end of each sequence, the film links the unleashing of graphic violence with a musical climax. In the second montage, this combination places the spectator in the position of being led to enjoy the onscreen brutality, even as it is happening unjustly to a character—Richie (Adrien Brody)—that the spectator identifies with throughout the film.

The poetry of Lee's montage sequence and the perfectly synchronized music track make this one of the most enjoyable moments in Lee's films. The Who's Roger Daltry screams triumphantly in "Won't Get Fooled Again" just as the Dead End gang assaults Richie (wrongly believing him to be the Son of Sam). By including the assault that we dread in a sequence that heightens our enjoyment, Lee demands that we confront our own enjoyment of this violence. As a result of Lee's depiction of the gaze here (through the use of montage and its link to the music), we experience our presence in what we see and our complicity with the enjoyment that the Dead End gang derives from its violent outburst.

In forcing the spectator to avow the excessive enjoyment that derives from hidden fantasies, Lee demonstrates the politics of the cinema of fantasy. His aim here is not to produce a feeling of guilt in spectators for their enjoyment of the violence. Such guilt would itself be part of the problem.

produces rather than stems violent outbursts: the subject feels guilt for the excess of enjoyment and then continues to keep this disgusting excess hidden. But Lee's film asks us to publicly avow this excess. Once publicly avowed, this enjoyment can no longer function as support for racist or paranoid violence.

Lee's cinema is a publicizing cinema, one that shines the camera's light not on a hidden piece of reality that we have failed to notice, but on the unseen fantasy support of our daily existence. It offers us an experience of the gaze—an opportunity to recognize our own involvement and investment in what we are seeing. The point of this recognition is not that we might actually attain the neutrality that excessive enjoyment disturbs, but that we might genuinely take up and publicly avow this excess. In doing so, we strip the excess of its power to quietly supplement the functioning of ideology.

7

Michael Mann and the Ethics of Excess

WHEREAS STANLEY KUBRICK and Spike Lee reveal the way in which a fantasmatic excess supplements the functioning of ideology, the films of Michael Mann focus on an excess that is the source of our ethical activity. That is to say, Mann uses cinematic fantasy in order to make ethical subjectivity visible for us. In Mann's films, we see what was merely suggested in the films of Kubrick and Lee: the radicality of fantasmatic cinema derives from its ability to facilitate identification with excess rather than retreat from it.

If there is a director whose films bear a profound resemblance to those of Spike Lee, it is Mann. Both directors emphasize the plenitude of the cinematic image in a way that reveals the excess that haunts the social order. As with Lee, reviewers and critics take Mann to task for the way in which this excess manifests itself in film form. For instance, according to Walter Goodman in his review of *Manhunter* (1986), the problem with Mann's direction is that "attention keeps being directed away from the story to the odd camera angles, the fancy lighting, the crashing music."[1] Mann and Lee use cinematic excesses not simply for their own sake but in order to manifest the distortion of the gaze. But whereas Lee's films indicate the role that this excess plays in providing support for ideology, Mann's films highlight it as a source for ethical action.[2] By showing us the link between excess and ethical action, they reveal the precise nature of ethical action itself. It derives not from obedience to the demands of the social order, but from adherence to and embrace of the enjoyment that exceeds that order. Mann's films demand that spectators embrace duty in the manner of the heroes they depict, heroes who devote themselves to duty regardless of any pathological considerations.

In creating this depiction of devotion to duty, Mann focuses on fomenting a fantasmatic investment in his films rather than engaging the desire of the spectator. This is why he can take on projects whose denouements are fully known by the viewing public, as is the case with both *The Insider* (1999) and *Ali* (2001). Neither film relies on stimulating desire through mystery or suspense. In each case, the narrative dimension of the film—concern over what will happen next—plays a minimal role. As spectators, we know full well what will happen next, and yet this in no way detracts from the impact of these films or from our investment in them. Instead, our investment occurs on the level of fantasy. Even Mann's crime films, such as *Thief* (1981) and *Heat* (1995), do not revolve around suspense, unlike most films in the genre. Whereas suspense films tend to attract the spectator's interest through their manipulation of lack (specifically, the spectator's lack of knowledge about what will happen next), Mann's films engage the spectator through the cinematic depiction of a fantasmatic excess.

The excess that exists at the heart of Mann's films is that of subjectivity itself, or, which is to say the same thing, the ability of the subject to attach itself excessively to its duty. The feature that defines subjectivity is its ability to value duty over all other concerns, and Mann's films call us to value duty in precisely this way. In attaching itself without restraint to duty, the subject elevates itself above the contingencies of its social and historical context. We cannot reduce this excessive attachment to any external chain of causality; instead, it marks a rupture in this chain, a point at which the subject breaks from what determines it. This is why Kant associates the subject's ability to give itself over to the moral law with the subject's freedom. According to Kant, the subject knows that he or she is free because of the inclination toward morality, that "he can do something because he is aware that he ought to do it."[3] The very structure of the subject's relationship to its duty is excessive.

Even though many of Mann's heroes are criminals, their devotion to duty nonetheless achieves Kantian proportions. For Kant, ethical subjects perform their duty for the sake of duty rather than for any pathological motivation. As he explains in the *Groundwork of the Metaphysics of Morals*, "In the case of what is to be morally good it is not enough that it *conform* with the moral law but it must also be done *for the sake of the law*; without this, that conformity is only very contingent and precarious."[4] In a strictly Kantian sense, Mann's heroes act for duty itself. In the last instance, they follow their duty regardless of how it might profit or harm them (or others). This singular devotion to duty refuses to acknowledge any external—and thus contingent—influences and in this way attains purity. Kant adds, "The proper worth of an absolutely good will—a worth raised above all price—consists just in the principle of action being free from all influences of contingent grounds."[5] In our everyday experience, we don't see instances of what Kant describes here. But through his use of cinematic fantasy, Mann is able to depict it and realize this ethical ideal.

The drive of Mann's heroes to perform their duty produces the hyper-realistic and overly cinematic style that annoys his critics. This becomes visible in one of the most memorable sequences in all of Mann's films: in *The Insider*, when *60 Minutes* producer Lowell Bergman (Al Pacino) telephones whistleblower Jeffrey Wigand (Russell Crowe) after executives at *60 Minutes* have refused to air Jeffrey's interview exposing the unethical practices of tobacco companies. Mann shoots and edits this conversation in a highly stylized and formally excessive way. These formal excesses emerge in response to—and attempt to capture—the excessiveness of Jeffrey's devotion to his duty even as he has lost everything because of it.

Through the phone conversation, Mann juxtaposes two dramatically different scenes—a picturesque beach and a hotel room. As Lowell is walking on the beach outside a beach house, we see him try to phone Jeffrey in his hotel room. At the moment of the call, Mann changes the music, using a soft, haunting chant that continues until Jeffrey and Lowell begin to speak to each other. When Jeffrey doesn't answer, Lowell calls the hotel manager, who carries a phone to the door of Jeffrey's room. In the middle of the conversation with the manager, the reception on Lowell's phone begins to fade, and Mann shoots him wading into the ocean in order to improve it. The extreme mise-en-scène here—the vastness of the ocean illuminated by a fading sunlight, with the strong wind hinting that a storm is impending—underlines the excessiveness that we see in both Lowell and Jeffrey. While the manager is outside the hotel room door, in the room we see a painting of a tropical scene in the background with Jeffrey in the foreground. Mann then depicts the painting morphing into a fantasmatic image of Jeffrey's children playing in his backyard.

The distortion becomes even more evident in the conversation that ensues between Lowell, the hotel manager, and Jeffrey. Lowell asks the manger to speak to Jeff through the door, and when the manager finally convinces Jeffrey to talk to Lowell, Mann immediately stops the chanting music, and the conversation begins between Lowell and Jeffrey without any music. This sequence utilizes many formal excesses—the mise-en-scène of Lowell's end of the conversation, Jeffrey's fantasy sequence, the dramatic score—and these excesses parallel the ethical excess in both Lowell and Jeffrey. Mann ends this sequence with a long shot of Lowell standing up to his knees in the ocean holding the phone in his hand as the sunlight fades. This final shot indicates the way in which Mann's highly stylized and highly fantasmatic cinema aims to depict the ethical subject as that which sticks out in its environment.

We can see another instance of this in a scene between Vincent Hanna (Al Pacino) and his wife Justine (Diane Venora) in *Heat*. In this case, Vincent's excessive devotion to his duty occasions a response by Justine that belongs in a tragedy rather than in a crime film. She says to him, "You don't live with me. You live with the remains of dead people. You sift through the detritus; you read the terrain; you search for signs of passing, for the scent of your prey, and then you hunt them down. That's the only thing you're committed to. The rest is the mess you leave as you pass through." Here, Justine's poetic language completely defies the conventions of realism that this genre of film operates within. Even critic Nick James, who appreciates both the film and this scene, points out that Venora must speak "these lines which no one could make sound natural."[6] And yet, the unnatural sound of the lines does not detract from their ability to impact the spectator because their impact derives from their excessiveness rather than from their realism. Justine's diction rises to this level of excess in order to register the disruption occasioned by Vincent's devotion to duty and neglect of every other aspect of his life.

The depiction of duty through filmic excess in this way reveals the excessive nature of duty itself. While watching a film such as *Heat*, our enjoyment derives in large part from this excess, which allows us to see the enjoyment in duty itself. We tend to view duty as a restriction of our ability to enjoy, and this taints our relationship to it. This is what Mann's films help to free us from through their alignment of devotion to duty with enjoyment. In *Heat*, Vincent (like all of Mann's heroes) clearly enjoys his duty, and this offers us the possibility of taking up a similar relationship to duty. But the film also makes clear that this enjoyment does not imply happiness; in fact, throughout Mann's films, devotion to duty, while it brings enjoyment, inevitably deprives the hero of happiness.

Like Vincent, Mann's heroes almost always end up alone and isolated. However, they are not simply alone, but alone because they adopt a sense of duty that brooks no compromise with the exigencies of society or even survival.[7] Their ethical drive leads them to refuse the false satisfaction that the symbolic order offers. Their ethos consists in a drive to abandon everything that would confine them within a symbolic identity. In *Heat*, Neil McCauley (Robert DeNiro) gives a succinct summary of this ethos that all of Mann's heroes share to some extent: "Have no attachments, have nothing in your life that you can't walk out on in thirty seconds flat." In abandoning everything that provides them a consistent identity within the social order, they emerge as subjects. As Slavoj Žižek argues, the subject "emerges not via subjectivization-narrativization, i.e., via the individual myth constructed from the decentered pieces of tradition; instead, the subject emerges *at the very moment when the individual loses its support in the network of tradition*."[8] At the moment one loses one's symbolically supported identity, one gains subjectivity, which is what we see in Mann's heroes. They face a social order that attempts to buy them off, to purchase their acquiescence, but they continue to refuse its inducements. Instead, they sustain a pure devotion to the duty that they have given themselves, and the films depict this purity as a possibility for us as spectators.

Ironically, it is through the pure and excessive devotion to duty that the subject attains its freedom. In this sense, Mann provides the foremost filmic illustration of Kant's contention that "a free will and a will under moral laws are one and the same."[9] This connection becomes clearest in the shocking conclusion of *Thief*. Frank (James Caan), a jewel thief and the film's protagonist, dreams throughout the film of retiring from his life of crime and settling down with his new wife Jessie (Tuesday Weld) and their adopted child while living off his car dealership and bar. However, when local godfather Leo (Robert Prosky) refuses to allow Frank to retire from criminality, Frank destroys everything that supports his own symbolic identity in order to free himself. Leo tells Frank, "You got a home, a car, businesses, family, and I own the paper on your whole fucking life. . . . You do what I say. I run you. There is no discussion." At this point, Frank realizes that the possessions and relationships that offer him a symbolic identity are also what deprive him of his freedom. In order to free himself, he must destroy everything that he values.

Mann depicts Frank's rampage as the ultimate display of devotion to duty. As he orders Jessie to take their son and leave his life forever, Frank acts mechanically, without any display of emotion. He ends their relationship in a totally matter-of-fact way and refuses to answer her questions about the abrupt parting. After getting rid of his wife and child, we see Frank blow up his house, the bar he owns, and his car dealership. After setting fire to the cars at his dealership, Frank performs the most important gesture of all: he crumples up and throws away a collage of magazine and newspaper images that he had assembled of the fantasy life he wanted for himself. In the act of discarding this fantasy, Frank evinces his complete freedom. Subsequently, he is able to kill Leo and his henchmen because he is free to risk himself, no longer weighed down by concerns about his symbolic identity or by his fantasy of future enjoyment. In the final shot of the film, the camera cranes up into the trees in front of Leo's house as it follows Frank walking alone down the sidewalk until he disappears into the darkness. The isolation of Frank in this final shot is the isolation of the ethical subject, a subject that refuses to allow any pathological considerations to interfere with duty. The film shows us that we can have the enjoyment inherent in a pure devotion to duty, but at the cost of our symbolic identity (which is why the enjoyment of one's duty is inimical to happiness).

Initially, the duty that Mann's heroes give themselves to is not entirely free of pathological elements. Frank in *Thief* and McCauley in *Heat* fantasize about using their devotion to duty in order to escape: Frank dreams of living out the American dream, and McCauley plans to live out his life in prosperity in New Zealand with Eady (Amy Brenneman). In short, it seems as if these characters fail Kant's test for morality completely because they use their devotion to duty as a means to a pathological, contingent end rather than as a pure end in itself. However, as we saw in the case of Frank, when the fantasy and the devotion to duty become at odds with each other, each character opts for duty and thereby destroys the possibility for realizing the fantasy. Though their devotion to duty begins with pathological fantasies of rewards, both Frank and McCauley reveal, in the end, that they are entirely willing to sacrifice such fantasies when duty is at stake. Thus, it becomes apparent that the fantasy existed for them as an excuse for following their duty rather than the other way around. This excessive devotion to duty—or, devotion to duty as itself an excess—locates them among Mann's heroes.

Through the portraits of these heroes, Mann uses the fantasmatic dimension of the cinema to depict the excess of ethical subjectivity, in which we see the gaze manifest itself. The key to taking up an ethical position lies in identifying fully with this excess and thereby disregarding the entire field of representation and the dictates of the symbolic order. Mann's films open up the possibility of taking up this ethical position by exposing the existence of the excess that our everyday reality works to obscure. By offering too much reality, his films encourage spectators to adopt an ethical position that places them irreconcilably at odds with the prevailing social reality.

8

The Bankruptcy of Fantasy in Fellini

THE EXPLORATION OF the fantasmatic dimension of cinema reaches an endpoint of sorts in the films of Federico Fellini. Even though (as we have seen) filmmakers after Fellini continued to exploit cinema's ability to publicly enact fantasies and to render the gaze fantasmatically, Fellini exposes the limits of the cinema of fantasy by creating films devoted to its logic.[1] His films obey the logic of fantasy to such an extent that they expose the tedium of the enjoyment that derives from fantasy. Like Kubrick, Lee, and Mann, Fellini immerses the spectator in filmic fantasy, but he does so toward radically different ends. Whereas these other incarnations of fantasmatic cinema force us to avow our hidden enjoyment, Fellini's films break the power of fantasy's hold on us by revealing, at the point where we would expect an experience of the ultimate enjoyment, a radical failure to enjoy.

Beginning with 8 1/2 (1963), Fellini's films focus explicitly on the barrenness of the fantasy world. This film depicts the struggles of a film director, Guido Anselmi (Marcello Mastroianni), who is unable to decide what film he wants to make. Throughout 8 1/2, Anselmi exists within a fantasy world in which he experiences no symbolic barriers to his ability to enjoy. 8 1/2 shows Anselmi able to have access to all the women he wants: his wife, his mistress, the lead actress in his film, and so on. And because the film is fantasmatic, even temporal barriers do not stand in his way. He relives childhood experiences with his mother and with a local prostitute. This total access to all women parallels the possibilities he has as a filmmaker. Anselmi has funding and a reputation, which frees him to make whatever film he chooses. But in this fantasmatic situation in which he can experience enjoyment without restriction, Anselmi experiences none. Instead, he is overcome with boredom and a sense that none of the infinite possibilities open to him are worth

63

exploring. The excess of enjoyment here corresponds to its complete absence. In this way, Fellini reveals that fantasmatic enjoyment necessarily remains imaginary and futural: when one attempts to actually obtain it—as Anselmi does throughout *8 1/2*—one winds up with nothing.

The film produces in the spectator the same sense of boredom that Anselmi experiences within the film. Because it is a film that leaves open every possibility, nothing of significance ever happens. One watches the film waiting for the actual events of the film to commence, not recognizing that nothing can happen in this situation of total openness. In this way, the film demands that the spectator bear the weight of fantasy and experience its ultimate vacuity. We succumb to fantasy because it seduces us with the lure of a complete, nonlacking enjoyment. But *8 1/2* shows us how far fantasy is from fulfilling its promises on this count. By exposing the emptiness of the fantasy scenario, Fellini helps to free us from its power. We fall for the seductiveness of fantasy because it presents with an image of plenitude that it doesn't actually have.

Fellini makes the monotony of excessive enjoyment the explicit subject of *Satyricon* (1969). In this film depicting Rome during the reign of Nero, we see numerous displays of excessive enjoyment: orgies, feasts, executions, gladiator games, and so on. But despite the unending depictions of enjoyment throughout the film, the predominant mood is boredom. Even the characters themselves seem bored as they are in the midst of "enjoying" themselves. We see this boredom, for instance, on the faces of the guests at Trimalchio's banquet, as they eat to excess. Though the film depicts eroticized images, it never manages to incite the spectator's desire. This failure of desire stems from the absence of narrativity in the film. As William Van Watson notes, the film's structure involves "loose plotting and the virtual breakdown of narrative and narrativity."[2] Whereas narrative structure relies on the absence—that is, the withholding—of enjoyment, *Satyricon* makes enjoyment present for the spectator. This overpresence of enjoyment in the film becomes suffocating and blocks the ability to enjoy. What this reveals is that the experience of enjoyment actually depends on its absence: too much enjoyment leaves us without any.

Fellini depicts the failure of enjoyment most straightforwardly through the impotence of Encolpio (Martin Potter). After a gladiator spares his life, Encolpio is awarded a woman for his sexual pleasure. Fellini shows Encolpio begin to caress the woman as she is lying on a bed in the middle of an arena, and with a crowd of people watching him, Encolpio attempts to have sex with the woman. But in the presence of this willing and beautiful woman, he remains unable to become aroused and enjoy himself. Here, the impotence of Encolpio functions as an objective correlative for the entire film. Amid the promises and displays of unlimited enjoyment, the subject is completely unable to enjoy.

Even after Encolpio finally recovers his potency later in the film, Fellini continues to emphasize his lack of enjoyment. In the final shot of the film, he sails back to Rome, and we see a close-up of his face during the journey. The close-up then becomes a freeze frame of the face, which quickly morphs into a rock painting of Encolpio. As the camera tracks back from the rock, the other characters from the film become visible in the painting and in paintings on other rocks. Through this denouement, Fellini depicts the absence of enjoyment in these characters. Rather than being vital, enjoying beings, they are nothing but static, lifeless images. This is the final shot of the film, and it underlines the barren nature of fantasy.

The films of Fellini's middle period—from 8 1/2 and Satyricon to Roma (1972) and Amarcord (1973)—confront the spectator with excess, with too much presence, and this leaves the spectator yearning for absence. Here, one suffocates from an overabundance of enjoyment that leaves one bored rather than enjoying. The films strip the mystery and the obscurity away from fantasy, and we thus see the fantasy fully illuminated. This deprives fantasy of the aura that generates its appeal. As a result, Fellini's films have the effect of pushing the spectator out of the experience of fantasy and igniting desire, which would be an experience of the gaze as an absence.

Looking for relief from the tedium of the fantasy scenario, we begin to desire what remains absent despite the excessive presence. We come to realize that no matter how much the cinema shows, there will always be something missing. Fellini submits us completely to the logic of fantasy only in order to free us from it. In this way, his films point toward the possibility of another kind of cinema—a cinema structured around absence and desire rather than excess and fantasy. This cinema of desire offers an alternative aesthetic and an alternative conception of politics to that which the cinema of fantasy articulates. Rather than focusing on the visibility of film—on what film does show—the cinema of desire focuses on what it cannot show.

The Cinema of Desire
Absence amid the
Plenitude of the Image

9

Desire and Not Showing Enough

THOUGH THERE IS no pure desire, no desire prior to its capture within a fantasmatic scenario, we can nonetheless conceptualize what desire might look like in its pure form. The desiring subject emerges through its entrance into the social order, its submission to the demands of a symbolic law, a process that constitutes the subject through lack. As a being becomes a subject through its entrance into language, need transforms into desire. Unlike need, which can be directly satisfied through obtaining its object, desire orients itself around the Other and what the Other wants. This renders desire much more complicated than need and impossible to satisfy with a mere object. The desiring subject seeks the key to its lack in the field of the Other—its desire is, as Lacan frequently says, the desire of the Other. But the path of desire is infinite because the subject's desire can never line up perfectly with what the Other offers the subject. In the visual field, for instance, the subject desires to see precisely what is not visible in the Other, and what results is that the subject continually seeks without ever finding.[1] In the experience of desire, the gaze remains a motivating absence: it triggers the movement of desire but remains an impossible object in the field of vision. Visually, desire concerns what we don't see, not what we see, and this allows us to contrast the cinema of desire with the cinema of fantasy.

The cinema of fantasy depends on the visibility of film—its ability to reveal more than we see and hear in our everyday lives outside the cinema. The fantasmatic dimension of cinema manifests itself in the extent to which cinematic experience exceeds our daily experience and allows us to recognize the excess (in the form of the gaze) that the everyday quality of our daily experience obscures. Film is fantasmatic because it overwhelms the spectator with image and sound. In a sense, an emphasis on fantasy in film represents an attempt to remain faithful to the exigencies of the filmic medium itself. Films

69

allow spectators to immerse themselves in the movement of images and to minimize—at least during the duration of the film—a sense of lack. The relief from lack and absence that film offers is one of its primary attractions.

Even in the way that cinema produces meaning, it takes the side of presence rather than absence, as the contrast between linguistic and filmic signification reveals. Whereas words derive their signification paradigmatically (through distinguishing themselves from an absent field of other possibilities), shots in a film do not. When we experience a particular shot in a film, we do not discover its meaning through contrasting it with other possible—and absent—shots; instead, we simply experience the shot in its overwhelming presence. In *Film Language*, Christian Metz explains,

> Only to a small extent does a shot assume its meaning in paradigmatic contrast to the other shots that might have occurred at the same point along the filmic chain (since the other possible shots are infinite in number), whereas a word is always part of at least one more or less organized semantic field. The important linguistic phenomenon of the clarification of present units by absent units hardly comes into play in the cinema. Semiologically, this confirms what the aestheticians of the cinema have frequently observed: namely, that the cinema is an "art of presence" (the dominance of the image, which "shuts out" everything external to itself).[2]

This is not to say that meaning in the cinema does not derive from the juxtaposition of shots in the editing process, but that even in this case the spectator does not so much contrast present shots with absent ones (ones that might have been used) as with other present ones.

Though this overpresence of the image in film renders film an ideal medium for the exploration and development of fantasy, it renders it much more difficult to interpret than, say, literature. Interpretation tends to depend on absence, on discovering meaning through the relationship between what is said (or shown) and what is not said. As Metz notes, "A film is difficult to explain because it is easy to understand. The image impresses itself on us, blocking everything that is not itself."[3] Not only does the overpresence of the image make the interpretation of a film difficult, it also—which is to say the same thing—leaves little room for a sustained development of desire in the filmic medium. However, despite this structural proclivity of film, there nonetheless exists an essential connection between the cinematic experience and desire.

Understanding how filmic narrative deploys knowledge can lead us to uncovering a second category of film—the cinema of desire. Whereas the cinema of fantasy renders the gaze manifest through a distortion of the filmic image, the cinema of desire sustains the gaze as a structuring absence and an impossibility.[4] Here, the gaze is not what distorts the field of the visible, but what can never be reduced to this field. The cinema of desire offers spectators the opportunity of recognizing and embracing their position as desiring subjects. It does not try to resolve desire through creating a fantasy scenario, but instead provides a filmic structure that reveals the impossibility of the objet petit a—the gaze—by depicting an absence in the visual field. By doing so, this type of cinema challenges the spectator in a way that typical Hollywood films do not.

While the cinema of fantasy can exist within (or at the margins of) Hollywood, the cinema of desire has a more tortured relationship. Because it sustains desire—and thus dissatisfaction—in the spectator, the cinema of desire is not often a popular cinema. Fantasmatic cinema allows spectators an experience of the gaze (even if this experience is traumatic), but a cinema of desire never grants the possibility of this type of enjoyment. To experience the cinema of desire is to experience what one doesn't have. This section of the book will explore the development of different emphases that filmic movements (and some individual filmmakers) have placed on desire, beginning with the French *nouvelle vague*, moving to Orson Welles, to Claire Denis, and finally ending with a discussion of Italian neorealism. As with the discussion of fantasy in the cinema in the previous chapter, the aim here is to uncover the political and philosophical importance of the cinema of desire. By preserving an absence within the image, this cinema aims at sustaining desire against the reconciliatory power of fantasy. Its importance lies in its refusal, to put it in Lacan's terms, to give ground relative to desire.

The cinema of desire manifests itself most directly in the revelation of the gaze through the absence of the object that would satisfy desire, an absence we see in the case of the French nouvelle vague. Welles's films complicate this refusal by showing how absence can be made tangible within the film through an object that stands in for this absence. Claire Denis illustrates precisely what the central absence consists of—the enjoyment of the Other—and her films work to combat fantasies about this enjoyment. With Denis, the political implications of the cinema of desire begin to become visible, but Italian neorealism foregrounds these implications as it reveals how sustaining the gaze as the source of an absence is the key to breaking the fantasy of individual exceptionalism and thereby fostering political commitment. Each set of films marks a further development and complication of a form that appears most baldly in the strict absence of the object of desire.

In this type of cinema, the objet petit a or gaze manifests itself through the absence of the object of desire. Thus, the cinema of desire reveals the difference between the objet petit a and the object of desire. The objet petit a causes the subject's desire, but it is not the object of desire. The latter is an ordinary object that holds out the promise of satisfaction for the subject who would obtain it, whereas the objet petit a offers the subject the satisfaction that comes from simply being a desiring subject and following the path of the drive. One might say that the objet petit a embodies the failure of any object of desire to satisfy the subject. For instance, when I desire to drink a can of Coca Cola, the particular can of Coca Cola itself is my object of desire. The objet petit a is the enigmatic quality I attribute to Coca Cola that raises it above all other drinks and renders the particular can desirable. I don't pursue this objet petit a—I pursue the particular can—and yet the objet petit a serves as the engine for my desire. Drinking a particular can of Coca Cola never satisfies me, but I can achieve the satisfaction that accompanies desire itself through this very failure. One rarely hears of desire's path—a path that misses the object—as satisfying, but this is how psychoanalysis conceives of desire. The objet petit a provides satisfaction through the way that the subject moves around it—it is satisfying only as an absence—and this is precisely the experience that the cinema of desire imposes on the spectator.

This cinematic experience is difficult to enact because film as such tends to allow spectators to come too close to the object of desire, thereby dissolving the objet petit a into the specular image. The objet petit a has a fundamental elusiveness: one must approach it through indirection and absence rather than proximity. Sustaining desire in the cinema thus involves subverting the inherent proximity of the filmic image, finding ways of producing absence amid its overpresence. It is almost as if one must violate something essential to the cinema in order to engender a cinema of desire.

Despite this seeming divorce between desire and the filmic medium, desire is inextricably linked to narrative structure as such, which means that narrative film must in some way appeal to and manipulate the desire of the spectator. The forward movement of narrative implicitly relies on desire as its engine.[5] In *Reading for the Plot*, narrative theorist Peter Brooks sees desire as constitutive of narrative. He claims that "we can . . . conceive of the reading of plot as a form of desire that carries us forward, onward, through the text. Narratives both tell of desire—typically present some story of desire—and arouse and make use of desire as a dynamic of signification."[6] Desire functions centrally both within narrative and in the relationship between narrative and audience. It is the key to the movement of the narrative: without desire within the narrative, the narrative can't move forward; without the desire of the spectator, the spectator will simply stop watching. Films—and narratives in general—engage us because they trigger a desire to experience what comes next.[7]

The structure of filmic narration reveals the central role it accords to desire. In creating a narrative, a filmmaker produces gaps in knowledge that stimulate the spectator's desire. Even though filmic images do not signify through absence, they nonetheless do not—and cannot—reveal everything. The frame itself and the exigencies of time represent limits on what film can reveal, producing gaps in the spectator's knowledge.[8] Narrative cinema relies on the introduction of absence to the spectator, convincing the spectator that the film itself conceals a secret, that there is some piece of knowledge yet to be revealed. Without absence, a narrative would have no structure and, what's more, would have no way of prompting spectators to invest themselves in the narrative events. Absence—what the filmic narrative does not reveal—triggers the spectator's desire.

The role of absence in filmic narrative is not arbitrary or contingent. Films regulate spectator desire through the manipulation of absence. This manipulation occurs, most obviously, in the relationship between the way that events are narrated and the story of the events themselves. Film theorists have used various terms from narrative theory in order to discuss this relationship: for David Bordwell (borrowing terms from the Russian formalists), it is the relationship between the *suyzhet* (plot) and the *fabula* (story); for Christian Metz (borrowing from linguist Emile Benveniste), it is the relationship between the *discours* (discourse) and *histoire* (story).[9] The former terms indicate what one sees happening on the screen, and the latter terms point to what has really happened in the universe that the film constructs. For instance, a suyzhet may depict the discovery of a murdered body without revealing the specifics of the murder, which the underlying (and unrevealed) fabula does include. In whatever terms one uses, desire in the cinema depends on this relationship insofar as absences on the level of the suyzhet lead the spectator to desire to construct the (not fully known) fabula.

The primary way in which this relationship between suyzhet and fabula plays itself out is through delay. The suyzhet withholds information—most commonly, the denouement itself—about the fabula, leaving the spectator desiring to reach an endpoint in which the fabula would be complete. In the typical mystery film, for example, we begin without knowing the identity of the killer, which is part of the fabula, because the structure of the suyzhet withholds it. As Bordwell points out in *Narration and the Fiction Film*, "Every suyzhet uses retardation to postpone complete construction of the fabula. At the very least, the end of the story, or the means whereby we arrive there, will be withheld. Thus the suyzhet aims not to let us construct the fabula in some logically pristine state but rather to guide us to construct the fabula in some specific way, by arousing in us particular expectations at this or that point, eliciting our curiosity or suspense, and pulling surprises along the way."[10] According to Bordwell's formulation, filmic narration remains tightly in control of absence and the flow of knowledge. He sees narrative in terms of a stable dialectic of absence and presence that successfully manipulates spectator desire. Here, film produces desire only in order to satisfy it through preestablished and socially acceptable paths. Rather than being a potential site of a disturbing or radical desire, the desire created in the cinema works in the service of docility (though Bordwell himself never puts it quite this way).

The problem with this conception of filmic narration lies in its inability to see the relationship between absence in film and the gaze. Film does not create and sustain desire simply through delaying the revelation of the complete fabula or story. When Edward Branigan claims that "narration involves *concealing* information as much as revealing it," he assumes that there is an Other of the Other, a force responsible for the filmic narration that *really* knows."[11] Such a schema reduces all desire produced in the cinema to manipulation: the film withholds and conceals in order to dupe spectators into investing themselves, and then it reveals the object that sates the spectators' desire. What psychoanalysis allows us to see, however, is that the relationship between film and desire is far more complicated than this.

In addition to withholding the missing details of the fabula, filmic narration also withholds the gaze, the absent object that constitutes the field of representation itself. This object is necessarily absent—not simply an empirical absence introduced by the filmic narration—and it remains constitutively unknowable. The importance of the gaze in filmic narration is the result of the gaze's resistance to all representation. The fabula may have the power to further conceal the gaze, but it lacks the power to reveal it.

Bordwell and Branigan miss the importance of the gaze in filmic narration because they see desire in terms of the desire for completion, for gaining knowledge of the whole fabula and filling in the blanks of the suyzhet. According to this view, even if a film ends without closure, closure or completion nonetheless represents the direction toward which desire moves. Even Peter Brooks, who theorizes narrative in psychoanalytic terms, shares this conception of desire. Conceiving desire as the desire to totalize and to complete the story fails to grasp, as Lacan insists, that "human desire is not directly implicated in a pure and simple relationship with the object that satisfies it."[12] What drives narrative is not simply the desire for an end. The simplification of this relationship between desire and the object is what leads so many theorists astray when discussing the role of desire in the narrative process.

Film can do more than simply manipulate the desire of the spectator; it can instead take a more radical path, encouraging and even fomenting a desire that cannot be contained within the filmic narrative. Filmic narrative produces desire in the spectator through the introduction of an impossible object that resists meaning—the objet petit a in the form of the gaze. The eroticism of the cinema—its ability to produce desire—stems from this object that remains, no matter how much the spectator understands, irreducible to meaning. If we understand desire in this way, we can rethink the way in which filmic narrative deploys knowledge.

The gaze is the absent point in the spectator's knowledge, the point at which a film attests to the limits of its knowledge as well as the spectator's. A filmic narrative conceals but doesn't necessarily know what it conceals. That is to say, in addition to concealing something—like, for instance, the identity of the murderer in a mystery film—narrative also conceals nothing, an emptiness that no empirical object can fill in. It is this emptiness, this object that the narrative doesn't itself have, that triggers the spectator's desire, not the object that the narrative does have and is holding back. No matter how thoroughly a film reveals itself to the spectator, it still cannot directly reveal the gaze because this object does not exist in the field of the visible except through distortion. However, film does have the ability to insist on the gaze as an absence rather than attempt to obscure it through the illusion of presence.

10

Theoretical Desiring

GIVEN THE RESISTANCE of the cinematic form to the creation of a cinema of desire, it should not be surprising that it took film theory many decades to begin to think about this possibility. As we saw in the previous chapter, early theorists of film directed their energy toward the fantasmatic dimension of the cinema, toward cinema's ability to aesthetically manipulate what it depicts. The idea that filmic distortion constituted the essence of film was the controlling thought (in some form or another) of almost every early film theorist. In the late 1940s and 1950s, this began to change. Another type of theorizing began to emerge, and it emphasized—in direct contrast to the early theorists—cinema's ability to free itself from highly stylized aesthetic manipulation.

André Bazin and Siegfried Kracauer are known primarily as the proponents of realist film theory. For both, the importance of cinema lies in its ability to depict reality without the kind of manipulation that occurs in the other arts. It offers us the prospect of a mechanical or automatic reproduction. This idea of cinema creating an automatic—and thus unmanipulated—reproduction of reality seems, to be sure, naïve to contemporary ears. We recognize that there is no such thing, that the very decision to start filming, to frame a shot in a certain way, to select a certain location, and so on, all represent layers of manipulation. If we can no longer take seriously Bazin and Kracauer's insistence on realism as such, however, this does not mean that we must completely discount their theoretical contribution. Before dismissing their realist proclivities as completely naïve, we should understand precisely what realism entails for each, which will allow us to see Bazin and Kracauer in a different way than usual—as the first theorists of a cinema of desire.

Bazin celebrates realistic cinema not for what it makes clear but for what it leaves ambiguous. His critique of montage—or, more correctly, the overuse of montage—stems from the same concern. Because montage creates meaning through editing together disparate shots in rapid succession, it directs the response of the spectator, leaving little room for uncertainty in relation to the film. In contrast, while looking at a shot with depth of field, the spectator cannot, according to Bazin, immediately make complete sense of the shot or even know precisely where to look within it in order to render it meaningful. A fundamental ambiguity and uncertainty attaches to depth of field, and this is why Bazin values it to the extent that he does. He argues that "what distinguishes reality from abstraction, the event from the idea, the credible character from the mere psychological equation, is the portion of mystery and ambiguity therein that resists any attempt at analysis."[1] By preserving ambiguity, a film forces the spectator into an attitude of questioning and probing— the kind of attitude Bazin would like to see proliferate (with the help of the cinema). Though he never makes reference to psychoanalysis, Bazin does stress what remains irreducible to meaning within the filmic image. He singles out precisely those films that sustain the gaze as a fundamental absence, those films that never offer us the fantasy of capturing the object of desire.

Bazin never talks about desire as such, but the presence of the gaze as an absent object in the cinema leads him to recognize an inherent eroticism in the cinematic medium. The ability to arouse the spectator in fact distinguishes film from other artistic forms. According to Bazin, "It is of the cinema alone that we can say that eroticism is there on purpose and is a basic ingredient. Not the sole ingredient, of course, for there are many films and good ones that owe it nothing, but a major, a specific, and even perhaps an essential one."[2] Eroticism is essential in the cinema because, amid the total presence of the image, we encounter an absence that the image cannot encompass. In this sense, desire is not antithetical to the basic structure of the cinema but equally, with fantasy, a product of it. It is as if the overpresence of the image has the function of highlighting the impossibility of representing the gaze—and thus allowing this absent object to produce desire in the spectator. In an experience of otherwise complete presence, the absence marked by the gaze stands out dramatically. The spectator cannot reduce this object to the field of the visible or the significant, and this leaves the spectator in a constant state of desire.[3] Bazin's emphasis on the ambiguity of the filmic image allows him to see a structure of desire that he lacks the terms to articulate.

Whereas Bazin stresses the inherent ambiguity of the cinematic form, Kracauer stresses the openness of the filmic image. Like Bazin, Kracauer uncovers the structure of the cinema of desire without having a psychoanalytic terminology to express it. The realism of cinema, for Kracauer, consists in directing our attention to what the filmic image cannot encompass rather than emphasizing what exists within the image. He notes that "cinematic films evoke a reality more inclusive than the one they actually picture. They point beyond the physical world to the extent that the shots or combination of shots from which they are built carry multiple meanings."[4] The filmic image demands that we posit a world beyond what it represents because the representation remains superficial. Kracauer stresses that the very limits of the filmic image—its inability to register depth or inwardness—are at once the measure of its fecundity.[5] This is the fundamental difference between film and other arts, such as literature or even theater, which can register depth. When watching a film, we are constantly reminded of what we cannot see, what the film cannot show us. In this way, film maintains an openness to the gaze as that which cannot be included in the image.

The openness of the cinema leads Kracauer to see cinema as the antithesis of tragedy. One cannot create a tragic film because tragedy demands closure—a point at which one can recognize and reflect on the tragic situation. Tragedy derives from the fact that there are no alternatives, that we reside in a fundamentally closed world. Even when a film ties together all the loose ends of its narrative, the medium of cinema itself produces an open ending, an ending that suggests events to come. This idea that the filmic ending is never really closed stems from Kracauer's understanding that the filmic image always indicates a beyond. Or, to put it in psychoanalytic terms, the filmic image always suggests an objet petit a that it cannot represent. The filmic image is structured around this missing object, and no effort can fully integrate it into the image. In this sense, for Kracauer, films are constitutively incapable of delivering ideological closure. There is inherent radicality in the cinema that stems from this resistance to closure, a resistance that aligns the cinema with desire.

Neither Bazin nor Kracauer develops fully the political dimension of the role of desire in the cinema. But it is clear that a certain conception of the politics of cinema lies implicit in their work. By producing and sustaining desire, cinema encourages spectators to refuse to accept the answers that ideology provides and to refuse the fantasies that promise to domesticate the gaze. A cinema that emphasizes desire—the kind of films that Bazin and Kracauer celebrate, such as those of Italian neorealism or of Orson Welles—helps to liberate subjects from the power of fantasy.[6] It is a political cinema in a different sense than the cinema of fantasy: rather than exposing hidden enjoyment, the cinema of desire allows us to experience lack and absence as fundamental—and thus to combat the fantasies that secure our position within ideology.

11

The Politics of Cinematic Desire

THE VERY EXISTENCE of desire indicates the subject's dissatisfaction with the social order, and this gives desire an incipient radicality. The desire of the subject emerges with subjectivity itself, as the effect of a being's subjection to social demands. No social order produces perfectly satisfied subjects, and if one did, it would cease to exist as a social order. The dissatisfaction of subjects is the result not just of social requirements (such as a society's need for productive labor) but also of every social order's foundation in language. If a society perpetuates itself through language, it will necessarily produce dissatisfied, desiring subjects.

When a subject enters into a social order, this order confronts the subject with a demand or law that directs the subject's behavior. No matter how straightforward this demand may be, the fact that it appears through words creates an ambiguity: the subject inevitably interprets the demand and sees something hidden underneath or behind it. The limitation of words lies in their fundamental opacity, an opacity that creates the illusion that they house a secret meaning. When an authority addresses us with a demand, we wonder what that authority really wants; we want to uncover the implicit desire lurking beneath the explicit demand. Our desire emerges through the act of positing a hidden desire in the figure of authority, in the Other representing the forces of society.

The subject's desire focuses on what it believes is the secret of the Other, but this secret has no positive content. It is merely an effect of language itself, the form in which the Other's demand arrives. If the Other told us its secret and revealed its hidden desire, we would find this dissatisfying and posit another desire beneath this revelation. The Other cannot satisfy the subject's desire simply by revealing what the subject appears to want. In the act of producing the subject of desire, the Other produces a subject that seeks something more than the Other has to offer. The subject seeks what is in the Other more than the Other—the objet petit a, the gaze, the object that the Other does not have. Though desire emerges in response to the demand of the Other or the social order (articulated through language), it nevertheless resists being reduced to the Other. This is why we can never put our desire into words. Language carries desire but cannot capture it, and as a result, desire represents a danger to the smooth functioning of the social order. This constitutes the political kernel of desire and of the desiring subject—and it is this kernel that the cinema of desire accentuates.

Because desire desires what the Other doesn't have—what is in the Other more than the Other—ideology cannot provide definitive answers for desire's questions. Desire thus moves around a fundamental impossibility. In the act of concerning itself with an impossibility, desire transcends (or seeks to transcend) the social order out of which it emerges. Even when the desiring subject seems to direct its desire completely within the orbit of the social order or the big Other—when, for example, the subject wants public recognition—desire always seeks an additional something that the social order cannot provide. This means that desire is never simply the desire for recognition and that no amount of recognition can ever fully satisfy the subject. Though it provides recognition for the subject, ideology necessarily produces dissatisfied subjects because it provides nothing but recognition.[1]

Since ideology cannot provide the definitive answers for desire and since desire radicalizes the subject, ideology requires fantasy to stabilize the desire of the subject. Every ideology relies on a fantasmatic supplement to offset the desire that ideology itself incites. Fantasy operates by seducing the subject with the lure of total enjoyment, an enjoyment free from all lack. Desire becomes ensnared by fantasy when it succumbs to the fantasmatic deception that there is an object capable of completely satisfying it. Fantasy allows subjects to avoid confronting the fundamental impossibility that characterizes desire. When subjects invest themselves in the fantasmatic idea of an actual object of desire hidden somewhere in the social order or big Other, they remain subjected to this order through this investment in what it seems to contain.

One key to breaking the power of the big Other over the subject consists in recognizing that the big Other does not hold the secret of desire, that it isn't actually hiding anything. This is the key not only to effective political action but also to the subject's freedom. The big Other seduces the subject through creating a sense of mystery and thus perpetuating the illusion that it contains a secret object. It is only when the subject recognizes that the big Other lacks in the same way that the subject itself does that the subject breaks the hold that the social order has over it. In making this recognition, the subject grasps that its desire is in fact interminable, that the big Other will never be able to provide the satisfaction that the subject lacks. Such a recognition is the act of following what Lacan calls the ethic of psychoanalysis.

In *Seminar VII*, Lacan formulates the fundamental ethic of psychoanalysis in the following way: "The only thing one can be guilty of is giving ground relative to one's desire."[2] Giving ground relative to one's desire involves failing to accept the impossible dimension of the objet petit a. It indicates that one has invested oneself in a fantasy that envisions an object of desire that one might obtain and find satisfying. The subject who follows this ethic, on the other hand, grasps the objet petit a in its impossibility and relates to it as an impossible object. This involves embracing the act of desiring and finding satisfaction in it rather than investing oneself in the lure of obtaining.

When one follows this ethic and remains true to one's desire, all support within the social order disappears. The authentic subject of desire rejects the symbolic identity that the big Other offers it because this identity (one's position or status within the social world) demands a compromise of desire. All social blandishments lose their meaning for this subject, who recognizes that the big Other lacks just as the subject itself does and, consequently, does not have any foundation on which to base the meaning that it offers. The ethical subject has given up its investment in public recognition and thus can no longer count on the guarantees and security that the ideology provides. Instead, this subject must face its existence alone, fully responsible and without alibi, which is, of course, a difficult position to sustain.[3]

The difficulty of not giving ground relative to one's desire stems not only from the loss of support in the social order that such an act entails, but from the relationship to lack that desire without its fantasmatic supplement forces us to recognize. Desire emerges through the loss of the object, and an ethic of desire demands that the subject embrace this loss as constitutive for both desire itself and for subjectivity.[4] Because desire originates through lack, it seeks to return continually to the experience of lack. Desire desires the object in its absence rather than in its presence, which means that the desiring subject must endure this absence without respite and without even the hope for respite. This is why fantasy remains a constant source of attraction for the subject: it doesn't eliminate loss as such, but it holds out the possibility of its elimination, the possibility that the subject could relate to the present object of desire rather than the absent objet petit a. Herein lies the difficulty of sustaining desire without recourse to fantasy. Fantasy relieves the subject from the burden of perpetual lack; within fantasy, lack magically becomes contingent rather than constitutive.

The cinema of desire, at its best, allows us to derive enjoyment from lack itself, to realize the perpetual nature of our desire and to embrace it. However, the most common relationship to desire in the cinema (especially in Hollywood cinema) involves proffering fantasies in which the objet petit a ceases to be an impossible object. Rather than presenting the gaze as an absence, most films present the fantasy of the presence of the object of desire, and in this way, they domesticate the gaze, bringing it within the world of representation as just another object. There is something momentarily satisfying about such films (which we will look at in part 3) insofar as they seem to fill in the lack that is desire itself. However, we soon realize that such fantasmatic answers do not, in the end, quell the dissatisfaction of desire. It is only the cinema of desire that allows us to find a way out of this dissatisfaction by embracing and enjoying desire itself. These films provide a more fundamental satisfaction insofar as they allow us to find satisfaction within the seemingly dissatisfied position of desire itself.

Because it fights against both the inherent tendency of the apparatus itself (its tendency toward visibility) and the ideological direction of Hollywood (its role in providing a fantasmatic supplement for late capitalist ideology), the cinema of desire has the odds stacked against it. This kind of cinema asks that we embrace what we don't have and what the filmic image cannot represent. It offers only lack where we are used to experiencing the illusion of total presence. The barriers in the way of a cinema of desire seem almost insurmountable, especially when Hollywood remains at the center of the filmic universe. However, despite Hollywood's hostility and popular resistance, a cinema of desire has flourished and has managed to appeal to the desire of some spectators. Most often, we watch films in order to find relief from our daily dissatisfaction, to find a fantasmatic answer for our desire. But we also watch them in order to desire.

12

The Impossible Object of the Nouvelle Vague

W E CAN BEGIN examining the cinema of desire by looking to its most obvious incarnation: films that create and sustain an absent and impossible object through narrative, editing, mise-en-scène, or framing. Such films use film structure to trigger spectator desire and to highlight the irreducibility of that desire. In the films of the French nouvelle vague, we find an exemplary instance of this type of aesthetic—an aesthetic that produces desire through a depiction of the gaze as an impossible object within the filmic image.

Whereas desire accentuates and thrives on what it cannot achieve, fantasy produces an imaginary scenario of what it can. This is how fantasy blinds the subject to the constitutive incompleteness of ideology. If the subject believes in the object as a possibility, the subject implicitly accepts an image of ideology as a whole that has the ability to deliver the ultimate enjoyment. Aware of ideology's constitutive incompleteness, the desiring subject has an inherent resistance to ideological demands. To recognize the impossibility of relating to the gaze as a present object in the cinema thus plays a crucial part in the struggle against the lure of fantasy. By constantly emphasizing the impossibility of the gaze as objet petit a, the nouvelle vague joins the project of struggling against the role that fantasy has in supplementing ideology.

The fidelity of the nouvelle vague to the path of desire becomes most apparent in the role that story plays in these films. Rather than creating films that follow a prescribed narrative trajectory, nouvelle vague films seem liberated from the structuring constraints of story. They stress instead the importance of contingency. A structured story regulates the desire that the act of narrative enunciation generates and offers a fantasmatic outlet for this desire. Story provides a way of organizing and directing desire, and this organizing of desire is precisely the activity of fantasy. Obviously, no narrative film can do without story—that is, without fantasy—altogether and remain a narrative film.

But the problem with story is that even if it concludes with a failed relation to the objet petit a, the very structure of story itself produces the object as a possibility rather than as an impossibility. Take, for instance, the heist film. Even—or perhaps especially—when the heist ends in failure, the heist story line suggests that the object of desire is a possible object (in the form of jewels or whatever object of the heist). Story suggests that there is a possible path to the resolution of desire—a way of ameliorating its fundamental deadlock. The very forward movement itself of story invokes the fantasy of escape from the repetition of desire. Though the stress on contingency in the nouvelle vague is in some sense illusory—a narrative filled with contingency remains the story of contingency—it nonetheless has the effect of depriving the spectator of scenarios in which the object seems approachable. Hence, the deemphasis on story in the films of the nouvelle vague has the effect of foregrounding the fundamental impossibility of the objet petit a.

François Truffaut's *Les quatre cents coups* (*400 Blows*, 1959) has a paradigmatic role in the nouvelle vague because it emphasizes the fundamental incompatibility between desire and the social order that generates that desire. The film depicts the fourteen-year-old Antoine Doinel (Jean-Pierre Léaud) as he gets into trouble with his parents and other social authority figures. Antoine's activity in the film centers around the desire of the Other: he is trying to act in a way that answers that desire, but it remains an impossible object for him. The opening credit sequence establishes the film's relationship to the objet petit a through its depiction of the Eiffel Tower. In many films (especially Hollywood films), the inclusion of the Eiffel Tower in a shot signifies Paris; it is a signifier with a clear signified, a signifier that clarifies meaning and setting. For Truffaut, it also serves as a signifier, but the opening credit sequence emphasizes the impossibility of sustaining a secure relationship with this signifier.

The first shot of *Les quatre cents coups* depicts the Eiffel Tower in the distance, and then, through a series of mobile shots, the camera circles the Eiffel Tower and keeps it relatively centered in the frame. Even when buildings block the camera's view of the Eiffel Tower, it continues to control the frame as an absent object (and it soon reappears when the moving camera passes the building that was blocking the view). After approaching in a circular fashion, the camera finally arrives almost directly below the landmark— just as Truffaut's name appears in the credits—but the camera continues to move as the image of the Eiffel Tower begins to recede. During the entire sequence, the camera is not able to successfully arrive at the Eiffel Tower or to establish a stable relationship with it. The best that it can do is to circulate in a tenuous path around this signifier and attempt to keep it in sight. This disjunction between the camera and the Eiffel Tower—between the subject and the signifier—creates the space in which the objet petit a emerges. The subject desires precisely because its relationship to the signifier is perpetually out of joint. Through the credit sequence, Truffaut makes clear that *Les quatre cents coups* will demand that the spectator take up the position of the desiring subject.

Through the character of Antoine, we see how desire originates in the fundamental, constitutive misunderstanding that occurs in the relationship between the subject and the social order. The adults that we see in the film single out Antoine as a thief and a troublemaker, and yet the film makes evident that this evaluation stems in large part from various misunderstandings. After the opening credit sequence, the film depicts the first glimpse of Antoine's brush with trouble and the role that misunderstanding plays in this encounter. We see a shot of a classroom in which the camera pans, following an erotic picture of a woman in a bathing suit as several boys stealthily pass it around. The teacher doesn't notice what the boys are doing until the moment when Antoine has the picture and attempts to pass it on. The teacher then singles him out and orders Antoine to stand in the corner, assuming—mistakenly—that Antoine is the source of the disruption of the class. Here, it is misunderstanding that constitutes the first relationship that we see between Antoine and the social order in which he exists.

Because the adult world misunderstands him and his intentions to such an extent, Antoine develops as a desiring subject. He is attuned to the lack in the Other—its failure to understand him—and this lack generates desire. To a greater extent than most children, Antoine sees what the Other lacks, and this absence propels him. No adult in the film is capable of properly responding to Antoine. This absence—this missing point in the Other—constitutes the subject of desire. As spectators, our desire emerges alongside Antoine's because we experience the lack in the Other at the moment he does.

In the final sequence of the film, Antoine escapes from the reform school he has been condemned to and begins to run. The camera follows his running through two extended tracking shots. The first follows him until he reaches a beach, and the second follows him as he runs toward the ocean after reaching the beach. The camera stops tracking alongside him when Antoine reaches the ocean, at which point he turns and looks back in the direction of the camera. We then see a freeze frame of Antoine looking as the camera zooms in to a close-up of his face, which closes the film. This final freeze frame suggests that Antoine's forward movement in the film has stopped, which seems also to suggest that desire itself has stopped. Here, *Les quatre cents coups* seems to abandon the logic of desire that has animated it throughout. But in fact, the turn away from movement at the end is in keeping with the overall mode of the film. If Truffaut had ended the film with Antoine still running, this might have indicated the continuing movement forward of desire, but it also would have betrayed an investment in a fantasmatic reprieve from desire. Fantasy does not simply provide an illusory scenario in which we can imagine the satisfaction of our desire; it also creates the illusion that desire is open to the future rather than locked in the movement of repetition. Truffaut interrupts the tracking shot of Antoine on the beach with a freeze frame, which suggests that desire does not confront an always open and ever-expanding future but turns back toward the past.

Even the decision to end Antoine's run and the film as a whole on the beach brings the idea of a limit to bear on the depiction of desire. We have seen that the social order itself cannot provide the object of desire for Antoine, but the image of the beach shows us that he cannot continue to move forward in a perpetual search for this object. The limiting quality of the beach indicates that this object is not simply absent, but structurally impossible. The concluding freeze frame of Antoine on the beach directly avows the impossible status of the objet petit a. By ending in this way, *Les quatre cents coups* underscores its recognition that desire circulates around this impossibility rather than continually moving forward toward a possibility. It reveals that possibility is a lure through which the social order seduces subjects into abandoning their desire for a fantasmatic reconciliation. The final freeze frame of Antoine encourages us to fight against this reconciliation.[1]

Truffaut's film contributes to the development of the cinema of desire both through both its form and its content. Like other films of the nouvelle vague, it emphasizes absence in the filmic content by the particular formal approach taken to this content. The very way that *Les quatre cents coups* depicts Antoine's refusal to reconcile himself to the social order makes evident the impossibility of this reconciliation. In this sense, Truffaut uses film form to underscore the desire engendered on the level of content, a move that other directors of the nouvelle vague would also make.[2]

Reconciliation is impossible because the object gaze exists beyond the Other's look at the subject. This is what dooms the project of seeking the Other's recognition. In seeking recognition, the subject is actually looking for the gaze, hoping to discover the gaze in the look of the Other. Subjects submit to the constraints of this look, striving in every way to meet its demands, in order to capture the gaze and thereby discover the secret of their own being. In this sense, submission to ideology stems from confounding the gaze with the look of the Other: no matter how well subjects comport themselves to the demands of this look, it will never see them in the way that they want to be seen, never look at them from the perspective of the gaze. No matter how fully the subject submits to the Other in order to gain recognition, this project is never successful. In *Cléo de 5 à 7* (1962), Agnès Varda depicts this failure through the character of Cléo (Corinne Marchand). The film makes clear how the Other's recognition fails to resolve the subject's relationship to the gaze, and it thus works to free us from the struggle for recognition.

The opening sequence of *Cléo de 5 à 7* reveals the irreducibility of the gaze to the Other by locating the gaze in a pack of tarot cards. Worried about possibly having stomach cancer, Cléo begins the film visiting a tarot-card reader. The film opens with a color shot looking directly down on a table where we see two pairs of hands, one of which is manipulating a deck of tarot cards. In this scene, Varda uses the opposition between color and black and white in order to make clear the impossible status of the gaze. Cléo desires to discover herself in the Other, to discover a point in the Other where the Other recognizes the truth of her being. But no one in the film is able to do this, which is why the entirety of the film, except for the opening shots of the cards themselves, is in black and white. Varda even shoots the tarot-card reader herself in black and white, which indicates that the cards see a truth that the reader herself does not. The cards shot in color represent the gaze: unlike the actual characters in the film, they see the truth of Cléo's being—her impending complete transformation. But of course tarot cards are inherently fanciful, and they cannot provide the assurance that the Other itself would. By opposing the tarot cards to the Other through the opposition of color and black and white film, Varda points toward the irreducibility of the gaze to the Other. The subject cannot find a fantasmatic resolution for desire because the Other cannot embody the gaze.

The majority of the film follows Cléo as she attempts to quiet the desire that a scheduled meeting with her doctor has prompted. Soon after the opening scene with the tarot-card reader, she enters a hat store and purchases a hat, and later she practices a new song with her song-writing team. Both of these activities leave her dissatisfied: the hat is not the perfect hat, and the song her partners have written for her is not the perfect song. Subsequently, she goes to a café where she plays one of her own songs on the jukebox, hoping to see the Other respond to her and her music in the way that she wants. Throughout this scene, Varda shoots Cléo walking among the different people in the café and looking for signs of recognition in their faces. But no one pays any attention to the music, except for one woman who complains about the excessive noise in the café. Just like the purchase of the hat and the practice session, Cléo's attempt to find respite from her desire in the café fails. She leaves the café even more alone with her desire than when she entered. The café scene once again emphasizes the inability of the subject to find the gaze through the recognition of the Other.

We desire because the Other never looks at us in the way that we want to be seen, and it is the failure of the Other to see us properly that sustains desire. As Lacan notes, "When . . . I solicit a look, what is profoundly unsatisfying and always missing is that—*You never look at me from the place from which I see you.*"[3] But rather than embrace this inherent antagonism of desire, we attempt to retreat from it into fantasy, trying to fantasize a way in which the Other's look—the look of recognition—and the gaze might coincide. It is the one of the main projects of the nouvelle vague to explode this fantasy and insist on the impossibility of the gaze as objet petit a, as the conclusion of *Cléo de 5 à 7* makes especially apparent.

The desire that underlies the entire film is Cléo's desire for her doctor's report. She hopes that her doctor will see her in the way that the tarot cards did: she wants him to identify the hidden kernel of her being—whether she will live or die. Cléo awaits this report throughout the film, and yet when it occurs, the encounter with the doctor, in contrast to that with the tarot cards, fails. When she arrives for her long-awaited appointment, Cléo learns that her doctor is out. When she finally does meet the doctor on the hospital grounds a few minutes later, this meeting is as unsuccessful as the earlier missed encounter. The doctor treats Cléo's condition and the treatment with nonchalance, telling her briefly that she will be fine after two months of treatment. He then quickly drives away.

This meeting with the doctor indicates the failure of Cléo's search for recognition even more decisively than the missed meeting. For Cléo, this meeting has a supreme importance because the doctor holds her fate in his hands. But the doctor's flippancy completely shatters Cléo's expectations, leaving her stuck in the position of the desiring subject. Varda suggests this through the way she depicts the doctor's departure and its aftermath. After the doctor drives away, Varda shoots a medium shot of Cléo and Antoine (Antoine Bourseiller), a man she met in the park. The camera then tracks away from Cléo and Antoine very rapidly, simulating the speed of the doctor's car and emphasizing the distance between the doctor's look and Cléo. Unlike the tarot cards, the doctor cannot see the truth of Cléo's being; Cléo is not important to him. After the rapid tracking shot, we see a closer shot of Cléo asking herself, "Pourquoi?" (Why?). Here, she expresses the shock of experiencing the failure of recognition. Throughout the entire film, she has sought the Other's recognition, but now she realizes that it will never provide her with what she wants. This realization frees Cléo from her dependence on the Other, and it reveals to the spectator the freedom that results from desire without its fantasmatic supplement.

The failure of the encounter with the doctor reveals to Cléo the impossible status of the objet petit a, and she quickly embraces this impossibility. Even the news that Antoine must return to his military unit the next day does not disappoint Cléo. She recognizes that she will never be able to successfully fantasize a resolution to her desire and that this recognition can be the source for her freedom. In the final moments of the film, Cléo tells herself, "Il me semble que je n'ai plus peur. Il me semble que je suis heureuse." (It seems to me that I am no longer afraid. It seems to me that I'm happy.) As the word "seems" suggests, Cléo continues to lack the certainty that she has lacked throughout the film, and yet this no longer bothers her. The film does not conclude with a return to the color photography of the opening, which means that Cléo has not discovered the gaze. But she has now embraced its absence.

This embrace of the gaze in its absence is not, as it might seem, a form of self-empowerment but a realization of the failure of power. This is the problem with Sandy Flitterman-Lewis's interpretation of Cléo's transformation. According to Flitterman-Lewis, "she ceases to be an object, constructed by the looks of men, and assumes the power of vision, a subjective vision of her own."[4] This way of seeing Cléo's transformation considers it in terms of the subjective look rather than the objective gaze. In doing so, it transforms the failure of the film's final scene into a success. And it is her failure to encounter the gaze, not her success, that frees Cléo. Rather than achieving power—"the power to direct her own life,"[5] as Flitterman-Lewis puts it— Varda shows Cléo freed from the seductions of power.

The end of *Cléo de 5 à 7* highlights the importance of recognizing the impossible status of the gaze.[6] In doing so, the subject frees herself from seeking the Other's recognition. As long as the Other seems to embody the gaze and hold the secret of the subject's being, it has power over the subject and leaves the subject in a state of unfreedom. With its emphasis on the impossibility of the gaze, the nouvelle vague points us in the direction of freedom by showing us the various failures of the Other to offer the subject what it wants.

13

The Banality of Orson Welles

ORSON WELLES CONTRIBUTES to the cinema of desire in a way that is very similar to the nouvelle vague. But Welles takes this cinema one step further through his treatment of the impossible object. By perpetually deferring the encounter with the object and stressing the filmic image's ultimate resistance to complete presence, the nouvelle vague thwarts the possibility for the fantasmatic resolution of desire. But it also risks creating the illusion that the satisfying object of desire does exist as a future possibility.

The very openness of the nouvelle vague relative to the gaze—its absolute refusal to depict the gaze as such—represents at the same time a potential openness to fantasy: one can still fantasize a scenario in which this absent object could become present.[1] This would be a misreading of these films, but it is the danger that accompanies their emphasis on openness. Herein lies the value of a cinema that renders the absence of the gaze present within the filmic image in order to underline its status as an impossible object. In this kind of film, the object of desire appears in the form of a banal object, thereby making clear that this object really is nothing. It is in the films of Orson Welles that we see again and again the object of desire in its full banality.

By depicting the object in this way, Welles enacts, *avant la lettre*, a Hegelian modification of the Kantianism of the nouvelle vague. The insistence of the nouvelle vague on the impossibility of the object follows Kant in his attitude toward transcendent objects. Kant devotes the Transcendental Dialectic of the *Critique of Pure Reason* to showing the impossibility of representing transcendent objects within a phenomenal field and revealing the tautologies and contradictions that inevitably result. If, for instance, one tries to prove logically the existence of God, one must have recourse to the ontological proof for the existence of God, which mistakenly establishes God's actual being on the basis of the idea of God. In this way, Kant establishes the limits of human understanding and representation. One cannot extend the operations of human understanding to objects—such as God or freedom—that lie outside the phenomenal field of appearances. Through the Transcendental Dialectic (which demonstrates our inability to prove the existence of these objects), Kant sustains them as sacrosanct. In doing so, he is trying to put an end to philosophical fantasizing about transcendent objects, to allow philosophy itself to hold fast to the path of desire and resist the lure of fantasy.

The problem with this procedure, according to Hegel, lies in the way that it deceives us into believing in the extramundane status of the transcendent object. The object is an impossible object; however, it is impossible not because it is out of reach but because it embodies nothing. Unlike Kant, Hegel accepts the ontological proof for the existence of God, with the caveat that God is nothing beyond the way that he manifests himself in the world. As he puts it in the greater *Logic*, "God, as the living God, and still more as absolute spirit, is known only in his *activity*; man was early instructed to recognize God in his *works*; only from these can proceed the *determinations*, which are called his properties, and in which, too, his *being* is contained."[2] Hegel's theism here stems from his rejection of any attempt to envision the ultimate object (God) as having an existence on a plane beyond our own. This marks his effort to correct the implicit danger he perceives in Kant's critical philosophy: by insisting on the impossibility of representing the object, Kant leaves the door open to fantasy just at the point at which he attempts to eliminate it from philosophy altogether. When the nouvelle vague sustains the gaze as an impossible object beyond the field of representation, it risks, like Kant, producing fantasies about the fullness of this object. The cinema of Orson Welles consistently allows us to see this object as the embodiment of nothing, thus forcing us to wrestle with its emptiness.

Given the cinema's resistance to desire and the deployment of absence, those who develop a cinema of desire often fit awkwardly within the world of film. This is true of no one more than Orson Welles, who, despite the near-universal acclaim that today surrounds his work, made only one film—his first, *Citizen Kane* (1941)—that was not damaged in some way by his tumultuous relationship with Hollywood.[3] Films structured around desire without the possibility of fantasmatic resolution tend to disturb audiences and, as a result, are often unpopular. On the one hand, desire draws us to such films, but on the other, we retreat from this desire and seek the assurances of fantasy. As Lacan points out in *Seminar VII*, no one ever has "a simple and unambiguous relationship to his wish. He rejects it, he censures it, he doesn't want it. Here we encounter the essential dimension of desire—it is always desire in the second degree, desire of desire."[4] The challenge that the cinema of desire presents is for spectators to embrace their desire, to opt for desire over the fantasmatic resolution of it.

Citizen Kane, like most of Welles's films, continually revolves around an impossible object (suggested by the signifier "Rosebud"). The film repeatedly brings the spectator close to an encounter with this object, but each time the encounter is missed. We see five different accounts of Kane's life, and each account adds elements to the total picture. But none can render the object visible: Kane's desire remains absent. The first account we see—the objective newsreel version of Kane's life in "News on the March"—is the most inadequate. By beginning with the newsreel, Welles emphasizes that an objective look can never see what is in Kane more than Kane, the objet petit a. But the film also makes clear the subsequent failure of every subjective perspective as well.

As spectators, we remain in a position of desire relative to Kane and his desire. The film offers us no anchoring point or way of securely positioning ourselves relative to the characters or events depicted. We encounter the limits of each perspective and thus have no clear way to direct our interpretation. The film leaves us desiring without resolution, though the end seems to offer some respite from our desire with the image of Kane's childhood sled with the name "Rosebud" being engulfed in flames. But here Welles does not solve the question of desire; he rather leaves us with its fundamental deadlock.

One must understand the precise nature of this deadlock. The perspicuity of *Citizen Kane* lies in the fact that it reveals that the gaze constantly eludes our grasp because it gives body to a void. The great secret of the Other—the Other's hidden enjoyment, the secret object-cause of desire that animates Kane—is that there is no secret. Which is to say, even the Other doesn't know what it wants. In this sense, the epigraph that Welles uses in *Mr. Arkadin* (1955) could apply to all of his films: "A certain great and powerful king once asked a poet, 'What can I give you, of all that I have?' He wisely replied, 'Anything sir . . . except your secret.'" Exposing the Other's secret reveals that the Other is hiding nothing—that desire merely circulates around a void. *Citizen Kane* avoids betraying the circulation of desire because it recognizes that there is no secret to the secret of the objet petit a.[5]

The mystery of "Rosebud" is important not in itself but for what it indicates about the role of desire in the film. It provides a structure for the film that places the spectator in the position of the desiring subject. According to Laura Mulvey, "While 'Rosebud' signifies 'the Kane mystery' within the story, Welles presents the spectator with a series of visual clues which transform the literal mystery into images on the screen. The enigmatic text that then gradually materialises appeals to an active, curious, spectator who takes pleasure in identifying, deciphering and interpreting signs."[6] The mystery of "Rosebud" allows Welles to create a filmic text that invites the spectator to probe its enigma. But the "Rosebud" mystery is not a conventional mystery; it is a mystery without a solution—in the same way that desire is a question that has no answer. There is no object that can prove adequate to the signifier "Rosebud," no object that can represent Kane's desire.[7] However, by attaching the childhood sled to the signifier "Rosebud" at the end of the film, Welles seems to suggest that ultimately one can in fact solve the enigma of the desire of the Other, that one can uncover the object of desire and look directly on the gaze.

When one experiences the revelation of the object of desire at the end of *Citizen Kane*, one must take care to resist two opposite temptations. On the one hand, one should avoid the commonsensical response of assuming that the sled explains everything about Kane's desire. According to this reading, all Kane desired was his mother, whom he lost in his youth as he gained as his fortune. All the money and objects that he amassed never compensated for this primordial loss. On the other hand, one should avoid completely dismissing the revelation that the image of the sled seems to promise. This is the reading advanced by D. N. Rodowick, who identifies the sled with the impossibility of ever representing *the* object.[8] For Rodowick (who is developing Deleuze's philosophy of the cinema in his book), the significance of the closing image of *Citizen Kane* lies in its distance from the object of desire, not in the answer it provides. Here, the point of the film's conclusion is that no object could ever finally end the quest to uncover the enigma of Kane's desire. The problem with both this reading and the commonsensical one is that they fail to grasp the nature of the objet petit a and its relationship to representation.

The concluding image of the sled in *Citizen Kane* identifies the gaze (the object-cause of Kane's desire) with an everyday object. In so doing, it doesn't domesticate the gaze in the manner of the typical Hollywood narrative, but instead renders its absence fully present. That is to say, in the image of the sled we see the void, the primordial emptiness, around which Kane's desire turns. An everyday object can, in part, embody the privileged objet petit a precisely because this object is nothing but a void. Hence, by stressing the banality of the object in the way that he does at the end of *Citizen Kane*, Welles exposes this void and demands that the spectator abandon the fantasy of an actual object that would satisfy desire. In this sense, the very insufficiency of the sled is to the point: the sled is an inadequate object—it doesn't provide a sense of completion or of total enjoyment—because every object of desire itself is inadequate. We invest this object with the promise of total enjoyment, but it inevitably betrays us and our investment in it. The fundamental emptiness of the object is what the conclusion of *Citizen Kane* attempts to make clear.[9] When we grasp and embrace this fundamental emptiness, we can desire without the idea of somehow escaping desire.

Welles's second film, *The Magnificent Ambersons* (1942), extends this treatment of the object to our images of the past. On one level, this is a film of nostalgia for a lost past. As Welles himself notes, "The basic intention was to portray a golden world—almost one of memory—and then show what it turns into. Having set up this dream town of the 'good old days,' the whole point was to show the automobile wrecking it—not only the family but the town."[10] Through its focus on the corrosive effects of the automobile and modernization, the film establishes the premodern past as the lost object and creates a desire for a return to the past. However, it embodies this desire (and the critique of modernization) in the figure of George Amberson Minafer (Tim Holt), which has the effect of exploding all the fantasies that we might associate with it.

Of all the characters in the film, George is by far the least likeable. He is arrogant, smug, and contrary; he treats those beneath him economically with contempt and refuses to work to earn a living.[11] In contrast, Eugene Morgan (Joseph Cotten), who introduces the automobile to the town, is one of the most likeable characters in the film. He is so good natured that he even accepts George's criticism of the automobile and agrees that it may be a destructive invention. And yet, the film associates its central desire with the unlikable George, not the likable Eugene. Though the film shows the damage done by the introduction of the automobile, it forces us to see our nostalgia for the preautomotive era represented in the unattractiveness of George. According to the logic of the film, George's aristocratic haughtiness and his disdain for work are not simply nostalgia's rough package, but rather something essential to the structure of nostalgic desire. He sustains the values of premodernity, and if we indulge in nostalgia for this lost epoch, *The Magnificent Ambersons* demands that we recognize the emptiness of this object as it manifests itself in a figure such as George. By embodying its nostalgia in George, the film works to deprive nostalgic desire of its support in nostalgic fantasies about the past. In this sense, it struggles against not so much the corrosive effects of modernization as those of the yearnings that modernization produces.

The Magnificent Ambersons also creates a desire to see George revenged. Throughout the film, we see George's arrogance and cruelty, but he really becomes detestable when, after the death of his father, he breaks up the impending marriage of his mother Isabel (Delores Costello) and her longtime admirer Eugene. This marriage would allow Isabel and Eugene to reunite and rekindle the love of their youth, which makes George's action all the more contemptible. Later, as Isabel lies on her deathbed, George goes so far as to deny Eugene access when he comes to see her, despite Isabel's desire to see him. As a result, the film creates a desire to see George punished for his actions, to see him receive his "comeuppance," as Welles's own voiceover narration in the film puts it.

Rather than leaving George's punishment as an impossible object, *The Magnificent Ambersons* depicts it. The end of the film shows George left penniless and alone, forced to do the work he once disdained in order to survive. George receives his comeuppance, but he receives it in a way that renders it empty and meaningless. As we see his destruction, the voiceover narration comments, "George Amberson Minafer had got his comeuppance. He got it three times filled and running over. But those who had so longed for it were not there to see it, and they never knew it. Those who were still living had forgotten all about it and all about him." The images of George's destitution and desperation in the last part of the film do not provide the enjoyment that we imagine they will. We fantasize an enjoyment that the missing object will deliver, but through forcing us to confront this object, the film reveals that this enjoyment is ultimately illusory. Even in satisfying our desire to see George receive his comeuppance we still must confront the emptiness of this object. As the film shows, to attain the object of our desire is to attain nothing.[12]

Of all Welles's films, *Touch of Evil* (1958) seems furthest removed from this project of desire. The noir characteristics of the film—the gritty border-town setting, the predominance of darkness, the larger-than-life figure of Hank Quinlan (Orson Welles), and so on—seem to suggest the excessive presence of the gaze and enjoyment rather than their absence. However, Welles is able to construct a film of desire despite all the characteristics of the noir universe that seem to work against it. He does this by using the predictability of noir to expose the monotony of desire when deprived of its fantasmatic supplement. Difference functions as a fantasy that accompanies our desire and spurs it forward. It is the basis for our sense of hope that we can discover a new object. But *Touch of Evil* thwarts this hope and our anticipation of difference. In this way, the film reveals the fundamental monotony of the path of desire.

The famous three-minute-and-twenty-second tracking shot that opens *Touch of Evil* establishes the central role that desire will play in the film. The shot begins with someone—we learn later it is Mañelo Sanchez (Victor Millan)—placing a bomb in the trunk of a car. As a couple begins to drive the car, the camera tracks its movement, though the car continually moves in and out of the frame. Soon after the car begins to move, we see a couple—the newly married Mike Vargas (Charlton Heston) and Susan Vargas (Janet Leigh)—walking alongside it. Once Mike and Susan enter the frame, the camera follows them rather than the car. At first, it slows to focus on them while the car moves ahead, and then, when goats in the road stop the progress of the car, the camera follows the couple as they move ahead of the car. This constant misalignment of the camera's attention and the central object (the car with the bomb in the trunk) points toward the attitude of desire that the film attempts to establish. The camera cannot simply follow its object but instead continually misses it, just as desire encircles its object without ever arriving at it. When the bomb finally goes off, the explosion occurs offscreen, as the camera closes in on Mike and Susan as they begin to kiss. Just after their lips meet, we hear the explosion, and this occasions the first cut in the film to a shot of the car in flames. Even though the entire tracking shot builds up to the explosion, we are unable to see it. The object itself must remain impossible in order to remain *the* object.

And yet, the explosion that concludes the opening tracking shot is not at all unexpected. We see the bomb placed in the car, and we watch the progress of the car knowing that it contains this bomb. But precisely because this is what we see, we also believe that some force may intervene to stop the impending explosion. We desire while watching this scene, but we also fantasize that the explosion will somehow be averted. Fantasy here is the fantasy of an alternate future, but *Touch of Evil* refuses to offer us any fantasmatic alternatives. Instead, the film follows our desire to its logical conclusion.

Throughout *Touch of Evil*, Welles shows that desire does not involve mystery. In fact, an investment in mystery represents a fantasmatic compromise of our desire. The objet petit a is not a mysterious object that we can never locate but a banal object that represents the emptiness around which desire circulates. The central desire for the spectator in the film involves the character of Hank Quinlan and his act of framing Mañelo Sanchez. Part of the reason we desire to see Quinlan exposed is that we want to see justice done and not see an innocent person be framed for a crime he didn't commit. But in the denouement of the film we find out that Quinlan actually framed the guilty man, which strips us of our belief that we might attain satisfaction through seeing "justice" done—precisely the fantasy that the vast majority of detective films proffer. If the exposure of Quinlan doesn't lead to anyone being exonerated, then this act loses much of its power to satisfy us on a fantasmatic level. Fantasy tries to convince us that desire can find satisfaction through finding its elusive object, but *Touch of Evil* reveals that there is no such object just beyond our reach. It shows us this object is not elusive but simply absent.

One of the great lures for the desiring subject is the image of an unapproachable object of desire, an object that possesses such riches that we cannot come near it. This image of the object of desire is every bit as fantasmatic as the reduction of the object of desire to the status of an empirical object that one can obtain. In fact, the former represents a greater danger insofar as its fantasmatic dimension is less evident. The films of Orson Welles disabuse us of this fantasmatic deception, demanding that we recognize the emptiness of the object where we anticipate its richness.[13] In this way, they allow us to desire for the sake of desiring itself rather than in anticipation of satisfaction. Welles's films encourage the subject to enjoy its desire rather than look for a way out of it. Desire involves lack, but lack can become a source of enjoyment for the subject rather than only representing a barrier to enjoyment. Through the cinema of desire, we can discover this mode of enjoying.

14

Claire Denis and the Other's Failure to Enjoy

THE PATH OF desire provides a certain enjoyment for the subject, and this is the enjoyment that Orson Welles's films champion. But the limitation of the enjoyment we find in the path of desire is its partiality. It is an enjoyment that acknowledges and embraces lack. Complete enjoyment almost always tends to look more attractive, especially when we see an image of the other appearing to enjoy itself completely. The films of Claire Denis contribute to the cinema of desire through their attempt to break the hold that this image has over us as subjects. They work to demolish fantasy at precisely the point of its greatest power over us—the image that fantasy provides of the enjoying other. The seductive dimension of fantasy is not visible in the films of the nouvelle vague or of Welles because of their stricter adherence to the constitutive absence of the gaze. Denis's films first show us what its illusory presence looks like in order to underline its status as absent and thus undermine fantasy's power over us.

Through fantasy, a subject does not experience its own enjoyment but experiences an imaginary enjoyment through fantasizing about the enjoying other. As Slavoj Žižek puts it in the *The Plague of Fantasies*, "Fantasy provides a *rationale* for the inherent deadlock of desire: it constructs the scene in which the *jouissance* we are deprived of is concentrated in the Other who stole it from us."[1] Because fantasy necessarily attributes our own enjoyment to the other, there is always a paranoid dimension to fantasy: underlying the typical fantasy scenario is the idea that the other enjoys in our stead because of a secret knowledge that she/he has illicitly obtained. The inherent paranoia of fantasy represents one of its chief dangers for the subject; it is one of the most difficult obstacles for the subject to overcome, simply because the subject rarely experiences the other's lack or failure to enjoy, which would contradict it. This paranoia also leads to racism, sexism, homophobia, and so on. We fantasize enjoyment in the other, and then we want to destroy it because this enjoyment often appears to come at our expense. But the image of complete enjoyment we see in the other is our own fantasmatic image, and when we invest ourselves in it, we miss the enjoyment that we can derive from the path of desire.

Through her films, Claire Denis both establishes and subsequently tears down the image of the enjoying other. She shows the power of this image and, subsequently, its ultimate illusoriness. Just as Welles shows the ultimate emptiness of the object of desire, Denis reveals the lack that exists where we posit enjoyment in the other, though she goes further than Welles in depicting its initial illusory fullness. For instance, *S'en fout la mort* (*No Fear, No Die*, 1990) reveals the absence of enjoyment in the underworld of Parisian cockfighting, a location that we would expect to be full of transgression and illicit enjoyment. Instead of producing the ultimate enjoyment, this underworld produces nothing but ennui in the film. By exposing this, Denis pushes us away from the lure of fantasy and back toward the path of desire.[2]

Denis's first feature, *Chocolat* (1988), depicts the return of France Dalens (Mireille Perrier) to Cameroon, where she lived as a young girl. Though she never states the reason for her return, it is clear that France hopes to rediscover a lost enjoyment that she associates with her childhood here. On this return trip, she carries her father's journal from their stay, which contains pictures of the landscape that he drew, and she looks at the contemporary landscape through these images. France's desire to recapture the lost enjoyment that she associates with Africa manifests itself in the flashback to her childhood here. This flashback takes up most of the film's running time, and it emphasizes the extent to which the fantasy of the enjoying other underlies the relationship between France and Africa.

The flashback section of *Chocolat* deals with the desire of France's mother Aimée (Giulia Boschi) for her African servant Protée (Isaach De Bankolé). Aimée desires Protée because she fantasizes an exoticness in him that her husband—an unexciting French colonialist—lacks. Eventually, her desire becomes so unbearable that she even has Protée banished from the house and sent to work in the garage. Unlike Aimée, the spectator sees beyond the fantasmatic image of Protée because Denis reveals the pain and humiliation that Protée suffers precisely at the point where Aimée sees his body at its most exotic. This becomes apparent when Aimée sees Protée takes a shower outside. Denis shoots this scene with a long shot of Protée, a shot that allows us to see in the background the arrival of Aimée and France. Aimée looks at Protée's naked body desirously, but as Protée hears her voice and realizes that Aimée has seen him, Denis registers the lack that Protée experiences here. The camera pans from a long shot of Aimée and France to Protée, and it simultaneously tracks to a close-up of him. The close-up captures the agony on his face, and a longer shot shows him beat his elbow against the wall in response to the humiliation. This brief scene communicates the overriding idea of the entire flashback section of the film: where the French-woman Aimée sees the ultimate enjoyment in the African Protée, Protée actually experiences humiliation and pain. In this sense, *Chocolat* represents Denis's attempt to explode the predominant European fantasy of Africa as a place where enjoyment flows naturally and repression does not exist.[3]

This is not to say that there is no enjoyment in Africa or that Protée never enjoys himself. Nor is the point that no Frenchwoman could possibly understand his mode of enjoyment. Instead, Denis's film stresses the partial nature of his enjoyment. Rather than escaping lack altogether, Protée's enjoyment has its basis in lack. This is what Aimée's fantasy—and all fantasies of exotic otherness—refuse to recognize. To acknowledge the lack in the other would be to abandon the image of a nonlacking, complete enjoyment. It would mean acknowledging that the other is in precisely the same boat as the subject when it comes to enjoyment, and this recognition is such anathema to the subject that it constructs a fantasy in order to sustain the nonlacking image of the other.

At the close of the flashback section, Protée attempts to show France the link between suffering and enjoyment. While he is working on the power generator, France approaches him and asks if a pipe is too hot to be touched. Through a close-up of his hand, we see Protée grab the pipe without speaking, indicating that one can touch it. However, when France places her hand on the pipe, it burns her. After France runs away in pain, Denis shows Protée's burned hand in close-up, taking note of his suffering. Rather than being a sadistic act or even an act of revenge against French colonialism, Protée's act here involves inviting France to experience his lack in a way that her mother never did. In this sense, the act sums up the flashback section of the film as it deprives Aimée's fantasy of the image of Protée's perfect body that sustains it. As Denis shows here, the enjoying body is necessarily a damaged body, not a complete or a natural one. When we recognize this, we free ourselves from the fantasy of the other's exotic and ultimate enjoyment.

The frame narrative concludes by moving beyond the character of France in order to challenge further the fantasy of Africa as a site of exotic enjoyment.[4] Mungo Park (Emmet Judson), a man whom France meets at the beginning of the film, relates his disappointment with Africa when he arrived as an African American émigré. Expecting to find home, he instead discovers a place in which he feels completely alienated. As he tells France, "Ici, je suis rien." (Here, I'm nothing.) Mungo comes to Africa expecting that it, unlike America, will allow him to escape the dissatisfaction of desire. His disappointment stems from the dissolution of this fantasy, a dissolution that compels him to remain in the position of the desiring subject. Just as the film demonstrates the lack in Protée that Aimée's fantasy fails to register, it also depicts Africa itself as a site of lack. Rather than embodying the elusive enjoyment of the gaze qua objet petit a, the Africa of *Chocolat* embodies its absence. When we recognize this absence—when we recognize the gaze as an absent object—we sustain the path of desire and resist the lure of fantasy.

This is the direction in which *Chocolat* points us, a direction that becomes even clearer in Denis's *J'ai pas sommeil* (*I Can't Sleep*, 1994). This film begins with a depiction of enjoyment that seems to have no narrative connection to the rest of the events in the film. After first just hearing laughter over a blank screen, we see two police officers laughing loudly while flying in a police helicopter over Paris. The film never explicitly refers back to this scene, and yet this show of enjoyment establishes the tone of the film that follows. The Paris that Denis depicts is a world in which enjoyment seems to proliferate everywhere, and yet on no occasion do the main characters in the film seem to enjoy themselves. They remain stuck in the position of the desiring subject despite existing in a world that bombards them with images of enjoyment.

The three primary characters in the film—Daïga (Yekaterina Golubeva), Camille (Richard Courcet), and Théo (Alex Descas)—all evince a sense of dissatisfaction that stems from their encounter with an enjoyment that they cannot access. The film follows Daïga's arrival in Paris from Lithuania, Théo's preparations to leave Paris for Martinique, and Camille's experiences as a transvestite dancer in the gay subculture of Paris. The dissatisfaction of all three manifests itself most conspicuously in the minimalism with which the actors play each character. At the same time, the predominance of scenes and images of enjoyment leave these characters feeling as if the ultimate enjoyment that others are experiencing is eluding them. As a result, they lash out with violence or resort to fantasy in order to discover this enjoyment for themselves. These paths fail because they succumb to the lure of an ultimate enjoyment or an enjoyment that doesn't lack anything, and it is through this lure that Paris—and global capitalism in general—seduces subjects.

Through its depiction of their failure, however, Denis's film reveals both the illusory nature of the image of ultimate enjoyment and the depth of its power over us. The film illustrates that there is no outside—no space beyond the world of dissatisfaction and lack—but this doesn't mean that we cannot enjoy. When we succumb to the image of an ultimate enjoyment that we lack, we miss the partial enjoyment that is accessible for us. In this sense, Denis here shows a path for desire that avoids the lure of fantasmatic images of the enjoying other. We can derive enjoyment from partial objects, objects that do not promise us completion.[5] But when the idea of a whole or an ultimate enjoyment has a hold on us, the possibility for this kind of partial enjoyment recedes.

All three main characters are outsiders in Paris (Daïga from Lithuania, Camille and Théo from Martinique), and this outsider status exacerbates their sense of missing the enjoyment that Paris contains. For instance, excessive enjoyment bombards Daïga during a sequence in which she is walking through the streets of Paris when a stranger accosts her and makes sexual advances. In her attempt to flee from him, she enters a movie theater. She soon discovers that this is a porn theater and that her flight from excessive enjoyment has led her into more. Here, enjoyment seems inescapable, and at the same time, it remains the enjoyment of the other.

It is this encounter with the enjoyment of the other that drives the actions of the main characters in the film. For instance, Théo's plan to go to Martinique derives from his fantasy that he can access there the kind of enjoyment that he sees but can't experience in Paris. He imagines a Martinique where everything is there for the taking, where one has no need for money or even clothes. Rather than fantasizing about Martinique as his brother Théo does, Camille reacts to the ubiquitous enjoyment with violence. Violence offers the subject a way of enjoying at the same time as it wipes out the enjoyment of the other. This is why it is so attractive for subjects who feel themselves on the outside of enjoyment. Both of these solutions, however, fail in the end because they remain blind to the illusoriness of any ultimate enjoyment.

Throughout *J'ai pas sommeil*, we are continually confronted with the illusion of an unrestrained, ubiquitous enjoyment, but in each encounter with this enjoyment, the film goes on to show its limits and its partiality—its incompleteness. Denis accomplishes this on a formal level through her use of sound and editing, as we see, for instance, in the scene just after the opening in the police helicopter. The camera tracks Daïga's car as she is driving into Paris while seemingly nondiegetic music plays over the credits. However, a subsequent shot inside the car depicts Daïga turning off her cassette player, which stops the music and thereby locates it within the diegesis. This shift indicates the partiality and localized nature of an enjoyment that first seemed unbound by any spatial restriction. While presenting music as initially nondiegetic and then revealing it to be diegetic is not wholly uncommon within contemporary cinema, here it relates to the fundamental structure of the film itself, which constantly emphasizes the partiality of enjoyment. Just as there is no ubiquitous music, there is no full or complete enjoyment (though there is the illusion of it). By exposing the illusory status of complete enjoyment in this way, Denis's films allow us to see the possibilities for enjoyment within the path of desire itself rather than within fantasy. The enjoyment linked to the path of desire remains partial: one enjoys the partiality of the objet petit a—the not having it as much as the having it.

This also becomes evident formally toward the end of the film just before the police apprehend Camille. A lengthy tracking shot follows Camille as he leaves a club and walks down a Paris street. As the camera follows Camille, it seems connected to no particular point of view. However, just after the tracking shot of Camille, Denis reverses the camera and allows us to see that a police car is driving slowly down the road and following Camille. The subsequent shot places the earlier tracking shot in relief, allowing us to understand that what seemed an objective tracking shot was actually a point of view shot from the perspective of the police. As with Denis's use of sound at the beginning of the film, this subjectivization of a seemingly objective shot occurs regularly in cinema, but here it emerges directly out of the filmic content. By attaching a seemingly objective shot to a point of view, Denis stresses the impossibility of an all-seeing look. The illusion of seeing without a localized perspective supports the fantasy of an unlimited enjoyment, and this is precisely what *J'ai pas sommeil* combats.

Denis's film leaves spectators in the same position as the characters in the film relative to enjoyment. Traditional Hollywood films—and especially mystery films—establish spectators in a position of desire with the promise of a denouement that will completely satisfy that desire: one lacks knowledge of the killer's identity, and the film's conclusion provides that knowledge and thereby delivers satisfaction. But *J'ai pas sommeil* does not regulate desire in this way. Instead, Denis creates a film with a trajectory that clearly rejects the fantasy of an ultimate enjoyment that the typical conclusion of a filmic narrative implies.

The film establishes a mystery surrounding the identity of the granny killer—a serial killer operating in Paris who targets old women—but does not present the solution as a way of quenching our desire. The spectator learns just over halfway into the film that Camille is the granny killer. This revelation comes without any buildup or suspense: the very matter-of-fact mode of the revelation—we simply see Camille and his lover in the midst of the criminal act—destroys any sense that it might provide satisfaction. The narrative trajectory of the film neither hints at a satisfying resolution nor delivers it.

The peripheral status of the mystery throughout the film further impairs our ability to fantasize about its solution. At no point prior to the depiction of Camille's guilt does the film explore directly the mystery or the main characters' involvement in it. Instead, we first hear about the mystery of the granny killer on the radio; then we see a newspaper headline about it and hear people discussing it. The mystery unites all of the different threads of the film together, and yet the ordinary events in the lives of the characters—Daïga looking for a place to stay, Camille dancing, Théo installing bookshelves—entirely overshadow it. By consigning the mystery of the granny killer to a peripheral status in the structure of the film, Denis implicitly cautions the viewer against expecting a satisfying resolution to our desire. The emphasis in the film is on desire itself rather than on the idea of its resolution in a moment of ultimate enjoyment.

The absence of any ultimate enjoyment becomes clearest in the way that the film characterizes Camille and his killings. Typically, cinema represents serial killers as enjoying themselves too much, as enjoying without any restraint. Killing provides the serial killer with the kind of horrible enjoyment that law-abiding citizens necessarily lack. This becomes most evident with a figure such as Hannibal Lecter in Jonathan Demme's *Silence of the Lambs* (1991), for whom eating his victims is a mode of the ultimate transgressive enjoyment. When watching Lecter on the screen, it is difficult not to love him for his seemingly unrestrained ability to enjoy himself. Camille, however, is completely unlike Hannibal Lecter. Rather than deriving extraordinary enjoyment from killing, he kills with the same sense of boredom that he lives the rest of his life.

The first time we see Camille attack an old woman, his partner knocks the woman to the floor just inside her apartment, and Camille removes his belt and strangles her with it. Camille performs this act disinterestedly, and Denis depicts the act through a long shot, which adds to the lack of enjoyment in the scene. Even the act of killing does not allow Camille to access the enjoyment that he feels himself to be missing. In fact, he is so uninvolved with his own act that he leaves the old woman alive, which allows the police to identify him. Even where we might imagine the ultimate transgressive enjoyment, *J'ai pas sommeil* depicts ordinariness.

Daïga, Théo, and Camille all believe in another place or another mode of existence that would deliver them entirely from this dissatisfaction, but this fantasy is what sustains their dissatisfaction. The recognition that there is no ultimate enjoyment does not imply that one must adapt to prevailing social forces and give up desire for the sake of the reality principle. In fact, the fantasy of an ultimate enjoyment beyond the symbolic structure is precisely what allows subjects to exist within the drabness of ordinary reality. By offering the illusion of another place or another time of full enjoyment, this fantasy encourages adjustment to current social conditions.

Through the brief connection that develops between Daïga and Camille, Denis indicates the kind of enjoyment that is possible—a partial enjoyment, an enjoyment of a partial object, an enjoyment of one's desire. After learning that Camille is the granny killer, Daïga follows him from the hotel to a café. At the café, she stands next to him at the counter and orders a coffee. When Camille passes her the sugar for her coffee, we see a close-up of their hands, which for a brief moment touch and remain together. After each quickly pulls away, Camille evinces a very slight smile and then tells the clerk that he will pay for Daïga's cup of coffee. But even in this moment of ostensible connection, Denis emphasizes the barrier that exists between them: when Camille leans forward to speak to the clerk, we see Camille and Daïga separated by a post. Here, the two characters are able to have a moment of enjoyment, but Denis uses the mise-en-scène in this scene to underline its partiality.

Through its sustained insistence on the inherent partiality of enjoyment, *J'ai pas sommeil* offers a path that avoids the dissatisfaction that seems always to accompany desire. This is a path that always remains open to the subject. There is no object that can satisfy desire—no ultimate enjoyment—but one can find satisfaction through desire itself and its partial object. The key to being able to enjoy one's desire lies in accepting the inherent partiality of enjoyment, and this is what the cinema of desire as a whole—and the films of Claire Denis in particular—encourage us to do. This cinema pushes us toward a kind of enjoyment, the enjoyment of desire, that most of us miss because of our turn to fantasy. To succumb to ideological fantasies is also to invest oneself in paranoia about the other, and this paranoia represents a barrier to becoming a political subject insofar as it transforms every other subject into a rival in enjoyment. Rather than enter into the political arena, one retreats into the shell of the ego (in order to safeguard one's own enjoyment from the other). It is this turn away from politicization that the cinema of desire struggles against.

15

Political Desire in Italian Neorealism

DESIRE ALWAYS HAS an incipient political dimension, though often in film this political dimension remains barely visible. Films tend to depict desire as a force that transcends rather than energizes political activity. Partially as a result of this practice, we tend to think of desire and political activity in opposed terms: desire is private, whereas political struggle is public. According to this schema, one's desire can run in the opposite direction from and actually transcend one's politics.[1] While this view attests to the power that we accord desire, it misses the role that desire has in energizing political struggle. Italian neorealism functions as a corrective. It develops the cinema of desire in the political direction that the nouvelle vague, Welles, and Denis only hint at, and it does this by showing the failure of fantasy to a greater extent than these other films.

Italian neorealism emphasizes the link between desire and political activity because it focuses on the oppressive societal conditions that generate the sense of dissatisfaction that is desire. Unlike the standard Hollywood film, the Italian neorealist film does not depict desiring subjects as isolated individuals, but as subjects implicated in the concrete struggles of their historical moment. The point is not that these films envision a collective subject—though they sometimes do—but that they show the effects of the social order itself on individual subjects. This is why Italian neorealism so often involves the Resistance movement. The Resistance film allows neorealism to emphasize the conditions against which the desiring subject struggles. For the neorealist film, desire always exists within a politicized context, even when political activity is not its explicit subject matter.

Italian neorealism also develops a narrative form in which desire continues without fantasmatic resolution. At each point where we discover some fantasmatic resolution to the desire that the filmic narrative creates, the neorealist

107

film undermines this resolution by creating another complication. The neorealist film forces us to continue to desire because it shows us the impossibility of
a successful resolution of desire.[2] Though neorealism situates desire within a
clearly defined political context, it does not offer the fantasy of a political resolution to desire, as we might expect from an explicitly politicized kind of filmmaking.[3] In this way, the neorealist film calls us toward a form of political
activity that refuses the sense of security that fantasy provides for the subject
and accepts the necessity of antagonism. By adopting this kind of political position, one can engage in political activity without believing that one can heal
the social order entirely. It is a form of politics that highlights and preserves the
existential isolation—and thus the freedom—of the subject. The subject politicized in this way struggles against injustice but also recognizes the necessity of
a certain ontological injustice.

In *Roma, città aperta* (*Rome: Open City*, 1945), Roberto Rossellini works
to develop the political subject constituted through the refusal of fantasmatic
reconciliation. Rossellini structures the film around the absence of the gaze,
and this absence prevents us from being able to arrest the movement of
desire. The film never makes clear what it wants from the spectator. It is never
clear precisely where we are supposed to direct our desire, and as a result, our
desire cannot find any stability or security. In this way, the film keeps desire
alive and does not permit its resolution in fantasy. While watching *Roma, città
aperta* we experience the deadlock of desire—the inability to discover
precisely what we want—and we see the connection between desire and the
political struggle that the film depicts.

The most obvious way in which the film sustains desire lies in its use of
multiple protagonists—all of whom it links to the resistance against fascist
rule. The beginning of the film follows Pina (Anna Magnani) until the Germans shoot her down. Then Giorgio Manfredi (Marcello Pagliero) dominates
the film until he dies as a result of German torture. And finally, the last third
of the film focuses on the priest Don Pietro (Aldo Fabrizi). But even as the
film concludes with Don Pietro's execution, it shifts attention away from him
and to a group of young boys who have watched the execution and are now
walking back to Rome. It is not that the film has no protagonist, but that it
creates a series of protagonists. Perhaps no film goes as far as Rossellini's in
establishing a character as the protagonist and then killing the character off.
Though Hitchcock does this with Marion (Janet Leigh) in *Psycho* (1960),
Rossellini actually repeats this gesture three times in *Roma, città aperta*, and
as a result the spectator's desire cannot rest with one character.

The film also sustains desire by continually disrupting the resolutions
that it seems to offer. These disruptions are the formal expression of the
film's sympathy with the Italian Resistance in specific and with resistance to
fascism in general. Fascism is itself a fantasy formation that envisions over-
coming the antagonism that motivates desire. Specifically, fascism offers the
subject an image of society that reconciles the advantages of modernity (tech-

nology, social structure, and so on) with the stability of traditional society (especially the connection to "blood and soil"). Within the fascist fantasy, there is no contradiction between modernization and sustaining tradition because it attributes all the social disruption that stems from modernization to the force that is contaminating the society (most often, the figure of the Jew). The resistance that *Roma, città aperta* depicts and evokes depends on the refusal to find satisfaction in the fascist fantasy.

This becomes apparent in the sequence that surrounds the death of Pina, a sequence that moves forward directly through the thwarting of fantasmatic resolution. At the beginning of this sequence, we see the Germans searching Pina's apartment building in order to find Giorgio and Francesco (Francesco Grandjacquet), who are hiding there. Giorgio and Francesco escape through a window into a hidden corridor. In a long shot, we see them escaping down the corridor in the background, while in the foreground a German soldier places his head into the corridor, looking for them in the other direction. As the shot indicates, if the soldier had turned his head in the opposite direction in order to see what we can see, he would have seen the fugitives. After this escape, Don Pietro arrives and informs the Germans that he has come to attend to a sick old man who remains in the building. He proceeds to the roof in order to encourage a boy who has a bomb to leave the building so that the Germans won't kill him. While waiting for Don Pietro, the German leader outside grows suspicious and enters the building in search of Don Pietro and the old man. At this point, the spectator expects to see Don Pietro's lie discovered and the boy apprehended. But it turns out that there really is an old man in the building, and Don Pietro goes to his room. Unable to convince the man to play along with the masquerade, Don Pietro is forced to knock him out with a frying pan, and then he pretends to give him last rites when the German soliders arrive. After arousing the spectator's desire concerning the fates of Giorgio and Francesco, and subsequently the fate of Don Pietro, the film seems to conclude the sequence and offer relief from desire with this comic moment in which Don Pietro completely averted danger with the aid of a frying pan. However, it is precisely at this point—when the film seems to have effected some resolution for our desire—that Rossellini propels our desire forward once again.

The death of Pina follows directly on the respite of the last-rites scene. Unlike the rest of the film (which consists primarily of long takes), Rossellini shoots Pina's death in a rapid montage sequence: there are two quick shots of her running after the truck carrying Francesco, a shot of Don Pietro comforting her son, Marcello, and then a shot of Francesco looking from the back of the truck. During the latter, we hear the sound of machine-gun fire, and a reverse shot of Pina reveals her collapsing on the ground. Pina's death upsets the movement of the narrative not only because she seemed to be, up to this point, the film's protagonist, but also because it directly follows the comic scene involving Don Pietro and the old man. As Peter Bondanella says, "This tragedy is

introduced by a slapstick comic scene worthy of the best vaudevillian tradi-
tions."[4] This rapid alternation of the comic and the tragic in the film sustains
the spectator in the troubled position of the desiring subject. The scene following Pina's death sequence furthers the sense of disruption when we see the Resistance rescue the prisoners (including Francesco and Giorgio) who had just
been captured. At the precise point where the film seems to arrest the movement of desire, it undermines the proffered resolution and reenergizes desire.
Absence in the narrative never becomes a stable absence that might allow the
spectator to escape the deadlock of desire. By leaving the spectator in this
position, Rossellini's film calls her/him to a politicized subjectivity.

    Roma, cittá aperta constitutes the spectator in a position of desire relative
to the fantasmatic inducements of fascism. Later neorealist films, such as
Ladri di biciclette (*Bicycle Thieves*, Vittorio de Sica, 1948), *La Terra trema*
(*The Earth Trembles*, Luchino Visconti, 1948), and *Riso amaro* (*Bitter Rice*,
Giuseppe de Santis, 1949), depict the fantasies of capitalism rather than those
of fascism as the primary danger. These films continue and develop neorealism's insistence on desire as a political position, and they ground desire in the
concrete political context of postwar Italian capitalism. In this context, the fantasy that seduces the subject away from the path of desire is that of individual
difference, of finding an object that will lift the subject out of the oppressive
situation of the masses in general. As these films make clear, this fantasy is essential to the functioning of capitalist ideology because it prevents the subject
from entering into a collective opposition to capitalism.

    In *Ladri di biciclette*, de Sica continually links the situation of the main
character, Antonio Ricci (Lamberto Maggiorani), to other members of the
working class. Antonio is not alone, despite his fantasy of elevating himself
above his peers. The film reveals Antonio's sense of his own exceptionalism
from its very opening: other workers are clamoring to hear their names called
for jobs while he sits across the street not paying attention to the job an-
nouncements (despite his eagerness for a job). In fact, he only learns about
the job when a friend comes running to tell him. But when Antonio obtains
the job, he convinces himself that he will pull himself above the crowd. Later,
we see this fantasy of exceptionalism remaining intact even after the loss of
his bicycle (and thus the job) when he is eating at a restaurant with his son,
Bruno (Enzo Staiola). Antonio fantasizes about having a job that would pay
enough to allow him to afford the opulent meal that he sees people eating at
a nearby table. For Antonio, escape from poverty is always an individualized
and private project. But in the face of Antonio's individualist fantasy, the film
highlights his ordinariness, the link between him and the other impoverished
people we see in the film.

    Antonio's kinship with the other members of his class becomes appar-
ent when he visits the pawnshop to pawn the family sheets and retrieve his
bicycle. After Antonio has pawned the sheets and is in the process of picking
up the bicycle, the camera pans, following the worker who is in the process of

storing the sheets. We see him climb a storage area several stories high, in which there are thousands of sheets that people have pawned. This pan does not advance the narrative movement of the film, but de Sica includes it in order to show that Antonio is not at all exceptional in the way that he fantasizes.[5] De Sica turns from narrative progression to social exposition in order to illustrate the illusory status of the individualist fantasy that leads the subject away from the path of desire and the possibility of politicized activity.

Ladri di biciclette pushes us in the direction of this politicization because it reveals the failure of capitalism to deliver the object that its fantasies promise.[6] After it has been stolen, the bicycle comes to function as the impossible object in the film, an object whose impossible status underscores capitalism's failure. De Sica emphasizes that the impossibility of the object stems not from its scarcity but from our inability to distinguish our particular object. That is to say, capitalism offers the subject the fantasy of the individualized object—the object that is one's own and that one can own—and at the same time, capitalism works, as a mode of production, to eliminate all difference between objects. In this sense, it becomes impossible to own *the* object. Hence, capitalism itself renders its own individualistic fantasy impossible.[7] This becomes most apparent in *Ladri di biciclette* when Antonio enlists the help of his friends to search for his stolen bicycle.

The day after the theft, Antonio and his friends go to the market where bicycles are sold in order to find Antonio's. As they walk amid the many vendors, de Sica shoots a series of tracking shots that reveal hundreds of indistinguishable bicycles that vendors are selling. Here, the tracking shot communicates the multitude and the similarity of the objects that the group must search through. The way that de Sica shoots this scene—depicting bicycle after bicycle—reveals the impossibility of isolating one particular object from the many. In addition, Antonio also learns that stolen bicycles are often sold in pieces, so that the group must identify the individual pieces of the Antonio's bicycle rather than the object as a whole. Such a task is impossible because its object is impossible: within the capitalist world that the film depicts, one cannot distinguish one's own privileged object from any other object. As a result, the subject cannot live out capitalism's individualist fantasy within the world that capitalism creates. It is this contradiction that *Ladri di biciclette* highlights.

For the subject who succumbs to it, capitalism's individualist fantasy transforms a political situation into a purely economic one. This is what befalls Antonio. He invests himself in this fantasy right up until his final act of the film, when he attempts to steal a bicycle to replace his own. This act indicates that Antonio remains within the capitalist fantasy, but as the film concludes, de Sica emphasizes—for the spectator, if not for Antonio—the illusoriness of this fantasy. After the owner of the bicycle declines to press charges against Antonio, de Sica ends the film with a shot of Antonio and Bruno disappearing into a mass of people as they walk away from the camera. This concluding shot shows that Antonio has not raised himself above the crowd, but in fact merges into it. Though he does not recognize it, the film's conclusion inserts Antonio back into the position of desire as it dissolves the last vestiges of his individualist fantasy. Only by traversing such fantasies and sustaining the path of desire, the film suggests, can we become politicized subjects.

By sustaining absence within the structure of narrative, Italian neorealism suggests a model for political action. Rather than basing political activity on a fantasy of the future that we work to realize, we can base it on desire's resistance to the commands of symbolic authority. This is not simply resistance for its own sake—a kind of anarchism—but instead resistance that insists on the subject's freedom. When the subject accepts the fantasmatic resolution of desire and obeys the strictures of symbolic authority, it cedes this freedom to a big Other that exists only through the subject's positing of it. In short, the abandonment of desire itself brings symbolic authority into existence: fascism emerges because subjects eschew the traumatic freedom of their desire. If Italian neorealism has one overriding idea, it is its insistence on the political importance of sustaining desire. This is a conception of politics that centers around the rejection of the respite that paternal authority—up to and including that of fascist authority—provides for the subject of desire.

But there is a danger inherent within the cinema of desire. Through its emphasis on the absence of the object, this type of cinema, even as it encourages us to resist the lure of fantasy, pushes us toward fantasizing a scenario that would resolve the deadlock within which it leaves us. Few have the ability to sustain the path of desire, and those who do, like Welles, often find insurmountable barriers placed along this path. The path of desire is not that of pleasure but its opposite. In *Seminar V*, Lacan makes this equation: "Desire has an eccentricity in relation to every satisfaction. It permits us to understand what is in general its profound affinity with pain. At the limit, it is to this that desire is confined, not so much in its developed and masked forms, but in its pure and simple form; it is the pain of existing."[5] To sustain the path of desire is to sustain the pain of existing—and this is difficult for both filmmakers and audiences. Even overtly political films like those of Italian neorealism often slip into a form that presents the gaze as a possible object, if only to provide hope for the spectator. When the cinema opts for this path and chooses to resolve the deadlock of desire, it produces a kind of film that functions ideologically by integrating desire and fantasy. This process results in what I call the "cinema of integration."

PART 3

The Cinema of Integration
The Marriage of
Desire and Fantasy

16

The Intermixing of Desire and Fantasy

As AN IMPOSSIBLE object that cannot be reduced to the visual field, the gaze energizes the cinema, infusing it with desire, and yet, the gaze also indicates the point at which cinema challenges the hold that ideology has over its subjects. If cinema is to function ideologically—which is to say, if it is to assist in reconciling subjects with the social order—it must in some way negate or counter the central role that the gaze plays in its very structure. Though parts 1 and 2 have focused on films that allow spectators to confront the gaze either as it distorts the field of the visible or as it is absent from that field, most films do not take up either of these ways of relating to the gaze. Instead, they tend to take a more ideological path—taming or domesticating the gaze rather than insisting on its disruptiveness. In these films, the gaze no longer stands out as an impossible object or objet petit a, but becomes just another empirical object that film can represent. This domesticated gaze is the result of a cinema of integration, a cinema that works hand in hand with the functioning of ideology.

The cinema of integration is the predominant cinema in the world today. Though it has its roots in the filmmaking practices of Hollywood, the cinema of integration exists throughout the world and manifests itself in both commercial and independent films. This type of cinema predominates not simply because the capitalist class controls the means of (filmic) production and demands an ideological cinema, but because it offers subjects the opportunity to experience the traumatic excitement of the gaze while remaining safely within the structure of fantasy.

The cinema of integration rarely avoids altogether the trauma of the gaze; instead, it utilizes the gaze in order to incite the desire of the spectator. But it

115

always effects a retreat from this trauma. This type of cinema allows us to believe that we can actually integrate the gaze successfully into our world without any of its disruptive effects. Whereas the cinemas of fantasy and desire highlight the disruptive power of the gaze, the cinema of integration provides for a smooth insertion of the gaze into the field of the visible, an insertion that causes the gaze to disappear. The elimination of all the disruptiveness of the gaze constitutes the chief deception of the cinema of integration.

In order to domesticate the gaze and eliminate its disruptiveness, films must deploy fantasy and desire in a specific way. Rather than stressing either the fantasmatic distortion of the gaze or the absence of the gaze in desire, the cinema of integration uses fantasy and desire in conjunction with each other. These films integrate desire and fantasy. They produce desire through presenting the gaze as an absence, and they depict a fantasmatic scenario that allows us to relate successfully to this absence. The key to this type of film lies in the overlapping of the realms of desire and fantasy. Such overlapping contrasts with the cinema of fantasy and of desire. Both of these types of cinema rely on isolating, as much as is possible, the functions of desire and fantasy, and this is what allows them to reveal the gaze as the hole within the structure of ideology. The cinema of integration supports the structure of ideology by obscuring this hole, covering over the absence of the gaze in the experience of desire and the overpresence of the gaze in the experience of fantasy.

The main focus of part 3 is on the various developments within the cinema of integration that discover new ways of blending the cinematic experience of desire and of fantasy in order to deliver spectators from the trauma of the gaze. We can see this through Ron Howard's attempt to render the impossible object possible, the role that the father plays in the later films of Steven Spielberg, and D. W. Griffith's development of parallel editing. The final chapter in this part examines films that create a visible division between the worlds of desire and fantasy only in order to reconcile these worlds in the end. Here, the exemplary case is *The Wizard of Oz* (Victor Fleming, 1939). Through each of these developments, the ability of the cinema of integration to marry desire and fantasy has the effect of disguising the constitutive role that absence plays in the cinema and in the structure of subjectivity itself.

Howard's films present the logic of the cinema of integration in its most basic form. They initially present the gaze as an impossible object and subsequently show that we can conquer the barrier of impossibility. Spielberg's films develop this logic by emphasizing the role that the father plays in conquering the trauma of the gaze. A completeness of representation—the elimination of the absence that marks the gaze—becomes the affirmation of the power of symbolic authority. Looking at Griffith's parallel editing, which was developed decades before Howard and Spielberg were even born, further refines our understanding of the cinema of integration by emphasizing its political ramifications. The group of films modeled on *The Wizard of Oz*, films that create an initial divided structure that eventually allows for the reconciliation of the worlds of desire and fantasy, push the reconciliatory power of film to its end point as they reveal the fantasmatic alternative only to highlight the attractiveness of the present social reality. Such films develop the ideological power of the cinema of integration beyond even that of Griffith's films.

The cinema of integration structures every absence that it mobilizes through a fantasmatic scenario that envisions the elimination of this absence. No absence, no gaze, disturbs the visual field in such a way that the spectator can't imagine correcting this disturbance. Hence, the absent object marks only a temporary absence or impossibility within the cinema of integration. That is to say, this cinema always approaches and depicts desire from the standpoint of desire's fantasmatic resolution. According to this schema, there is no question of desire that fantasy cannot answer successfully. Films of this type might, for example, depict an impossible object within the mise-en-scène (as with the tarot cards in Agnès Varda's *Cléo de 5 à 7*), construct this object through the structure of the filmic narrative (as with the sled in *Citizen Kane*), or indicate the object's present absence through editing (as François Truffaut does at the beginning of *Les quatre cents coups*). But in the cinema of integration, these deployments of the impossible object always point toward a future triumph over impossibility in which the objet petit a disappears as the film presents the spectator with an attainable object of desire (that is, an object that seemingly could satisfy desire). The absence exists in the film form not as a constitutive or ontological feature, but as an empirical quality that the form itself has the ability to remedy. The cinema of integration accomplishes this deontologizing of the impossible object through the specific way in which it overlaps the realms of desire and fantasy.

The central impossible object that the cinema of integration deontologizes is the successful sexual relationship. The one intractable limit that desire encounters is the failure of the sexual relationship, a failure that results from the absolute divide between the sexes. In the process of entering the order of language, the subject must take up a sexed identity, must place itself on one side or the other. In doing so, the subject accepts an identity that lacks: sexual difference is the manifestation of lack or absence in the subject. To say that one must exist as a sexed subject is only to say that one cannot exist as a complete being when one is a subject of language. The subject then looks to the other in romantic love to provide what it is lacking. The problem is that desires do not line up perfectly: the other never has what the subject lacks, nor does the subject have what the other lacks—and this becomes especially apparent in the conflict between the desires associated with masculine and feminine structures. The dissymmetry places desires constitutively at odds with each other, and fantasy tries to find a way to reconcile these antagonistic desires. Fantasy does this not just for the sake of the subject's satisfaction, but also for the security of the social order itself.

The failure of the sexual relationship destabilizes every social order because it indicates the existence of a foundational rift in this order. In *Seminar*

XX, Lacan makes this claim: "What constitutes the basis of life, in effect, is that for everything having to do with relations between men and women, what is called collectivity, it's not working out."[1] No matter how tightly organized a society is, no matter how much a society tries to smooth over this barrier, it cannot overcome the antagonism made evident by the failed sexual relationship. This antagonism means that there will never be a resolution of desire. Consequently, every social order has an inherent fragility at the point of this antagonism, which is why the cinema of integration commits so much of its energy to the fantasy of the successful sexual relationship.

Though the failure of the sexual relationship is an antagonism that no society can escape, it nonetheless marks the point at which the seductive power of fantasy is the greatest. This is because of the enjoyment that we associate with this relationship. The idea of the successful sexual relationship embodies the ultimate enjoyment—an impossible relationship with an object that remains always out of reach. The successful version of this relationship would sustain the link with the object and the status of the object as beyond all relationality, which is why the very idea is impossible. In the face of the failure of the sexual relationship, the subject finds every other form of satisfaction inadequate. The chief ideological function of fantasy involves envisioning a way out of this impasse for the subject. This is why the fantasmatic depiction of the successful sexual relationship is the foundation of the cinema of integration. It dominates not only the romance genre, but action films, dramas, comedies, and science fiction as well. Its power transcends all generic boundaries. By sustaining our investment in this fantasy, the cinema of integration helps to convince us to accept the authority of ideology.[2]

The creation of the romantic couple also functions ideologically in the way that it resolves or obscures other antagonisms that a film presents. That is to say, a film may depict a class antagonism or race antagonism, but the concluding fantasmatic image of the successful couple diminishes the impact of this depiction.[3] In reconciling the sexual antagonism, the cinema of integration reconciles all other antagonisms as well.[4] Films that conclude with the romantic couple highlight it to the exclusion of all other narrative developments, thereby erasing the power of other antagonisms. This resolution requires the careful blending of desire and fantasy. The cinema of integration generates desire through a focus on sexual antagonism, but then it supplies just enough fantasy to suggest—rather than fully present—the reconciliation of this desire. The romantic union functions ideologically only if it is the result of this type of blending together of desire and fantasy.

Those films that blend desire and fantasy attempt to strike a compromise and achieve a balance between desire's insistence on the absence of the gaze and fantasy's insistence on its distorting presence. The problem with compromise and balance is that they dilute both desire and fantasy, thereby depriving us of the authentic experience of either one.[5] The compromised status of films in the cinema of integration facilitates their popularity. Their balanced filmic worlds that blend desire and fantasy correspond to the everyday experiences of most subjects. Thus, the problem isn't that most films are too much like dreams, but that most films are too much like real life.

The real life that the cinema of integration proffers is a neuroticized reality. Blending of desire and fantasy is, according to Freud, characteristic of the neurotic. Neurotics supplement their experience of desire with fantasy because they cannot endure the dissatisfaction that accompanies the experience of desire. They refuse to accept without question the sacrifice of enjoyment that the social law demands. Their illness is actually an attempt to find a way to enjoy while remaining within the confines of the social law. The problem with this strategy, however, stems from the specific way that it has recourse to fantasy. Neurosis allows subjects to continue to exist under the strictures of the social law while fantasizing that they are violating these strictures. Rather than acting to change their situation or even their society, neurotics content themselves with a fantasmatic revolt. Neurosis allows subjects to supplement the desiring world of the social reality with their private fantasmatic world.

This conception of neurosis determines the nature of the psychoanalytic cure. When at the end of *Studies on Hysteria* Freud and Breuer explain their goal as one of transforming "hysterical misery into common unhappiness," they suggest—though they wouldn't have put it this way—eliminating the blending of desire and fantasy, and allowing the hysteric to confront the traumatic real of the gaze rather than diluting this object through fantasy.[6] The attractiveness of neurosis stems from its ability to offer a solution to the problem of "common unhappiness," which is precisely what the cinema of integration promises.

The association of the cinema of integration with neurosis seems, at first glance, confusing. After all, the cinema of integration is an ideological cinema that aims to normalize subjects, not create a distorted relationship to the social reality. In addition, neurotics have, to some degree, an incipient radicality due to their quest for knowledge about the real. It would seem, then, that producing neurosis would violate the ideological function of this cinema. However, a limited dose of neurosis does not disrupt the subject's insertion into ideology; it provides only an imaginary transgression. In fact, a certain amount of neurosis is imperative for the ideologically interpellated subject because it allows the subject to deceive itself concerning its actual status within ideology. Unlike normal subjects, neurotics never grasp the extent of their subjection, nor do they recognize the absence of any foundation for that subjection. Without some neurosis, without some blending of desire and fantasy, the subject would experience the gaze in all of its traumatic power.

Freud's description of normality makes this clear. For Freud, the normal subject sustains an absolute divide between the worlds of desire and fantasy—what he calls the external and the internal—and can distinguish between them. In the experience of this hypothetical normal subject, "what is unreal, merely a presentation and subjective, is only internal; what is real is also there *outside*."[7] Here, "normal" indicates that the subject does not confuse external and internal, desire and fantasy. Such normality, however, is impossible: no one experiences the world of desire (the social reality) without some fantasmatic investment. Nonetheless, according to the strict psychoanalytic definition, normality allows no such confusion, which is why psychoanalysis also recognizes that we never encounter a normal subject. There is always some slippage between normality on the one hand and neurosis on the other. Unlike normal subjects, neurotics don't experience things so clearly. Neurotics seek in fantasy a substitute satisfaction for what they do not find in the world of desire. Hence, for the neurotic every experience has at least a hint of the fantasmatic. There is a blurring of the lines that allows the neurotic to domesticate the trauma of the gaze, which is why the cinema of integration aligns itself with neurosis.

In contrast to the cinema of integration, psychoanalysis aims at normalizing subjects in the precise sense that Freud defines the term. The psychoanalytic process works not to eliminate fantasy, but to create the strict separation between desire and fantasy that will allow the subject to experience the gaze and that will stop fantasy from supplementing the subject's experience of social reality. Psychoanalysis brings subjects to the point where they can identity with the gaze and thus experience fully the failure of ideology. That is to say, normality as Freud understands it thus marks a threat to the functioning of ideology. Freud's normal subjects have an experience of the gaze as ideology's constitutive failure, and they see the point at which fantasy attempts to compensate for this failure.[8] Whereas other subjects also experience this fantasmatic compensation, they do not recognize that it addresses an ideological failure. The cinema of integration feeds this ideological mode of subjectivity. In these films, we cannot see the point at which fantasy takes over for ideology and fills in the gaps of ideology, and as a result, we cannot see any indication of incompleteness within the ideological structure.

Fantasy has the ability to function as a supplement to ideology only insofar as it remains unseen. This is why the cinema of fantasy developed by someone like Spike Lee actually undermines the power of fantasy over us: in exposing the fantasy, Lee deprives it of the obscurity within which it operates. But films that integrate desire and fantasy help to keep the ideological work of fantasy hidden. In this sense, they replicate and support our everyday experience, in which fantasy silently works to fill in the gaps within our social reality and to provide our experience with the image of coherence. In fact, the coherence of our experience depends on the extent to which fantasy supports this experience without our awareness. The cinema of integration works to further obscure the role that fantasy plays in our experience and thus to increase the sense of coherence in our experience.

The fundamental feature of films within the cinema of integration is their coherence. They often disrupt the experience of the spectator through the type of shots they employ, the mise-en-scène, the use of sound, and the editing, but these disruptions always occur within a narrative and formal trajectory that promise the elimination of disruption as such. This produces an experience in which nothing is missing and nothing sticks out. Not only that, but this experience also assures spectators that any seeming incoherence in their lives outside the cinema will achieve the same kind of resolution. In this way, the cinema of integration helps subjects to live with the contradictions of ideology without experiencing them as contradictions. It teaches us to see and experience coherence where none actually exists. This is how fantasy provides an indispensable supplement to ideology. Without fantasy, we would come face to face with ideology's contradictions and have no means for sustaining a coherent sense of our own reality or identity.

In the cinema of integration, even the gaze—the object that stains the field of the visible and disrupts our vision—becomes an ordinary object that fits into our world of representation and meaning. By sustaining fantasy's domestication of the gaze, film allows us to believe in the possibility of escaping trauma through recourse to ideology. For the cinema of integration, there is trauma in its filmic universe, but one can always find a way of resolving this trauma. And when we can resolve a trauma, trauma loses its ability to shake us loose from our immersion within ideology.

17

The Theoretical Opposition

T HOUGH NO THEORISTS ever said as much, the emergence of traditional Lacanian film theory in the late 1960s and 1970s occurs in response to the predominance of the cinema of integration in classical Hollywood. This strain of film theory is first and foremost a political theory that targets the prevailing mode of representation in popular cinema. The complicity between ideology and cinematic representation, according to this theory, demands that theory take up an almost entirely negative role—opposing itself to and deconstructing the dominant cinematic representations. For most traditional Lacanian film theorists, the task of theory involves exposing what popular cinema works to hide.

This theory is critical of cinema—especially classical Hollywood cinema—for its mystifying deployment of fantasy.[1] According to this position, classical Hollywood cinema functions ideologically because it uses fantasy to deceive spectators about their own status in the cinema and in society in general. Jean-Louis Baudry, for one, claims that cinema's "precise ideological effect" involves "creating a fantasmatization of the subject."[2] This critique focuses on how cinema's investment in fantasy serves to hide the social structures that produce the fantasy. As Laura Mulvey points out, "In *reality* the phantasy world of the screen is subject to the law which produces it."[3] Cinematic fantasy produces the illusion of freedom and agency for the spectator, and when spectators invest themselves in this illusion, they fail to see the ideological system within which they actually exist. This is, for Baudry, Mulvey, and other traditional Lacanian film theorists, the product of cinema's fantasmatic power.

Cinema represents a danger insofar as it mirrors the process of ideological interpellation as described by Louis Althusser. For Althusser, ideology hails individuals as subjects, which means that it convinces them of their agency while simultaneously blinding them to the constitutive power of the social order over them. According to traditional Lacanian film theory, the cinema reproduces the moment of ideological interpellation when it employs continuity editing, uses high-key lighting, relies on synchronous sound, and so on. These widespread filmic techniques help to deceive spectators into viewing the events on the screen as the objects of their mastering look. The fantasmatic dimension of cinema—the way that it distorts spectators' sense of their own look—becomes the linchpin in the ideological work that the cinema performs.

However, the problem with classical Hollywood cinema, according to traditional Lacanian film theory, is not simply its fantasmatic dimension, but rather the way in which the cinematic situation impairs the spectator's ability to distinguish the world of fantasy from the social reality. According to Baudry, the filmic apparatus is responsible for this situation. As he points out, "The cinematographic apparatus brings about a state of artificial regression," and this state involves a "return toward a relative narcissism, and even more toward a mode of relating to reality which could be defined as enveloping and in which the separation between one's own body and the exterior world is not well defined."[4] In other words, cinema tends to confuse the internal and the external—fantasy and desire—leaving the spectator unable to distinguish effectively between them while viewing a film. It is in this sense that the target of traditional Lacanian film theory's attack is nothing other than the cinema of integration. This type of cinema relies on the blurring of the lines between desire and fantasy in order to seduce the spectator into believing in the seamlessness of ideology, and traditional Lacanian film theorists constantly take pains to point out the constructed nature of this seamlessness.

While in the cinema we become even more neurotic, losing the ability to distinguish the world of fantasy from the world of our social reality. Classical Hollywood cinema presents a fantasy as if it were actual, disguising the indications of its fantasmatic status. The danger of film lies in what traditional Lacanian film theory calls its "reality effect." Cinema creates this effect by hiding the act of production through the relationship it establishes with the spectator. While watching a film, the spectator doesn't see the film's artifice. The typical Hollywood film severs the productive act of making a film from the act of consuming it.[5] Because spectators' attention is wholly devoted to the images on the screen and because spectators accept them as real, they never reflect on the producer of these images—or on the ideological agenda of this producer. Instead, the form in which they are presented allows the screen images to shape the spectator without prompting questions. The pleasure that we derive from the filmic experience is thus a deceptive pleasure, for it situates us within ideology and mutes any efforts at questioning the truths that ideology proffers.

Here again, the target of traditional Lacanian film theory becomes visible as the cinema of integration. This cinema, as the analyses that follow aim to show, works to stifle the process of questioning that the cinematic gaze raises in spectators. The films of the cinema of integration provide fantasmatic answers to the questions that they raise, which has the effect of producing docile rather than curious subjects. These films refuse to sustain any empty spaces within their formal structure because such spaces would unsettle the state of satisfaction that they aim to produce.

18

The Politics of the Cinema of Integration

N O SOCIAL ORDER—even the most authoritarian—can eliminate the gaps within its ideological structure in which the forms of the objet petit a are situated. And in fact, no order would want to eliminate these gaps. Though blank spaces within an ideological structure attest to the vulnerability of that structure (and hence its potential modification or even overthrow), they also serve to energize the desire of subjects within the social order. For example, contemporary capitalist ideology tells subjects that they have a right to uninterrupted happiness, and yet the capitalist mode of production functions on the basis of the constant dissatisfaction of subjects. A similar paradox lies at the heart of every social order, and it gives rise to oppositional and even revolutionary movements. Without the gaps that make possible its overthrow, a social order would not give rise to the desiring and productive subjects that it requires to perpetuate itself.

In order to keep subjects desiring and satisfied at the same time, ideology simultaneously utilizes both desire and fantasy. Desire drives subjects to work to change their world, while fantasy creates a sense of satisfaction with the world as it is. Desire is the subject's mode of challenging and questioning its world, and fantasy is a way of finding an answer that appears satisfying. In this sense, desire and fantasy are opposing forces, and yet ideological stability requires that they operate together, existing in a perpetual balance. If subjects desire too much, they will revolt against the social order that oppresses them. If subjects fantasize too much, they will cease to invest themselves productively in the perpetuation of this order. This is why the extremes of the cinema of fantasy and the cinema of desire threaten to disrupt the normal functioning of ideology. This functioning depends on sustaining a balance between the dissatisfaction of desire and the imaginary satisfaction of fantasy. If a film swings too far in either direction, it shatters this balance and allows the spectator to experience the failure of ideology. The cinema of integration sustains a balance between desire and fantasy, and this is what allows it to function ideologically.[1]

Most often, the cinema of integration opens with the gaze as an absence—a lack in the Other—and then depicts the absence becoming a presence—a process of repairing the lack. In this way, the gaze is neither an impossible object nor an excessive one, but an object-cause of desire that becomes a present object of desire in the way that the Ark of the Covenant becomes present at the conclusion of Steven Spielberg's *Raiders of the Lost Ark* (1981), an exemplary film in the cinema of integration. Even though Indiana Jones (Harrison Ford) doesn't end up with the Ark, the film nonetheless chronicles the transformation of the Ark from an impossible absent object to a present one. This very transformation eliminates the point of impossibility in the Other and creates the image of a complete Other. By repairing the lack in the Other, this cinema disguises the source of the subject's radical freedom. The subject is free because the Other is incomplete and cannot provide a foundation for the subject. But the cinema of integration allows the subject to find support for its identity in the image of the nonlacking Other. This offers the subject a sense of security, but at the cost of the space for the subject's freedom. The subject has freedom on the basis of the constitutive incompleteness of the Other—an incompleteness that disappears in this type of cinema.

The cinema of integration allows us to experience the absence within the symbolic order where the gaze emerges, but it presents this absence as empirical rather than ontological. That is to say, no absence exists that we could not imagine filling in. Here, the impossible object of desire does not exist; every object is a possible object. Though the Other in the cinema of integration may lack, there is always a nonlacking Other that emerges to provide a sense of completion. The world of the nonlacking Other—the result of the disappearance of the gaze—is a world in which everything is controlled and in which agency belongs to the Other rather than the subject.

According to the logic implicit in the cinema of integration, if the impossible object-cause of desire does not exist and there are only a series of possible objects, then there must a reason why we are not enjoying this object ourselves. In denying the impossible status of the objet petit a, this cinema places the subject's failure to enjoy itself in the forefront of the filmic experience and often suggests an agency responsible for that failure. For instance, to return to *Raiders of the Lost Ark*, the film depicts first the Nazis and then the American government holding the Ark and hording the enjoyment that it embodies. The final image of the film—the Ark being stored in a crate anonymously in a U.S.-government warehouse amid thousands of other crates—suggests that the U.S. government knows the secret of the impossible object and will protect us from it. But ultimately the idea of the nonlacking Other in the film runs even deeper: the actual Other of the Other in the film is God himself, as testified to by the living power of the Ark.

The Ark does not simply memorialize God in his absence like every other religious icon, but embodies his presence in the world (which is why the Ark kills all who look in it). Through this characterization of God, the film suggests that God is a secret power operating behind the scenes who really has the ability to access the Ark (the privileged impossible object). By transforming the impossible object into a possible one, *Raiders of the Lost Ark* tries to convince us that the ultimate enjoyment exists and that some agency has the ability to access and manipulate it.

Through the fantasmatic resolution of desire, the cinema of integration shows us the image of the ultimate enjoyment as a possibility. If we lack this enjoyment—as we inevitably do—it often offers an explanation for our lack: there is secret agency responsible for stealing this enjoyment from us or at least depriving us of it. Even when this agency is not identified in a film as it is in *Raiders of the Lost Ark*, it is nonetheless implicitly present whenever a film obscures the gaze. The traumatic gaze (as a present absence or as an excess) assures us that the Other is lacking, that there is no fully realized and satisfied Other. But without the gaze, this lack becomes invisible and a nonlacking Other emerges in its stead. Hence, though spectators do not always leave the cinema of integration feeling duped, they do tend to leave with a sense of missing out on what the Other has.

By working to produce subjects with this view of the Other, the cinema of integration helps to stabilize symbolic authority in the face of the subject's radical freedom. Spectators of the cinema of integration seek an authority to follow because they believe that there is—somewhere—an authority with the ability to access and control the impossible object. Insofar as it imagines the impossible object replaced by a possible one, the cinema of integration thus pushes subjects away from their freedom.

19

The Ordinary Cinema of Ron Howard

Through its deployment of fantasy, the cinema of integration offers the spectator hope in the face of the impossible. Its unbridled hopefulness is one of the primary sources of this cinema's attractiveness. Subjects long to hope because hope suggests that they are not simply condemned to the path of desire, that there is something beyond the dissatisfaction of desire. If it sustains subjects in this way, hope seems beneficial, or at least innocuous. Where does the danger lie? Why does Nietzsche proclaim that "hope . . . is in truth the worst of all evils"?[1] The problem with hope is that it justifies our submission to the dictates of ideology. We submit to ideology hoping that the future will provide the enjoyment that the present denies us.

Ideology sustains its control on the basis of the hopes it engenders, hopes that no subject can ever realize. All hope for the realization of our desire is in vain because we cannot access—either now or in the future—the impossible object around which desire revolves. Even revolutionary or utopian hopes, insofar as they envision a future without lack, deceive us concerning the impossible status of the object.[2] Refusing hope, however, does not imply the quiet acceptance of present conditions. In fact, refusing hope represents the basis for political contestation. Rather than having faith in the possibility of a different future, we can act in order to transform the current situation. Subjects who sustain fidelity to the path of pure desire act because they recognize that no amount of obedience and no amount of waiting will bring the impossible object. In contrast, the hopeful subject obeys and waits, which is why the ideological cinema of integration focuses to such an extent on films that engender hope.

The films of Ron Howard are, above all, hopeful. They depict a marriage of the realms of desire and fantasy that eliminates the impossible object and produces an accessible object of desire in its stead. In the typical Howard film, we encounter an impossible object-cause of desire, and then, through the course of the film, we discover that we can actually achieve the impossible. Howard shows us that we can realize our desire and attain an object that would satisfy our desire—or that such an object exists. Because they enact the most elementary function of fantasy—transforming an absence into a presence—Howard's films represent the most basic manifestation of the cinema of integration.

Splash (1984) depicts Madison (Daryl Hannah) as an impossible object (a mermaid) who later becomes an accessible object of desire; *Cocoon* (1985) depicts three old men confronting death and then transcending it through joining an alien civilization; *Ransom* (1996) shows Tom Mullen (Mel Gibson) save his son from kidnappers determined to kill him even after Mullen agrees to pay the ransom; and *A Beautiful Mind* (2001) presents John Nash (Russell Crowe) facing his psychosis and conquering it through reason. Each of these films begins by stressing the impossibility of the object driving the hero's desire in order to maximize the enjoyment that we feel when we discover that the impossible is actually possible. By taking up this trajectory, these films create a seamless image of ideology, and they work to produce spectators invested in the rewards that ideology promises.[3]

Cocoon begins by emphasizing the dissatisfaction that Ben Luckett (Wilford Brimley), Art Selwyn (Don Ameche), and Joe Finley (Hume Cronyn) experience as a result of the aging process. Living in a retirement community surrounded by other elderly people, they feel their lives winding down and sense the proximity of death. This becomes evident in the first sequence introducing them, as Ben and Art see another resident of the community die. Howard establishes the gaze as a structuring absence in this scene. Watching this death, the two men experience the gaze insofar as they see the point in the visible field that includes them: as they look at this scene of death, they see their own impending demise. Howard shoots the scene in a way that places the death of this anonymous resident of the retirement community into the position of the gaze for the spectator as well.

The scene begins with a shot of Ben and Art looking in the distance with distraught looks on their faces. A subsequent long shot of the resident's room shows doctors and nurses working frantically to revive the person. This shot is brief, however, and the film quickly returns to another shot of Ben and Art. Just as they begin to walk away, we hear a doctor pronounce the resident's death while the camera stays with Ben and Art. Here, Howard indicates through the shot sequence and the timing of the death announcement the precise status of the resident's death. It is the gaze, the point at which Ben and Art—and the spectator—are not just objective onlookers but involved in what they see. The verbal pronouncement stains the visual image and functions as a present absence within that image. The presence of death as an absent object in this scene indicates that it is the truth of both Ben and Art's being. Death is the inescapable obstacle in the face of their desire, and at the same time, it is what animates this desire.

In the scene immediately following this encounter with death, Joe joins Ben and Art as they walk to the neighboring abandoned mansion where they often swim clandestinely in the pool. Ben asks Joe about the results of his visit to the doctor, and Joe responds evasively, suggesting that his illness is severe. He finally concludes by saying, "Doctors don't know everything," a statement that implicitly affirms the terminal nature of his illness. As in the prior scene, death—here the mention of it—functions as an absent presence. Joe knows he is going to die, and yet he cannot smoothly integrate this fact into his conceptual universe. Through these two scenes, the film establishes a world of desire, a world in which the absence of the gaze leaves subjects in a constant state of dissatisfaction, a world in which subjects feel their mortality impinging on them. Ben, Art, and Joe avoid directly confronting their impending death, but nonetheless the dissatisfaction that death produces structures their experience. With the spectator, they feel the lack that death and the aging process introduce.

The beginning of the film establishes a world of desire in which Ben, Art, and Joe exist as dissatisfied subjects. Their desire here centers around an impossible object, since they cannot escape death or counteract the effects of the aging process. However, the film constructs a fantasy scenario that allows the three men to relate successfully to this impossibility. This fantasy scenario is triggered when aliens (disguised as humans) rent the mansion and the pool as a hatchery for the cocoons of fellow aliens who were left behind on earth from an earlier visit. Because of the life energy that the aliens impart into the swimming pool in order to hatch the cocoons they place there, the pool acquires curative powers. The first time that Ben, Art, and Joe swim in the pool after the aliens have placed the cocoons in it, the pool rejuvenates them. Howard depicts this rejuvenation through a fantasmatic montage sequence. We see slow-motion shots of each of the men exuberantly diving into the pool as upbeat music plays on the soundtrack. This display of vitality suggests that they have found a way to resolve their desire. In this way, the film provides a fantasmatic supplement for the desiring subject, showing that the desiring subject can actually find a solution to its lack.

This turn from impossibility to possibility manifests itself even further in the subsequent behavior of the three men. After the swim in the energized pool, Ben, Art, and Joe display renewed sexual energy. When walking back to the retirement community, they all notice that they have erections, and that evening, they all have sex with their partners. The surprise evinced by each partner suggests that this is not a regular practice. Later, Joe learns from his doctor that his cancer is in complete remission, and Ben passes the eye test that he earlier failed in order regain his driver's license. After the three men introduce their partners to the life-enhancing pool, the film depicts them all dancing and displaying the energy of young people. At the end of the film, the three men, along with their spouses and many of their friends from the retirement community, depart in the alien spaceship for a life without death or aging. With this denouement, the film offers us a fantasy that perfectly addresses the desire that its opening establishes. Used in this way, fantasy disguises the impossible situation of the desiring subject and renders invisible the absences within the structure of ideology. *Cocoon* creates a fantasy that releases us from the trauma of death and aging, but at the same time, this fantasy also works to cement our position within ideology. This dimension of the film becomes even more pronounced in the final sequence.

Rather than concluding the film with the departure of the elderly group and the aliens from earth, Howard adds a coda. This coda—a mass funeral for the group—is perhaps the most important scene in the film because it emphasizes the link between the fantasy world and the world of desire. The minister presiding over the funeral says to the mourners, "Do not fear. Your loved ones are in safekeeping. They have moved on to a higher expression of life, not life as we know it, but in the spirit everlasting. Our loved ones are in good hands—now and forever more." Here, the minister offers the standard nebulous description of heaven that is meant to offer the families fantasmatic consolation. If they will never see their lost family members again, at least they can fantasize that their loved ones are in a better place.

But *Cocoon* gives a new twist to the standard consolation: while he undoubtedly thinks he is describing heaven, the minister unwittingly describes the actual life that the aliens have given to those who went with them. Though they are no longer visible in the image, we experience their presence through the unintended irony of the minister's words. The lost family members are here present even in their absence from the image. This conclusion is thus the precise opposite of *Citizen Kane*: for Welles, the object is absent even when it is present, but for Howard, the object is present even when it is absent. *Cocoon* demands that we see even the absences that do exist in the visual field as obscuring a hidden presence.

The film reveals to the spectator that fantasy is not a separate realm apart from the world of desire; there is no radical divide between the two. This lack of a divide allows fantasy to intervene clandestinely in the world of desire. As a result, the subject continues to experience the dissatisfaction of desire but does not experience this dissatisfaction as constitutive. Instead, dissatisfaction becomes empirical, an obstacle that one might overcome. In Howard's films, the impossible object that produces the world of desire disappears and an attainable object of desire appears in its stead, and this transformation dramatically undermines the subject's ability to recognize the hold that ideology has over it.

In the first instance, *A Beautiful Mind* seems to represent a break in Howard's filmmaking. Rather than hiding the gaze and its distorting power, it forces the spectator to confront the way in which our look—which we share with the main character, John Nash—distorts the field of representation in the film. At almost its midpoint, the film makes us aware that much of what we have seen in the first half of the film (John's top-secret government work, his congenial roommate, the roommate's niece) is nothing but the product of John's delusion. In the manner of David Fincher's *Fight Club* (1999), the film thereby demands that we recognize how our acceptance of John's delusional fantasy structure shaped our experience of the filmic world. Like John's, our view of reality in the film has been stained. We become aware that the filmic world wasn't simply there for us to see; instead, it included our look in the form of the object gaze distorting the visible field. By depicting the gaze as a distortion in the visible field, *A Beautiful Mind* places the spectator, with John, in the position of the desiring subject. However, the film quickly provides fantasmatic relief from desire.[4]

After he receives medication and becomes aware of his illness, John must endure the antagonism that accompanies the experience of desire. The subject of desire always confronts antagonism insofar as desire relates to an impossible object. When faced with antagonistic alternatives, the desiring subject cannot simply opt for one path or the other: either choice would fail to resolve desire. Either choice would leave the subject lacking something essential. Likewise, John is faced with an impossible choice: either he can take medication and lose his genius, or he can stop taking his medication and become delusional again. The impossible nature of this choice indicates the fundamental problem for the subject of desire.

But the film is unable to leave John—or the spectator—in the position of the desiring subject. Frustrated with his inability to think clearly, John opts to stop taking his medicine, and the results are disastrous. Again believing in his nonexistent college roommate, John almost allows his infant son to drown while the roommate is "watching" him in the bathtub. Unable to continue to live with the danger that John's illness presents to her and her son, Alicia quickly takes their child in the car and begins to drive away. As she drives away, the film shows John flash in front of the car. His abrupt appearance in the image seems to identify him here as a threatening figure—he has just almost allowed his child to drown—but the film quickly reveals the opposite: John has taken the first step to recovery. He proclaims to Alicia, "She never gets old. Marcy can't be real. She never gets old." By telling Alicia this, John informs her that he is able to control his delusions. Through the use of his reason, he can overcome the way delusion stains his sense of reality. He later says, "All I have to do is apply my mind." By applying his mind to the problem instead of using medication, John surmounts the antagonism and resolves his desire. When he is faced with an impossible choice—sanity or genius—the film depicts John having it both ways. This fantasy transforms the nature of the antagonism. Rather than signaling an impossibility, the antagonism becomes nothing but the site of a difficult problem.[5]

By first depicting the antagonism and then stripping it of its impossible dimension, *A Beautiful Mind* shows us that social antagonism doesn't really exist—or exists only insofar as it can be overcome. In doing this, the film helps to accommodate the spectator to ideology. The experience of antagonism is the key to developing resistance to ideology in the subject (which is why Marx constantly stresses the antagonism between classes that capitalist ideology attempts to obscure). The antagonism that the subject of desire experiences marks the point at which ideological explanations break down; it is a rift in the fabric of the social order. By obscuring the antagonism, the film disguises this rift. The disturbance in the visual field that we experience earlier in the film—the gaze—loses its disruptive power as John gains control of his delusions. Rather than depicting the gaze as an irreducible stain in the field of the visible, *A Beautiful Mind* domesticates the gaze.

The gaze does not disappear from the film altogether, however. John and the spectator continue to see his delusions: we often see them looking at him in the distance or walking alongside him as he is walking. But at the end of the film, a dramatic change occurs in the ontological status of these delusions. John is able to distinguish clearly between his delusions and reality. As he explains to someone who questions him about them, "I still see things that are not here, but I choose not to acknowledge them." With John, the spectator also gains, by the conclusion of the film, a firm sense of what is real and what is delusion. As a result, the gaze no longer represents a barrier to the experience of reality. John can—and does—treat the gaze as just another object in the field of the visible rather than allowing that object to stain the entire field. The film has transformed it from impossible object to just another possible object in the visual field. The end of the film thus marks a total victory over the gaze and desire, accomplished through the merging of the worlds of desire and fantasy.

The victories over the gaze in Ron Howard's films attest to the indefatigable hopefulness of these films. The gaze marks the limit of our ability to hope. As an impossible object in the field of the visible, it constantly reminds us of what we lack and what is absent. The films of Ron Howard work to convince us that we can overcome this lack, that we can hope even in the face of what seems impossible. The hope that they provide comes with a cost, however. When we embrace the hope that Howard's films offer, our social reality becomes whole and unquestionable. The loss of the trauma of the gaze is at once the loss of the possibility of freedom.

20

Steven Spielberg's
Search for the Father

HOPEFULNESS FOR A victory over the trauma of the gaze characterizes the cinema of integration as such. In order to achieve this victory and create a balance between desire and fantasy, the cinema of integration often relies on the sense of stability that the Name of the Father offers. "The Name of the Father" is Lacan's term for the symbolic father or paternal metaphor, the signifier that authorizes the law and the system of signification. Through its authority, this one signifier arrests the inherent sliding of signification and stabilizes social relations. The symbolic father's show of authority obscures the threat of the gaze; he seems able to control and domesticate this threat. But the power of the Name of the Father is nothing but a performative power of the signifier itself, which means that the problem with the symbolic father is that he is only symbolic and not real. As Lacan notes, "The father inasmuch as he promulgates the law is the dead father, that is to say, the symbol of the father."[1] Because the symbolic father is the dead father, he lacks the ability in actuality to eliminate the trauma of the gaze. Thus, when we invest ourselves in the authority of the symbolic father, we invest ourselves in an authority that consistently fails to provide the security he promises.

Grasping the incapacity of the symbolic father—recognizing that paternal authority is a dead letter—traumatizes the subject. The fact that the symbolic father is dead means that there is nothing to fill in the void in the heart of signification where the gaze emerges. The subject must thus navigate this void alone. But in an effort to avoid the traumatic encounter with the gaze, the subject turns to fantasy to resurrect the father, transforming a pure signifier (the symbolic father) into a powerful image. The fantasized father protects the subject because he seems to know the secret of the gaze, and having

137

this secret, he seduces the subject into obedience. This is what the cinema of integration offers spectators: it erects a fantasized father at precisely the point where the spectator encounters the trauma of the gaze.

This fantasized father also seduces us because he offers happiness—which is just another way of saying that he offers us freedom from desire. Without the sense of security that the father provides, the subject suffers from desire and cannot attain happiness.[2] Whereas the dead father lacks the power to stabilize the subject's symbolic identity, the fantasy of the living father has this power. He assures us that we are not alone and that we have a substantive identity, which allows us to be happy.

The recognition that the symbolic father is a dead father frees the subject from this father's authority. One need not obey a dead authority. The fantasy of the living father, in contrast, serves to increase the subject's tendency to obey. By propagating the fantasy of the living father, the cinema of integration pushes the spectator in the direction of obedience insofar as it convinces us that symbolic authority has some potency. The films of the cinema of integration offer us the pleasure of feeling safe from the traumatic gaze, but at the cost of the freedom that has its source in this trauma.

Even when the figure of paternal authority seems to be absent, he always informs the fantasmatic resolutions of the cinema of integration. In the later films of Steven Spielberg, however, this figure moves into the foreground. Here, the impossible doesn't just become possible (as is the case in Howard's films); it becomes possible through the agency of the symbolic father. Spielberg's films lack the ideological clarity of Howard's, but this is because they hope to do a more profound ideological work: to demonstrate again and again that the symbolic father is not dead but alive and well. As such, he is capable of providing the security that the fathers in Spielberg's first two films—David Mann (Dennis Weaver) in *Duel* (1971) and Clovis (William Atherton) in *Sugarland Express* (1974)—could not provide.

These first films stress the abject failure of the father to domesticate the gaze: rather than obscuring the void within the Other, the fathers here expose this void through their inability to control it.[3] However, after *Sugarland Express* (1974), Spielberg transitions from the cinema of desire to the cinema of integration, and his films begin to erect a father capable of controlling the desire of the Other as manifested in the gaze. The trauma of the gaze in the first films reappears in the later films, but a powerful father also appears, a father who knows the secret that the gaze embodies. Through the transition from the inadequate father to the powerful father, Spielberg joins Hollywood as such.[4]

It is almost as if Spielberg's entire career as a filmmaker represents a flight from the trauma of the gaze as manifested in his first film. In *Jaws* (1975), for example, Spielberg enacts what becomes a standard pattern in his films: an initial confrontation with a traumatic gaze, followed by a fantasized depiction of a father figure who would master the gaze and protect us from it. *Jaws* marks the first point in Spielberg's films where the father is able to master the gaze, and in this film, the father has the most difficult time. In this sense, it marks the highpoint of Spielberg's work within the cinema of integration.

Jaws begins by establishing the gaze in the form of the attacking shark. In the three attacks that we see in the first part of the film, the shark is an impossible object, and its traumatic impact stems from its impossible status. Spielberg creates this effect through the use of John Williams's threatening theme music and underwater shots from the shark's perspective. In the first two attacks (of a woman swimming at night and a boy playing on a raft), we never see the shark itself, and in the third, it appears only briefly. The attacking shark is an impossible object that we can experience only as an absence in the field of the visible. In the second attack, we see how this absence disrupts the form of the film. After a brief montage of shots showing Alex Kintner (Jeffrey Voorhees) under attack, the film focuses on police chief Martin Brody (Roy Scheider), who sees the attack. Just after the attack begins, we see Martin from the ocean as he sits on the beach looking out toward Alex. In what is known as a trombone shot, the camera rapidly tracks backward with Martin and simultaneously zooms slightly toward him, making it seem as if Martin's head is moving forward while the background recedes—an effect that registers the trauma of the attack formally. The attack traumatizes us as spectators as well because it indicates our vulnerability, marking the point at which our mastery and control of the world break down.

Each shark attack testifies to a gap in our knowledge. We never know who or where the shark will strike, nor when the attack will begin or end. In her discussion of the first two attacks, Antonia Quirke notes, "Both attacks are filmed *through* the moments of contact. For Chrissie the music never attained its climax by the time she was bitten, and Alex's end is filmed with an almost unruffled rhythm. This gives the attacks such reality. You are not allowed to think *Ah, the worst is over. The knife is in.* The moment of catharsis doesn't really come, and so the horror is never diffused, it's regretful and transfixed."[5] Spielberg films the attacks in a way that highlights our nonknowledge of what drives the shark to attack, and because it remains this point of nonknowledge, the shark embodies the gaze. As the gaze in the film, the attacking shark includes us in the picture: we experience the trauma of each attack because the attacks attest to our shared experience of the inadequacy of our mastery of the world.

The film points to our fundamental vulnerability even in the places where we feel safest. Spielberg sets the film in an idyllic island community in order to emphasize that there is nowhere we can go to escape this vulnerability. The beginning of the film takes pains to establish the lack of serious danger here. In the town of Amity, police chief Brody deals with inconsequential problems such as karate students chopping people's fences, not with serious crime.

When we first see him head off to work, his wife, Ellen (Lorraine Gary), asks him to be careful, and Martin responds, "In this town?" suggesting how dull and safe the small town is. Later, Martin points out that "in twenty-five years, there's never been a shooting or a murder in this town." The film also communicates the tranquility of the town visually: early on, we see Martin walking down the main street, where there are crowds of people walking in the street and children biking as the sun glistens down on them. We can hear the sound of a marching band in the background preparing for the Independence Day celebration (which a sign stretched across the street announces). All of this filmic emphasis on the peacefulness of the town serves only as a backdrop to the attacks. Even the most peaceful and secure place—even a town such as Amity—is vulnerable to the threat that of the gaze. One cannot construct a town immune to it.[6]

Just as the first part of *Jaws* shows us our vulnerability to the gaze, it also shows the failure of paternal authority—and masculinity in general—to protect us from it. In the first attack, the film depicts a woman leaving a beach party and running into the ocean to swim. A young man from the party follows her, eager to swim naked in the ocean with her. As she begins to swim, however, the man collapses on the beach, overcome by drunkenness. During this initial shark attack, the film stresses the complete inability of the masculine figure to protect the woman. Spielberg cuts between the woman struggling against the shark and shots of the man lying passed out on the beach, oblivious to the woman's cries for help. After the shark kills the woman, the sequence ends with a shot of the man still lying on the beach. Here, we see the first indication of the inadequacy of masculinity in the face of the gaze.

If the man on the beach fails to protect the woman from the gaze (or even notice that she's under attack), the town fathers of Amity actually exacerbate the dangers of the shark. After discovering the body of the woman killed in the first attack, Martin decides to close the island's beaches, but Mayor Larry Vaughn (Murray Hamilton) and other business owners in the community dissuade him from this course of action. The mayor even convinces the coroner to rule that the woman, an obvious victim of a shark attack, was killed in a boating accident in order not to incite fear. Even after the subsequent attack on Alex Kintner, the mayor refuses to close the beaches for an extended period of time. His concern is the island's tourist industry, not protecting the island from the threat of the shark. He wants Martin to punish the vandals who painted a shark fin on the island's welcome sign, but he actively discourages Martin from doing anything about the actual shark. The paternal authority's concern with image and capital, as the film shows, renders him feckless as a protector. The aftermath of the third attack highlights the fecklessness of the mayor, as we see him break down and recognize his complete failure. But the failure of the mayor is not the only such failure.

The first part of the film establishes Martin Brody as the central paternal authority in Amity, but it also stresses his weakness and his inability to protect the town from the shark. Even though Martin wants to close the beaches after the first attack, he fails to stand up to the mayor and insist. After the death of her son, the film shows Alex Kintner's mother (Lee Fierro) approach Martin and slap him for his failure. The film emphasizes her outrage as we see her face in a close-up without a cut as she confronts him. She says, "I just found out that a girl got killed here last week, and you knew. You knew there was a shark out there. You know it was dangerous, but you let people go swimming anyway. You knew all these things, but still my boy is dead now. And there's nothing you can do about it. My boy is dead. I wanted you to know that." Brody recognizes and acknowledges, as we do, the truth of her indictment. He fails as a figure of paternal authority, and a third attack that injures his own son causes Brody to feel his failure even more. In contrast to the mayor and the other town leaders, the film depicts Martin as a conscientious and capable authority, but even he cannot provide protection from the traumatic gaze. By emphasizing his failure and the inability of paternal authority as such to protect us, *Jaws* works to free us from this authority.

But *Jaws* does not sustain its indictment of the father's weakness. The conclusion of the film depicts Martin becoming a paternal authority capable of mastering the gaze in the way that he cannot throughout the rest of the film. After the third attack, Martin hires an old fisherman, the hypermasculine Quint (Robert Shaw), to hunt the shark for him. As Martin prepares to depart to hunt the shark with Quint and Matt Hooper (Richard Dreyfus), a shark expert from an oceanographic institute, the contrast between Martin's failed masculinity and Quint's hypermasculinity becomes evident. Spielberg follows Martin and his wife Ellen with a pan as they walk through a boathouse toward Quint's boat. As they walk, Ellen's efforts to prepare Martin for the voyage have the effect of revealing his vulnerability. She says, "Did you take your Dramamine? I put an extra pair of glasses in your . . . black socks, and there's the stuff for your nose, the zinc oxide, the Blistex is in the kit." As she speaks, we hear Quint's deep voice in the background yelling at the men preparing his boat. Overhearing him, Ellen says, "That's gotta be Quint," and Martin replies, "Colorful, isn't he?" Ellen's response—"He scares me"—indicates the distance between Quint and Martin as authority figures: Quint inspires Ellen's fear while Martin inspires her worry. As Ellen and Martin stand face to face in the foreground, we see Quint between them on his boat in the background, further emphasizing this contrast. Though Martin has proven an inadequate paternal authority, through the figure of Quint the film presents a stronger alternative.

In the end, however, the shark kills Quint, thereby suggesting the failure of even this hypermasculine authority. But as Quint dies, the film establishes Martin as the capable father that he has failed to be earlier. Martin begins the quest for the shark bumbling through every task aboard the boat, but he ends up single-handedly destroying the shark after it kills Quint and incapacitates Matt Hooper. Martin even overcomes his fear of the water in the act of killing the shark and asserting his paternal authority. The conclusion of the film shows Matt and Martin swimming toward shore, and we hear Martin proclaim, "I used to hate the water." He has here become a capable father. The seemingly indestructible object no longer terrorizes Amity because Martin has overcome all the weakness that stained his character. This denouement forces us to rethink the earlier depictions of paternal failure, to think of them not as failures but as temporary obstacles on the father's path toward his symbolic role. That is to say, the initial failures serve to highlight the father's final success. *Jaws* allows us to believe in the father's mastery: not even the trauma of the gaze can undermine his authority.

The idea of a paternal authority figure who offers us protection from the gaze becomes the central motif in almost every film that Spielberg makes after *Jaws*. For instance, in *Indiana Jones and the Last Crusade* (1989), Henry Jones (Sean Connery) takes up the paternal role that he has disdained throughout his life. At the end of the film, he reaches out to his son Indiana (Harrison Ford) and pulls him out of a chasm to safety, displaying concern for his son instead of for the Holy Grail—the now-accessible impossible object—lying just beyond Indiana's reach. This show of concern that Indiana has never seen before convinces Indiana not to risk his life in an attempt to access the object. In *Jurassic Park* (1993), reluctant father Alan Grant (Sam Neill) finally assumes a paternal role and protects the grandchildren of John Hammond (Richard Attenborough) from the dinosaurs that Hammond has created. In each of these cases, the father undergoes a transformation like Martin Brody does in *Jaws*. This transformation moves us from insecure world of desire to the protected world of fantasy. The image of the capable father allows us to fantasize a relationship to the gaze in which the gaze no longer disrupts our experience of the world. The symbolic father creates a coherent world for the subject—a world in which no trauma has the ability to cause a fundamental disturbance. By constituting this father, Spielberg's films try to create a sense of stability in this subject.

Not only do Spielberg's films tend to constitute an image of the father as he becomes a protective force, but they also depict the redemption of the failed father. By showing the father who initially fails to protect us and then succeeds in doing so, these films do even more to increase the power of paternal authority. We fantasmatically invest ourselves all the more in this authority because we see the process of failure and recovery. We do not simply see the strength of the father, but see this strength in light of his earlier weakness. The redemption of the father reaches its high point in *The Lost World: Jurassic Park* (1997). As in many of Spielberg's films, *Lost World* begins by highlighting the failure of paternal authority to protect children from the gaze.

In the opening scene, we see a wealthy family picnicking on a remote tropical island, and a confrontation develops between the young girl and her mother when the girl begs her mother to allow her to go off on her own. Though the mother worries about her daughter running off alone on the island, Spielberg stresses the indifference of the father: he tells the mother to stop being overprotective and to let the girl enjoy herself. We see the father sitting absorbed in the act of reading a newspaper while he says this, indicating that he says it not so much out of concern for his daughter but in order to end the squabbling that is disturbing his peaceful lunch on the beach. Through this depiction of the father, the film implies that his indifference to his daughter's activity leads to the attack she suffers as she leaves the picnic area on the beach. Several small dinosaurs attack the girl, and though the film doesn't show the attack itself, it does show the horrified expression on her mother's face as she runs to help her daughter after the girl screams for help. The attack on the girl is the absence—the impossible object—that haunts the scene. It marks the point of the child's vulnerability and the point at which the father's authority fails to provide protection. By beginning with an image of the inadequate father, Spielberg sets up the redemption of the father that will follow.

Lost World depicts the redemption of the father by chronicling the trajectory of three figures of paternal authority. Ian Malcolm (Jeff Goldblum) begins the film as a father who fails to give his daughter enough time and attention, but he ends up saving her from the threat of the dinosaurs. John Hammond, who in Jurassic Park was responsible for the destruction that the dinosaurs caused, becomes a benevolent and protective authority in the sequel. The film ends with John speaking on television about the need to keep the dinosaurs separate from human interference, thereby protecting both the dinosaurs and humanity from the trauma of their interaction. The third father that the film redeems is the Tyrannosaurus rex itself. Whereas the first film depicts the Tyrannosaurus rex as a brutal killer, Lost World depicts it—especially the male—as a nurturing and protective parent. In fact, scientist Sarah Harding (Julianne Moore) spends the entire film trying to overcome, as she says, the "resistance to the idea of [tyrannosauruses] as nurturing parents." The film proves the truth of her claims.

On both occasions when a Tyrannosaurus rex attacks humans in the film, it is searching for the baby tyrannosaurus that the humans have taken. The chase scene through the city of San Diego at the end of the film shows the Tyrannosaurus rex father pursuing Ian and Sarah's car because this car contains his child. In the fantasmatic world that the film creates, even the male Tyrannosaurus rex can find redemption as a figure of paternal authority. This redemption of the father establishes a fantasmatic image of unparalleled paternal authority in the psyche of the subject. We first experience the father as weak and vulnerable, unable to protect us—or as himself embodying the gaze, as in the case of the Tyrannosaurus rex. When the father subsequently shows that he can offer protection, his ability to overcome his earlier failure renders him even more attractive. Spielberg's image of the father is not simply an image of pure protection from the gaze; it is also an image of failure that the father has overcome. This is the fantasy that seduces us into accepting the father's authority.[7]

In one sense, *Schindler's List* (1993) marks a change in Spielberg's film-making. The trauma that the film addresses is here an actual historical trauma rather than a shark, a dinosaur, or the arrival of aliens. Just as *Amistad* (1997) would focus on the trauma of the middle passage and *Saving Private Ryan* (1998) would focus on the trauma of World War II, *Schindler's List* centers around the trauma of the Holocaust. Spielberg's film correctly perceives that the horror of the Holocaust stems not only from mass extermination but also from the encounter with the Nazi gaze. As a victim of the Nazis, one experiences this gaze as an inexplicable trauma, a desire that makes no sense within the world of meaning. Nothing that one does can assuage the Nazi gaze and render it navigable. It destroys regardless of how much one tries to capitulate to its desire.[8]

In *Schindler's List*, Spielberg locates the gaze in Nazi commandant Amon Goeth (Ralph Fiennes). In one of the film's great scenes, we see Goeth embody this object gaze as he arbitrarily shoots Jews from the veranda of his quarters above a newly erected concentration camp. The gaze here is not the mastery involved in Goeth's look over the compound. We don't experience the gaze when we share his look; instead, we experience it when we must confront his desire. Spielberg shoots much of this scene from the perspective of Goeth's look, but this look is not the gaze. When Goeth searches out his first victim, Spielberg uses a point-of-view shot and pans across the compound to indicate the movement of Goeth's eyes over possible targets. However, this shot is merely preparatory to our experience of the gaze, which occurs when Spielberg cuts from Goeth's seemingly omnipotent look to a series of objective shots from ground level in the camp. After Goeth fires his gun the first time, we see the camp at ground level (rather than from Goeth's veranda above), and in the background, Goeth appears as a barely recognizable blur: we see not Goeth himself, but the veranda from which he fires. As in *Duel* and *Jaws*, it is these brief shots of the absent point in the Other that manifest the gaze. The camera looks up at Goeth, but the picture does not capture his gaze. The spectator cannot experience mastery here, but must instead endure the indecipherable desire of the Other.

Here we have the gaze in all its traumatic horror: Goeth shoots, and we have no idea why he is shooting or why he shoots particular people. Just prior to Goeth's shooting spree, one of the camp inmates says to another, "The worst is over. We are workers now." It is precisely at this moment of seeming calm and respite that the gaze manifests itself, disturbing the stable picture. When Goeth fires his first shot, it unleashes a whirlwind of frenetic activity within the camp. The inmates begin to run and to work at an increasingly rapid pace. Spielberg even uses a handheld camera to shoot this portion of the scene, thereby conveying the frantic movement that Goeth's shot occasions. This accelerated pace on the ground of the camp represents an effort to avoid becoming the subject of the lethal gaze. Those in the camp have no idea what this unseen gaze wants from them; hence, they turn to frenetic activity and work in hopes of finding the answer and appeasing the gaze. What terrifies in this scene is not Goeth's total domination and mastery over those in the camp, but rather the real of his desire: why does he decide to shoot those whom he shoots? As one watches, it is clear that no one, not even Goeth himself, could answer. This absence is the gaze, and *Schindler's List* demands that we endure it.

But Goeth's gaze does not remain an impossible object throughout the film. Through the figure of Oskar Schindler (Liam Neeson), Spielberg domesticates this gaze and thereby deflects its trauma. With subterfuge and payoffs, Schindler is able to figure out the desire of the Other—the desire of Goeth— and make it bearable. Instead of continuing to confront us with a lethal gaze, Goeth accommodates Schindler, freeing over a thousand Jews from certain death. Schindler is thus a fundamental fantasy figure—a father strong enough to protect us from the traumatic real. As he emerges as a strong paternal presence in the film, the trauma of Goeth disappears. As Paul Eisenstein points out in his definitive reading of the film, *Schindler's List* ends by envisioning the mastering of desire itself. He writes, "From the standpoint of satisfied desire, which is to say the standpoint of no (self-interested) desire, we see only the Good—only Schindler and not Goeth. In disallowing the enigma of desire, the split in spirit that *is* its identity, Spielberg's film has the effect of getting rid of desire."[9] In *Schindler's List*, Spielberg takes us to the point of an encounter with the real of the gaze, but then he turns away, shielding us from the real through the enactment of a fantasy screen.

Many critics have taken *Schindler's List* to task for its ending. Omer Bartov, for one, contends that "since it is a Hollywood production, *Schindler's List* inevitably has a plot and a 'happy' end. Unfortunately, the positively repulsive kitsch of the last two scenes seriously undermines much of the film's previous merits."[10] Bartov takes exception to Spielberg's depiction of Schindler's tearful breakdown concerning his failure to save more Jews and the film's final shot in Israel (which suggests that Israel is the compensation for the Holocaust). With these two scenes, the ending of the film, as another disappointed viewer puts it, "descends headlong into an irredeemable sentimentalism."[11] The problem with this line of critique stems from where it locates the film's misstep.

It is not just that Spielberg tacks on a happy ending; a film can have a happy ending and nonetheless sustains the gaze in its absence, as the case of *Duel* testifies to. The retreat from the gaze in *Schindler's List* occurs in the construction of Schindler as a viable and effective paternal authority. The sentimentalism of the film's ending simply follows from the emergence of Schindler as a capable father. When he manages to assuage Goeth by grasping the latter's desire, the cinematic experience undergoes a complete transformation. Where we once endured the impossibility of the gaze, we now feel the protective power of the father.

This is precisely the ideological dimension of Spielberg's later films: by replacing the encounter with the gaze with a fantasmatic construction of a strong paternal authority figure and thereby covering over the gaps within ideology, they leave us securely within the structure of ideology. Rather than experiencing the failure of ideology to protect us, we learn to accept the illusion of protection that ideology offers. Spielberg's later films move us further away from the experience of the impossible object after initially allowing us a taste of this experience.

21

D. W. Griffith's Suspense

BOTH HOWARD AND Spielberg work to domesticate the gaze largely through the narrative structure of their films, but the cinema of integration also manifests itself prominently in the very construction of individual scenes. We can see this in the editing process that D. W. Griffith uses to create suspense. Films often use suspense to create spectator desire. Whereas surprise provides a brief moment of presence when a film confronts the spectator with an unforeseen object, suspense relies on an extended experience of absence. As Alfred Hitchcock notes in an interview with François Truffaut, we have a choice between "fifteen seconds of *surprise*" and "fifteen minutes of *suspense*."[1] Suspense allows the spectator to experience the object in its absence and to enjoy that experience of absence. In this way, it helps to develop and sustain the spectator as a desiring subject. Suspense derives from the absence of the gaze in the filmic image and our confrontation with this absence. When we enjoy suspense in a film, we enjoy this experience of absence. And yet, suspense almost always provides fantasmatic respite for the desiring subject.

Fantasy dilutes the desire that suspense creates in the way that it frames the alternatives of the suspenseful situation. Rather than allowing the denouement of the suspenseful situation to be indecipherable, fantasy creates an image of a possible successful resolution. According to Noël Carroll's definition of filmic suspense, this fantasmatic diluting represents an intrinsic part of the suspense itself. Carroll argues, "In film, suspense generally obtains when the question that arises from earlier scenes has two possible, opposed answers which have specific ratings in terms of morality and probability. . . . Specifically, suspense in the film generally results when the possible outcomes of the situation set down by the film are such that the outcome which is morally correct in terms of the values inherent in the film is the less likely outcome (or, at least, only as likely as the evil outcome)."[2] Carroll's definition of filmic suspense includes the possibility of the successful resolution of the desire that suspense creates. Without this possibility, according to this view, a film could not produce suspense. However, such a definition attests not to the nature of suspense as such, but to the power of the specific model of suspense that D. W. Griffith and classical Hollywood cinema set forth.

Not coincidentally, the first example that Carroll cites to support his theory of suspense is a film by Griffith, *Way Down East* (1920). For Griffith, suspense always operates within the realm of fantasy. Suspense always aims at resolution, at what Carroll calls the "morally correct" outcome, even when it does not necessarily arrive at this outcome. By diluting suspense with fantasy—with the idea that the suspenseful situation can somehow be successfully resolved—film overshadows our enjoyment of the absent gaze with the fantasy of its presence. This is one way the cinema of integration convinces us to compromise our desire, and this manifestation reveals the clear political valence of this kind of cinema. With Griffith, the politics that Howard and Spielberg imply becomes obvious. We see the necessarily reactionary result of the retreat from the gaze that marks the cinema of integration, but we also see how this politics entwines itself within even editing processes. Locating Griffith within the logic of the cinema of integration offers us a way of thinking about the link between his cinematic innovativeness and his racism.[3]

Griffith seems to confound the effort to link revolutionary film form to radical—or even democratic—politics. At its formal high point, *The Birth of a Nation* (1915), Griffith's cinema reaches its political nadir.[4] Though it may not be possible, as Sartre claims, "to write a good novel in praise of anti-Semitism," Griffith seems to prove that one can create a good film in praise of racism.[5] The coincidence between formal innovation and racism becomes especially poignant because Griffith's revolutionary use of parallel editing occurs in the most pronounced way when Griffith depicts the Ku Klux Klan coming to the rescue at the end of the film. Hence, when most theorists discuss Griffith, they tend to highlight either the formal qualities of his filmmaking or his racism rather than finding a connection between the two. In order to sustain the link between revolutionary film form and progressive politics, Béla Balázs simply ignores the racist content of *Birth of a Nation*. He contends, "It is by no means an accident that the initiator of the revolution in cinematography, the genius David Griffith, made films which were not only new in their form but radically democratic and progressive in their content."[6] While Balázs admirably attempts to sustain the connection between form and content here, it requires silence about the racism of *Birth of a Nation* when conceiving of Griffith's films as "progressive in their content."

One theorist who is not silent about Griffith's racism is Sergei Eisenstein. Unlike other theorists, who fail to grasp the interconnections between Griffith's racism and the form of his films, Eisenstein does see a link. Noting that Griffith is at times "an open apologist for racism," he contends that "the structure that is reflected in the concept of Griffith montage is the structure of bourgeois society."[7] The racism implicit in Griffith's cinema is that of bourgeois society itself—its inability to exist without the racist fantasy that obscures its fundamental class antagonism. Racism limits the form of Griffith's films, and it manifests itself in the particular way that Griffith conceives of parallel montage. Parallel montage—or, more precisely, Griffith's particular development of parallel montage—betrays an investment in the fantasmatic resolution of desire.[8]

The problem with Griffith's use of parallel editing is not that it leads to a resolution of the antagonism it creates, but that it suggests the possibility of this resolution through its structure. From the beginning of the parallel editing sequence, it is clear that the alternating shots are leading toward a possible resolution. Hence, even if the resolution fails—even if, for instance, the rescuer does not arrive in time—the fantasy remains secure because the resolution might have happened. Rather than remaining an impossibility, the resolution of desire becomes a possibility, whether it is achieved or not. For instance, in the Babylon section of *Intolerance* (1916), the parallel editing sequence leading up to the fall of Babylon—the crosscutting between the attacking troops of Cyrus (George Siegmann) and the chariot of the Mountain Girl (Constance Talmadge) heading to warn Babylon—suggests that the Mountain Girl might arrive in time, though she in fact does not. Even though Babylon falls and disaster ensues, the film preserves the idea of a successful resolution of desire. This alone indicates its hidden investment in fantasy: fantasy isn't necessarily the fantasy of success, but of possibility.[9]

The reliance on fantasy in his editing structure indicates the limit of Griffith's politics and the link between his aesthetic practices and the content of his films. Racism is always fantasmatic—the construction of a scenario that depicts the other enjoying itself in the stead of the subject. As we saw in the discussion of Claire Denis in part 2, the racist subject envies the enjoyment of the other and believes that this enjoyment rightfully belongs to it. But unlike Denis's films, Griffith's development of suspense supports and exacerbates the idea of the illicitly enjoying other. It is thus completely apropos that Griffith's most famous use of parallel editing involves a panegyric to the Klan.

On two occasions in *Birth of a Nation*, the Klan rides to rescue isolated white individuals endangered by black groups. These two overlapping incidents are the climactic sequences in the film, and as such, they lay bare the film's investment in the fantasmatic resolution of desire. Griffith shoots each incident through a parallel editing sequence that builds to the Klan's heroic rescue. In these sequences, the film reveals that the Klan has the ability to effect a resolution of desire and to domesticate the gaze. The Klan dissipates the threat that the desire of the Other brings to the stability of the social reality, and it can do this because of the way that the film establishes the gaze.

Throughout *Birth of a Nation*, the desire of the Other—the gaze—is located in the black men (especially the black Union soldiers) who desire white Southern women. However, we don't encounter this desire as an absent gaze. In the film, it is not an absence but a presence, and there is no uncertainty about it. It drives Gus (Walter Long) to pursue Flora Cameron (Mae Marsh); it drives the black-dominated legislature to pass a law sanctioning interracial marriage; and it drives Silas Lynch (George Siegmann) to woo Elsie Stoneman (Lilian Gish). In each case, the film allows for no question concerning the desire of the black male subject.

This desire is the central concern of the film; it is the gaze that the film addresses. And at the same time, it is the gaze stripped of its impossible status, which means that it is not the gaze in the proper sense of the term. When we see a shot of Gus looking at Flora, we have no doubt about what he wants. This is the measure of Griffith's racism: racism fantasizes a traumatic enjoyment in the desire of the Other and thus allows the subject to avoid encountering this desire as a traumatic, impossible object. For Griffith's film, the gaze becomes just another object. And because the desire of the Other is clear—black men simply want to have sex with (or rape) white Southern women—the figure of the Klan can emerge to domesticate this desire.

Birth of a Nation never presents us with the gaze in its pure form. From the beginning of the film, Griffith produces a fantasy in which the gaze becomes a knowable object. His use of parallel editing to depict the elimination of the gaze as a threat follows directly from this fantasy. Just after Silas Lynch (a black man) asks Elsie Stoneman (a white woman) to marry him, we see a shot of the Klan beginning to mobilize to rescue her and other endangered whites. Later in the sequence, the film cuts back and forth between a black mob outside Elsie's house attacking whites and Elsie imprisoned inside. Finally, as the Klan closes in, the shot sequence begins to build to the rescue. We see the Klan riding in an extreme long shot, followed by a shot of the angry black mob outside the house. Griffith cuts back and forth between the Klan and the mob, using successively closer shots of the Klan to depict their increasing proximity. When they arrive, we see several Klan members riding on the horses in a medium shot, and they soon rout the black group and rescue the whites, including Elsie. The resolution that the film produces here derives its power from the ability of the Klan to control a threatened and disruptive desire. The building crescendo of the parallel editing sequence suggests this control—or at least the capacity for it—throughout the struggle that it depicts.

During this crosscutting sequence, Griffith intersperses shots of the Cameron family trapped in a cabin under assault by black Union soldiers. After the rescue of Elsie, this scene becomes the sole focus of the film. Again, Griffith shoots this second rescue through parallel editing. The film depicts rapidly alternating shots of the Camerons in the cabin, the black soldiers outside the cabin, and the Klan riding to the rescue. After the soldiers gain entry into one room, we see alternating shots of their struggle to open a door into the adjoining room, the Camerons and their allies trying to hold the door shut, and the Klan riding. These alternating scenes prepare for the eventual arrival of the Klan to save the family.

These two parallel editing sequences that conclude *Birth of a Nation* present a fantasy scenario in which the Klan can control the gaze. The racism of these sequences is not simply confined to the celebration of the Klan or the negative black images in the content of the film. Racism pervades the form as well: Griffith's use of parallel editing never allows us to experience the gaze as such. There is a direct link between this form and the film's racist content. *Birth of a Nation* allows us to watch from a distance. As a result, we never see ourselves as spectators implicated in what we see on the screen. We experience a threat in the film, but this threat remains only an external threat. It thus never becomes traumatic. In saving us from the trauma of the gaze, Griffith feeds the racism of the spectator, even when he moves away from directly racist images in the content of his films.[10]

By making the film *Intolerance*, Griffith hoped to clear himself of the charges of racism that *Birth of a Nation* brought about. And while it is true that *Intolerance* lacks the overt racist depictions of the earlier film, it continues the formal structure that underlies those racist depictions. Griffith continues the use of parallel editing in a way that suggests our ability to control the gaze. Though parallel editing occurs in each of the film's four stories, it appears pervasively in the modern story. At the end of this story, a young woman, the Dear One (Mae Marsh), works with the aid of a police officer to save her husband, the Boy (Robert Harron), from an unjust execution. Griffith depicts the events leading up to his rescue and the rescue itself in a series of parallel editing sequences. These sequences unfold in response to a clearly identified threat, and they point toward a stable resolution. They help to obscure the gaze by supplementing the experience of desire with that of fantasy.

Though the film leaves the success of her efforts in question, it is clear that the Dear One's efforts to save the Boy at least create the possibility of resolving the desire occasioned by the parallel editing sequences. After the assisting police officer obtains the confession of the actual killer, he and the Dear One pursue the train carrying the governor (who could pardon the Boy) out of town. The film cuts from the moving train to the Boy receiving last rites to the car carrying the Dear One and the police officer chasing the train. This crosscutting ends with the car catching up with the train and thus producing an initial fantasmatic resolution. The final parallel editing sequence in the film juxtaposes shots of the police officer rushing to the site of the execution and shots of the Boy on the verge of being hanged. Again, the sequence leads to a conclusion that resolves the desire that the crosscutting elicits. As in *Birth of a Nation*, this fantasmatic resolution—the Dear One's rescue of the Boy—informs the entirety of the parallel editing sequence. *Intolerance* generates suspense in such a way that it appears resolvable. By doing so, the film blurs the line between desire and fantasy, and it allows us to experience the desire that suspense produces without the experience of impossibility that accompanies desire. This is the primary ideological gesture that the film makes.

Though the modern story of *Intolerance* does not incorporate explicit racism into its suspense in the way that *Birth of a Nation* does, it nonetheless sustains the idea that the desire of the Other represents a specific threat that the suspense sequence must overcome. In *Intolerance*, the danger is not lusting black men but virginal old maids. The film shows the chain of events that lead to the Boy's near execution, and at the origin lies the activity of a group of female reformers (who inveigh against alcohol, tobacco, and other vices). These reformers drain money from the local factory in order to finance their efforts, causing layoffs at the factory that cost the Boy his job (and his father) and lead him into a life of crime. Even though he is innocent of the murder charge that earns him the death penalty, his involvement in criminal activity places him in the position where he appears guilty. The film provides this back story leading up to the Boy's trip to the gallows in order to indict the female reformers as the party responsible for his situation. By doing this, *Intolerance* supplements the racism of *Birth of a Nation* with a dose of sexism. Here, women have a clear desire, and this desire aims at destroying enjoyment.

Griffith's depiction of the female reformers performs a kind of reductive psychoanalysis of them and their motives. An intertitle makes clear where the desire for reform originates. It baldly proclaims, "When women cease to attract men they often turn to reform as a second choice." After this intertitle, the film shows a series of shots depicting unattractive older women to support its claim. According to the film, these women campaign for reform because they fail to enjoy themselves sexually. By placing the blame of the Boy's demise on these women and their "intolerance," Griffith fantasmatically identifies the threatening desire of the Other. Because this desire is clear, the suspense sequences at the end of the film can depict the subjugation of this desire through the efforts of the Dear One and the police officer who assists her. Parallel editing cannot lead to a fantasmatic resolution if the desire of the Other is not clearly established. In this sense, fantasy's primary task involves eliminating the ambiguity of desire.

Even in films where neither racism nor sexism play a role in the suspense, Griffith nonetheless creates suspense in a way that eliminates the impossible status of the objet petit a. The villain in *Way Down East* is neither a threatening black man nor a repressed white woman. And yet, the film's use of parallel editing in the famous ice sequence produces the same dynamic that we find in *Birth of a Nation* and *Intolerance*. The sequence depicts the rescue of Anna Moore (Lilian Gish) by David Bartlett (Richard Barthelmess) as she floats unconsciously on a sheet of ice toward a waterfall. Griffith shoots this long sequence by crosscutting between the threatening waterfall, long shots of Anna lying on the floating ice, close-ups of Anna, and shots of David's frantic pursuit of her. The very structure of the parallel editing throughout the sequence points toward David's rescue, a rescue that fantasmatically resolves the difficulties of desire. Even though the film establishes the impossibility of a marriage between David and Anna (because of her earlier sexual relationship), the rescue sequence eliminates this impossibility and paves the way for their marriage. The resolution prompts David's father, a stern Puritan who had thrown Anna out of his house when he learned of her past indiscretions, to beg her for forgiveness. Here, the antagonism that kept Anna and David apart no longer holds as the fantasmatic structure of Griffith's parallel editing creates a world in which antagonism is nothing but a temporary barrier.

Griffith's suspense plays a crucial role in the development of Hollywood cinema because of its ability to merge the realms of desire and fantasy. Griffith's parallel editing disguises the impossibility of the object and the traumatic dimension of desire that results from this impossibility. When his conception of desire seduces us, the path of desire seems to become easier. However, in escaping the difficulty of desire, we also lose out on its rewards as well. When we follow the cinema of integration and rely on fantasy to avoid an experience of the impossibility of the object, we fail to enjoy our desire.

22

Films That Separate

IN ITS EFFORT to produce the most seductive fantasies, at times the cinema of integration extends the relationship between desire and fantasy in ways that almost lay bare the ideological function of this relationship. In its boldest development, the cinema of integration creates a visible filmic division between the world of desire and the world of fantasy. Through differences in mise-en-scène, editing, narrative structure, shot style, color, or sound, such films offer two distinct filmic experiences. By separating desire and fantasy, these films threaten to expose the workings of fantasy even as they seduce us with it. They are some of the most powerful films in the cinema of integration, and, at the same time, they come close to undermining the ideology that they work to support.

Films that initially create separate worlds of desire and fantasy include *The Wizard of Oz* (Victor Fleming, 1939), *It's a Wonderful Life* (Frank Capra, 1946), *Back to the Future* (Robert Zemeckis, 1985), *Titanic* (James Cameron, 1998), and *Family Man* (Brett Ratner, 2000). These films explain the separation by invoking the idea of a dream (*The Wizard of Oz*), a supernatural intervention (*It's a Wonderful Life* and *Family Man*), technological wizardry (*Back to the Future*), or simply memory (*Titanic*). Through whatever narrative justification the film uses, what results is a dramatic divide between two different modes of filmic experience. Each of these films initially presents a world of desire and then subsequently transports us as spectators into a world of fantasy. We move from a world of lack and dissatisfaction into a world that replaces the impossible object with an accessible object of desire. The separation allows us to see the way that fantasy attempts to provide an imaginary compensation for lack. However, our insight into the ideological role of fantasy becomes blurred as these films conclude by muddying the one-time stark divide that they initially establish between the world of desire and that of fantasy.

155

In the end, these films belong to the cinema of integration because they provide reconciliation. While they begin by presenting the worlds of desire and fantasy as radically disparate, the denouements betray this division and allow the world of fantasy to infiltrate the world of desire, thereby hiding once again the function of fantasy and occluding the gaze. But these films do hint at the possibility of another kind of cinema, a cinema that might sustain the world of desire and the world of fantasy as separate and distinct worlds. This cinema, which part 4 will examine, is the opposite of the cinema of integration insofar as it rejects any melding of desire and fantasy. Though films like *The Wizard of Oz* don't go this far, they do point the way.[1]

The Wizard of Oz establishes the difference between the world of desire and the world of fantasy by giving each a radically different form. As even those who haven't seen the film know, Victor Fleming shoots the world of desire and dissatisfaction in black and white, and the fantasmatic world of Oz in color. This formal contrast highlights the distinctiveness that manifests itself also in the filmic narrative. The first twenty minutes of the film depict a world of dissatisfaction. Dorothy (Judy Garland) opens the film complaining to her Aunt Em (Clara Blandick) and Uncle Henry (Charley Grapewin) about the threats that Almira Gulch (Margaret Hamilton) has made against her dog, Toto. Not only is Toto in danger, but no one pays attention to Dorothy. Ignored in Kansas, Dorothy dreams of a place "where there isn't any trouble," a place "beyond the moon, beyond the rain . . . somewhere over the rainbow." Just after Dorothy sings about this alternative world, Miss Gulch arrives, armed with an order from the sheriff, and seizes Toto from Dorothy in order to have him destroyed. The events that occur in the beginning of the film parallel the absence of color in the black and white image: here, we experience the absence of enjoyment that characterizes the world of desire.

The first transition between the world of desire and the world of fantasy in *The Wizard of Oz* is a dramatic one. The film shifts when a tornado strikes Kansas, as the storm causes Dorothy to fall and hit her head. After hitting her head, Dorothy dreams that the tornado picks up the house and carries it through the air, eventually setting it down in an unknown land. The use of the tornado as the vehicle for shifting from the world of desire to the world of fantasy suggests the disparity between these worlds and the barrier that exists between them.[2] The stark difference between the two worlds becomes most evident as Dorothy opens the front door of her house after it lands. As she opens the door, the camera tracks forward out of the black and white house toward the colorful outside world. During this brief moment when the door opens, both the black and white image and the color image share the screen. What Dorothy says at this point—"Toto, I've a feeling we're not in Kansas anymore"—underlines the difference.

By establishing the world of Oz as a separate fantasmatic realm, the film allows us to see how fantasy resolves desire. Rather than ignoring her as in

Kansas, the characters in Oz celebrate Dorothy as a hero (for killing the Wicked Witch of the East when Dorothy's house landed on her). She also gains three devoted friends (the Scarecrow, the Tin Man, and the Lion) as she journeys to meet the Wizard of Oz. Most importantly, in the fantasy Dorothy is able to destroy the threat that Almira Gulch represents when she melts the Wicked Witch of the West (also played by Margaret Hamilton). This fantasy scenario allows Dorothy to escape the dissatisfaction that plagues her in the first part of the film. Whereas other films in the cinema of integration disguise their use of fantasy, *The Wizard of Oz* openly displays its turn to fantasy and the role that fantasy plays in creating an imaginary satisfaction. This open avowal of the fantasy threatens to destroy the assurances that fantasy usually provides for the subject in the cinema of integration. But the film cannot sustain this attitude.

Though the film separates the world of desire from the world of fantasy, it concludes by smoothing over the intersection between these worlds. In doing so, *The Wizard of Oz* hides the gaze that its very form threatens to expose. The ease of Dorothy's return to Kansas reveals that there is no longer a traumatic barrier between the fantasmatic world of Oz and the world of desire. Dorothy simply clicks her heels, and she returns, waking up in her bed. In this way, the film fully integrates the experience of fantasy and desire. This blending of fantasy and desire informs the conclusion of the film as well. Back in Kansas, Dorothy no longer experiences the dissatisfaction that she felt prior to the fantasy. Almira Gulch no longer threatens, and rather than ignoring Dorothy, everyone on the farm pays attention to her just as people did in the land of Oz.

The fantasy has the effect of reconciling Dorothy to the world of desire, convincing her that "there's no place like home." Even though the film reverts to black and white when Dorothy returns to Kansas, postfantasy Kansas has nonetheless become a more colorful—which is to say more fantasmatic—place. Here, fantasy resolves the difficulties of desire. The problem is not just that "Dorothy has swallowed patriarchy's prescription for woman" and returned "to the familiar, worn path of home and security," as Linda Rohrer Paige laments, but that she has returned to a home that now basks in the glow of fantasy.[3] By concluding with a return the world of desire and coloring this world with fantasy, *Wizard of Oz* masks the ideological function of fantasy and works to produce spectator investment in fantasy.[4]

Like *The Wizard of Oz*, *Back to the Future* initially creates a rigid separation between the world of desire and the world of fantasy. In the present, Marty McFly (Michael J. Fox) experiences the same kind of dissatisfaction that Dorothy experiences in Kansas. The present world is a world of desire in which Marty encounters numerous barriers to his desire: in the first part of the film, we see the school principal label him a failure just like his father George (Crispin Glover); his band fails to qualify for playing at the school dance; and Marty's plans for a weekend at the lake with his girlfriend Jennifer

(Claudia Wells) are derailed when Biff (Thomas F. Wilson) wrecks the family car. Much of Marty's dissatisfaction in this world stems from his father's lack of self-confidence, a lack that Marty seems to have inherited from him. But when Marty leaves the present and enters the past with the help of a time machine that his friend Doc Brown (Christopher Lloyd) has invented, he enters a world of fantasy which provides a milieu where he can resolve the problems of desire. In *Back to the Future*, fantasy becomes the vehicle through which one can restructure the world and cure it of its absences.

Whereas *Wizard of Oz* depicts the divide between the world of desire and the world of fantasy by alternating between black and white and color photography, in *Back to the Future* this divide manifests itself through differences in mise-en-scène. The film contrasts the setting, costumes, and props of the 1980s in the world of desire with those from the 1950s in the world of fantasy. This world of fantasy gives Marty the opportunity to accomplish the impossible and to change the family into which he was born. Marty's dissatisfaction in the world of desire stems primarily from his family, and this is one obstacle that no one can circumvent. The subject is born into a family situation that is never of the subject's own choosing. But through Marty's immersion in the world of fantasy, the film allows him to arrange his own conception. Though his voyage to the past initially interrupts the onset of the relationship between his parents and threatens to annul his very existence, in the end Marty is able to create a different kind of relationship for them. He trains his father to act in the ways that he wants him to act and helps him to acquire self-confidence, thereby completely transforming his father's life. Because this takes place in a clearly delineated fantasmatic past, the film exposes the workings of fantasy, revealing how fantasy provides an imaginary scenario through which we resolve the impossibilities of desire. However, when the distinction between the fantasy world and the world of desire breaks down, the film begins to disguise the role that fantasy plays.[5]

As with Dorothy's return to Kansas, Marty's return to the present is a return to a changed present. His voyage into the fantasy world of the past has the effect of transforming the world of desire. Because of Marty's intervention, his family rises in economic status and emotional well-being. His father, George, is no longer bullied by Biff but now has Biff working for him (waxing his car), and he becomes a published science-fiction author. Marty's advice to George in the fantasy world—"If you put your mind to it, you can accomplish anything"—has had a remarkable effect. The whole family shows the signs of this transformation. Marty's mother becomes thin and healthier. His brother and sister are both dressed in much nicer clothes than they were before Marty left. Marty himself discovers that he owns the truck we saw him dream of owning (but unable to afford) in the first part of the film. Perhaps most importantly, Doc Brown, having read Marty's letter concerning his fate, wears a bulletproof vest on the night he is shot and thus survives. These changes indicate that the fantasy world of the past has bled into the world of desire and filled in the absences of this world. At the end of the film, the world of desire is no longer a world of impossibility. When Marty returns to the present, the film uses the absence of desire and the presence of fantasy to complement one another. Hence, at the end of *Back to the Future*, we avoid experiencing the gaze either in its absence or in its distorting presence. Instead, we experience the gaze as a temporary limit that we can overcome.

Though the final images of a reconciliation between the worlds of desire and fantasy disguise the gaze, films such as *The Wizard of Oz* and *Back to the Future* nonetheless point toward the possibility of a kind of cinema that would sustain the separation between these worlds. Such a cinema would emphasize even more than these films the contrast between the experience of desire and the experience of fantasy. What's more, it would allow us to encounter the gaze at the points where fantasy emerges out of and intrudes upon the world of desire. Rather than experiencing the integration of desire and fantasy, we would experience their intersection. Rather than domesticating the gaze in the manner of the cinema of integration, this other kind of cinema—a cinema of intersection—would facilitate a traumatic encounter with the gaze.

The Cinema of Intersection

Collisions of Desire and Fantasy

23

The Separation of Desire and Fantasy

IN PARTS 1 and 2 we saw how cinema can deploy the gaze as a distorting presence or as a constitutive absence. Both of these ways of presenting the gaze rely on indirection to allow the spectator to experience it. In part 3, we saw how the attempt to provide direct access to the object of desire has the effect of transforming the gaze qua privileged object into an ordinary object. What I have called the "cinema of integration" fails to sustain its rendering of the gaze because it wants to give the spectator a complete experience—and thereby the gaze, which must remain a partial object, disappears. In light of these three options, it seems that cinema's approach to the gaze must confine itself to creating an experience of the gaze at a distance if cinema is to facilitate any experience of it at all.

But there is another possibility that films such as *The Wizard of Oz* and *Back to the Future* point toward. This possibility involves bringing the cinematic depiction of an experience of desire (where the gaze is absent) and an experience of fantasy (where the gaze is a distorting presence) into the same film and sustaining a separation between them in order to reveal what occurs when they collide. In the moment of collision or intersection, these films produce a direct experience of the gaze: as spectators, we encounter an object that does not fit within the filmic field of representation and yet by that very fact indicates our involvement in that field. The direct experience of the gaze collapses the distance between subject and object, and it thereby forces spectators to experience themselves as directly implicated in what they see.

This occurs, for instance, when the naked and beaten body of Dorothy Vallens (Isabella Rossellini) appears in an idyllic neighborhood at the end of David Lynch's *Blue Velvet* (1986). In addition to her appearance, Dorothy's

163

mere presence in the scene disturbs Jeffrey (Kyle McLaughlan), who has been enthralled with her and has had an affair with her. Now, however, he is on a date with his new girlfriend, Sandy (Laura Dern). When Dorothy gradually enters from the side of the frame, Sandy's former boyfriend has forced Sandy and Jeffrey off the road in order to pick a fight with Jeffrey for stealing Sandy from him. Dorothy seems to appear out of thin air, and at first no one notices her. When the other characters do notice her, however, they become completely disoriented. As an embodiment of the gaze or objet petit a, Dorothy intrudes into this fantasmatic realm and completely disrupts it, ripping apart the fantasy structure. Her appearance comes from another world altogether, which is why it is so jarring. Such a disruption is possible through the extreme separation between the experience of desire and the experience of fantasy that Lynch produces in the film.

Sandy's ex-boyfriend quickly abandons any notion of fighting with Jeffrey because he correctly infers that Dorothy's presence changes everything. The threat of the fight suddenly seems absurdly insignificant in comparison with the trauma of the gaze. The fantasy screen suddenly breaks down because Dorothy's body has no proper place within the fantasmatic world. The form in which she appears—publicly naked and begging for Jeffrey's help— reveals the spectator's investment in the fantasy and demands that the spectator confront her as object gaze. She doesn't fit in the picture, which is why we become so uncomfortable watching her naked body in the middle of the suburban neighborhood. When Jeffrey and Sandy take Dorothy into Sandy's house, Dorothy clings to Jeffrey and repeats, "He put his disease in me." Dorothy's presence is unbearable both for characters in the film—Sandy begins to break down, and her mother retrieves a coat to cover Dorothy— and for the spectator.

Here the realm of desire intersects with that of fantasy, forcing an encounter with the real of the gaze. The fantasy structure of the town of Lumberton's public world can only maintain its consistency as long as it excludes desire. Hence, when Dorothy's desire intrudes into this structure, she shatters it, and at the same time shatters the spectator's distance from what's happening. As a foreign body in this mise-en-scène, Dorothy embodies the gaze, and our anxiety in seeing her indicates our encounter with it, revealing that we are in the picture at its nonspecular point, the point of the gaze. Here, the object looks back at us, and the film includes us in what it shows.

This experience becomes possible through the separation that films such as *Blue Velvet* enact. The worlds of desire and fantasy are opposed because desire thrives on the absence of the gaze and fantasy thrives on its excessive presence. The world of desire is a world without open displays of enjoyment, whereas fantasy facilitates such displays. The absence of enjoyment sustains desire, which is why the world of desire cannot simply tolerate fantasmatic intrusions. When open displays of enjoyment enter the world of desire, they throw it out of balance and highlight its fundamental instability. Blended together, desire and fantasy create an experience of stability that protects the subject from the traumatic real. In exchange for this protection, however, the subject sacrifices its access to its enjoyment.

In our everyday lives, we never experience separate worlds of desire and fantasy. We veer toward one and then the other but remain within a terrain marked by the experience of both. In contrast, cinema has the ability to create separate worlds of desire and fantasy and to hold them separate. By using the formal qualities of film to construct two distinct types of cinematic experience within the same film, films can separate desire and fantasy in a way that is impossible outside the cinema. The fundamental achievement of the cinema of intersection involves its ability to access the impossible and to thereby reveal to us the impossible as a possibility. Ironically, one of the most common criticisms of Hollywood films centers around Hollywood's proclivity for depicting the impossible as a possibility. According to this line of thought, Hollywood disguises the horrible reality of our real-life situation by offering us fantasmatic scenarios in which we can accomplish the impossible and escape this situation (by working hard, by falling in love, and so on). However, the deeper problem with Hollywood's fantasies lies in their failure to envision the impossible as such. Hollywood remains in the domain of the possible, even when it colors this domain with the image of impossibility. Hollywood's escapist films, for the most part, belong to the cinema of integration rather than the cinema of intersection because they transform the impossible object into an ordinary object. Cinema truly realizes its radical potential when it treats the ordinary object as an impossible one.

Unlike the cinema of integration, the cinema of intersection does not offer us access to the impossible by reducing the impossible to the status of the possible—by reducing the gaze to an empirical object of desire, as we saw occurring in films like *Cocoon* or *A Beautiful Mind*. When the impossible object becomes an empirical object, one can experience it integrated within the field of vision without a disruption of that field. In the cinema of intersection, however, the encounter with the impossible object completely shatters the field of vision. The gaze and the field of vision cannot simply coexist: the emergence of one implies the shattering of the other. If we think back to Hans Holbein's *The Ambassadors*, we can see this same either/or alternative in the recognition of the skull in the middle of the painting. Either one sees the skull as simply a blob at the feet of the two ambassadors, or one sees the skull and not the rest of the painting. Apprehending the gaze means losing one's rootedness within the field of vision and giving oneself over to the object itself.

The experience of the impossible in the cinema of intersection reveals not simply the possibility of the impossible but also its disruptiveness and its inability to be assimilated to the everyday order of things. This cinema thus represents the antithesis of the cinema of integration. Whereas the latter attempts to expand the reach of ideology, the former attempts to highlight the hole in its midst. This hole becomes evident in each of the films that this chapter will examine. We can see it in Andrei Tarkovsky's depiction of different worlds overlapping and intruding into each other, in Alain Resnais's insertion of the past into the present as a foreign body, in Wim Wenders's revelation of the turn to fantasy as an ethical gesture, and in David Lynch's divided portraits of failure of the sexual relationship. Tarkovsky takes this cinema in the direction of religion; Resnais takes it in the direction of history; Wenders takes it in the direction of ethics; and Lynch takes it in the direction of erotics. In each case, a filmic separation creates the possibility of a traumatic intersection.

Whereas the filmmakers of the cinema of fantasy can exist within Hollywood and the filmmakers of the cinema of desire tend to exist outside it, the filmmakers of the cinema of intersection often straddle the line, as is clearest in the cases of Wenders and Lynch. They often make films that Hollywood partially funds, but their films almost never receive the backing or distribution of the typical Hollywood film. When they do, usually disappointment ensues for both the filmmaker and Hollywood, as was the case with Lynch's *Dune* (1984).

The films of the cinema of intersection signal the difference between the two very distinctive cinematic experiences with changes in editing, mise-en-scène, film stock, framing, shot selection, or sound. But unlike films such as *The Wizard of Oz* and *Back to the Future*, films in the cinema of intersection sustain the rigid distinction between the two experiences throughout, without allowing them to bleed into each other, even in their conclusions.[1] Because it attempts to envision an encounter with the gaze, the cinema of intersection represents the furthest that film has gone in the attempt to address the gaze and to respond to the traumatic power of this impossible object.

The cinema of intersection allows us to examine what happens when fantasy emerges in response to the dissatisfaction of desire. Even though fantasy supplements the functioning of ideology, the turn to fantasy—the turn that helps to obscure the gaze in the cinema of integration—does not always work in the service of ideology. The very fact that fantasy exists reveals an opening within ideology. Through the recourse to fantasy, ideology shows itself to be fissured, to be in need of fantasy's support for it to function effectively. If ideology and the symbolic order were not haunted by a real—that is, if they were self-enclosed and self-sustaining structures—there would be no need for fantasy to keep subjects within them. In this sense, even the most ideological film testifies to ideology's point of failure, its need for a fantasmatic supplement. But this point of failure becomes especially evident in the cinema of intersection, which highlights the turn from desire to fantasy rather than hiding it.

The cinema of intersection aims at producing a normal subject in the way that psychoanalysis itself does. Understood in this way, normal subjects are not those who fit comfortably into their society but the ones who are able to avoid blending together the experience of desire and fantasy. Keeping these experiences distinct doesn't, as we might expect, ensure a healthy ability to distinguish reality from illusion, but it does allow the subject to have a direct experience of the traumatic real. The normal subject, for Freud, is the subject who embraces traumatic enjoyment instead of sacrificing it in the name of a demand made by the social law. The successful analysis, like the successful experience of the cinema of intersection, concludes with the subject opting for and embracing her or his particular mode of enjoyment, embracing the stain in the field of the visible that is the gaze. Such a subject does not use the turn to fantasy to supplement desire and to escape the path of desire, but instead uses it to discover the impossible object—the gaze—that supports this subject.

The encounter with the gaze occurs only when we sustain desire and fantasy as separate realms. As we have seen, the gaze is not an actually existing object; it is the distortion in the subject's visible field caused by the subject's perspective on that field. Consequently, when the cinema of fantasy allows us to see the gaze, we see it indirectly, through the distortions in the filmic image. When watching the films of this type of cinema, we do not experience traumatic shock of a direct encounter with this object. The cinema of fantasy allows us to recognize our involvement in what we see, but it doesn't confront us with this involvement in the form of a traumatic encounter. In the cinema of intersection, on the other hand, we do experience the shock of an encounter with the impossible object.

Fantasy, unlike our sense of reality, is always incomplete; it breaks down and loses its consistency at its edges. This incompleteness derives from fantasy's function for the subject: it provides the subject with a way of accessing an impossible object while sustaining its impossible status.[2] We fantasize scenarios in which we are excluded and thereby denied the object, but, at the same time, it is through these scenarios that we access the object for ourselves. In this way, fantasy violates the law of noncontradiction. In fantasy, the object is simultaneously there and not there; it is simultaneously denied to us and available to us. Consequently, the structure of fantasy lacks consistency and wholeness. Fantasy can provides access to the impossible object only insofar as its structure involves contradiction and breaks down at certain points. Because of fantasy's constitutive incompleteness, even though it domesticates the gaze, it also allows for an experience of the gaze that would otherwise be impossible to come by. This experience occurs at the edge of fantasy—when it emerges and when it breaks apart. Usually, we tend to retreat from fantasy precisely at the point when it would break apart and reveal the gaze to us. This is why, according to Lacan, we awaken from dreams at the moment we do. He writes, "A dream awakens just at the moment when it could unleash the truth, so that one awakens only in order to continue to dream—to dream in the real, or to be more exact, in reality."[3] The cinema of intersection forces us to remain within the fantasy to its endpoint in order that we might experience the gaze. When the cinema of intersection employs fantasy but at the same time reveals the limit that fantasy comes up against, it takes us to an encounter with the traumatic real.

We glimpse the impossible object through the filmic juxtaposition of the worlds of desire and fantasy, through the point at which one emerges out of the other. Because the cinema of intersection juxtaposes the worlds of desire and fantasy, it reveals the gaze as it becomes present and as it disappears, which is the only time that we can experience the gaze as such. That is to say, we experience the full traumatic impact of the gaze at the moment of its emergence and the moment of its disappearance. When it is simply distorting the visual field, it ceases to disturb us in the same way. This is why the cinema of intersection holds the key to the subject's encounter with the gaze: through the act of depicting the movement out of desire and into fantasy (and vice versa), this cinema shows us the distorting power of the gaze as it is actually occurring. In this experience, we undergo a shift from the uncertain world of desire to the clarity of fantasy. Fantasy fills in the empty space in the world of desire and provides an answer to the question of that world, but as we watch this process unfold in the cinema of intersection, we can come to understand the true nature of this answer.

The cinema of intersection forces us to experience not simply the empty space in the Other (like the cinema of desire) or how our subjectivity—our enjoyment—distorts the visual field (like the cinema of fantasy). Instead, we experience our own enjoyment as the answer to the question of the Other's desire. Through this type of cinema, we can recognize our own role in filling in the lack in the Other. When we experience the turn from the realm of desire to that of fantasy in the cinema of intersection, we see that our fantasy—not some secret buried within the Other itself—provides the support for the Other at its point of lack. The desire of the Other ceases to be mysterious and becomes visible as our own mode of enjoyment.

In short, the encounter with the gaze reveals the link between the impossible object and the subject itself. The trauma of the encounter with the gaze as a real—which is to say, impossible—object stems from this object's connection with the subject. The real is not the radical difference of the Other, but identity in difference, what the subject cannot escape. The real always returns to the same place, as Lacan puts it, because it is the subject's own mode of enjoyment that accompanies the subject wherever the subject goes. The key to the subject's freedom from dependence on the Other stems from its ability to embrace the gaze and identify itself with this impossible object. But such an identification costs the subject its support in the Other, which is why neurosis develops as a form of resistance to identification with the gaze. As Lacan notes in his seminar on identification, "The subject inasmuch as it is structured by the signifier can become the cut (*a*) itself. But this is precisely what the neurotic's fantasy does not accede to because it searches for the routes and the paths in an erroneous way."[4] Neurosis represents a barrier to the subject's identification with the gaze because it is a refusal to sacrifice the hope that the Other holds some ultimate enjoyment that the subject itself lacks.[5] The neurotic needs to believe in the otherness of the Other. This seemingly mysterious otherness provides what the neurotic seeks in the gaze, which is why the neurotic demands the object of its desire from the Other. Neurosis derives from a belief that the Other has the object—that the Other has a hidden mode of enjoyment inaccessible by the subject—and this belief sustains the enjoyment that the neurotic obtains from fantasy. But neurosis is a self-defeating enterprise.

Seeking the object in the Other necessarily runs aground because the object emerges out of the Other's inability to respond to the subject's demand. Lacan points out that "the object itself as such, insofar as it is the object of desire, is the effect of the impossibility of the Other responding to the demand."[6] In short, the Other cannot give the neurotic what the neurotic wants. And as we remain within a neurotic relation to the object of desire (as most subjects do), we will continually run up against the barrier of demanding that the Other give us what it doesn't have and what only we ourselves have. It is at this point that the cinema of intersection intervenes as a corrective.

By offering spectators a traumatic encounter with the gaze, the cinema of intersection attempts its own version of the psychoanalytic cure. It allows spectators to see what subjects ordinarily never see: to see themselves rather than the secret of the Other in the fantasy. In doing so, this type of cinema hopes to shock the spectator into the freedom that derives from identifying oneself with the gaze. Rather than neurotically identifying the gaze with the secret otherness of the Other, the spectator can recognize its own enjoyment in the form of the gaze. Subjects who do this become able to embrace their own mode of enjoying instead of continually seeking enjoyment elsewhere in the Other. In this way, the cinema of intersection aims at creating an enjoying subject. But because they involve a traumatic encounter with an impossible object, the films of the cinema of intersection are often some of the most disturbing films to watch. At the same time, these films develop an aesthetic that points us in the direction of an enjoyment that we rarely notice outside of the cinema.

24

Theorizing the Real

A s we saw in the first chapter, beginning in the 1990s a new form of Lacanian film theory emerges. Led by Joan Copjec and Slavoj Žižek, this new theory represents a dramatic departure from traditional Lacanian film theory. Whereas early Lacanian film theory exposes and criticizes the ideological function of cinema, the new version most often celebrates cinema's ability to depict that which disturbs rather than supports ideology. In this sense, the two forms of Lacanian film theory are very much at odds. Their divergence stems from opposing conceptions of film art and this art's relationship to ideology. For early Lacanian film theorists, the primary function of film art—at least as it manifests itself in a capitalist economy—centers around its ability to coerce spectators into accepting relations of power that run against their self-interest.

For the new Lacanian film theorists, the primary function of film art lies in revealing the failures and gaps within the structure of power. Rather than seducing us into accepting our symbolic prison, film tends to show us the real openings within that prison. In short, new Lacanian film theorists extend to the medium of film Walter Davis's idea that "the way artists know is not only different; it liberates a knowledge of the Real."[1] Because of its ability to deploy the gaze, film art facilitates an encounter with the real that deprives spectators of their symbolic support and thereby forces them to experience their radical freedom. By focusing on the real dimension of film instead of its imaginary qualities (in the manner of early Lacanian film theory), new Lacanian film theory discovers how cinema challenges our ideological interpellation rather than supporting it.

This is not to say that new Lacanian film theorists do not attribute any ideological function to the cinema. On the contrary, these theorists often pay a great deal of attention to the way that ideology functions in, say, Hollywood film. But according to this perspective, the ideological use of cinema always involves an attempt to escape or mask the power of the gaze in the cinema, a power that has primacy in relation to the ideological use of cinema. In other words, cinema is first and foremost a site for the revelation of the gaze, and an ideological cinema—what I call a cinema of integration—emerges as if in response to this situation. In order to create an ideological cinema, one must work to contain the gaze, which always threatens to erupt within the cinema. Early Lacanian film theory, in contrast, views ideological cinema as the primary state of the filmic medium because it implicitly views the medium as a superstructural expression of a capitalist infrastructure.[2]

The transition away from this position involves a rethinking of the role of cinema in society. According to the earlier view, we go to the cinema in order to procure an imaginary pleasure, a pleasure that simply smoothes over the dissatisfaction that accompanies existence in an unjust social order. The desire to attend the cinema is here a misleading desire, a desire given to us by ideology. According to the new Lacanian film theory, however, we go to the cinema in search of an enjoyment that cannot be confined to the structures of ideology. The great thrill of the cinema comes from the experience of the disruptive gaze, even if a film thoroughly disguises and blurs that experience, as is the case in a film like *Schindler's List*. What engages us about *Schindler's List* is the figure of Goeth (Ralph Fiennes) qua object gaze, though we need the comfort of Schindler (Liam Neeson)—and his final victory over Goeth's desire—to render our enjoyment of Goeth more palatable. What is primary for the spectator's enjoyment in the cinema is the gaze. We seek the real that ideology fails to provide. In this sense, the turn to the new Lacanian film theory represents an increase in respect for the cinema as such.

The emergence of the new Lacanian film theory also involves a revision of the popular understanding of ideology derived from Althusser. For traditional Lacanian film theory, the story of ideology and ideological interpellation is primarily, if not completely, a success story. To put it in Althusser's terms, ideology succeeds in interpellating individuals as subjects. In a similar fashion, film succeeds in giving subjects an illusory sense of their own autonomy and mastery. The enjoyment that spectators derive from cinema is thus an illusory enjoyment, an enjoyment that testifies to their subjugation and to ideology's success. According to this view, ideology functions smoothly and without interruption. It involves a call and a response, and even the misunderstandings between the call and the response do nothing to subvert—and in fact feed—the system of ideological interpellation. That is to say, the subject accedes to the call of ideology not when it recognizes the call as directed toward it, but when it *misrecognizes* the call and adopts the proffered identity as its own. In this sense, for Althusser and early Lacanian film theory, ideological interpellation succeeds when it fails. No subject manages to escape its trap. The new Lacanian film theory challenges this vision of ideological interpellation by emphasizing the possibility of its actual failure. For this latter theory, we might say that ideological interpellation fails when it succeeds.

The problem with Althusser's vision of ideological interpellation resides in its inability to account for the theorist who recognizes the process. If ideological interpellation succeeds even when it fails, what enables the theorist see it happening? If all subjects were in fact successfully interpellated, no subject could escape the process of interpellation enough to theorize the process itself.[3] When we exist wholly within a particular structure, we cannot recognize this structure but instead remain completely blind to it. The moment at which one recognizes a power structure, the structure has already lost its total control. This means that if we have the ability to theorize a power structure, we know on the basis of this ability that the structure has some weakness and is subject to failure. The theory of ideological interpellation advanced by Althusser and adopted by early Lacanian film theory allows no space for the very recognition implicit in the theory itself.

Althusser himself attempts to respond to this problem by appealing to Marxist science as alternate terrain, distinct from that of ideology, which the theorist, when theorizing, accesses. But this leaves unanswered the question of how the subject arrives at this new terrain if ideological interpellation has in fact been successful. In the end, Althusser's emphasis on the success of ideological interpellation has the effect of creating a theory without a theorist—a theory for which one cannot imagine a theorist capable of arriving at it.[4] One of the virtues of the new Lacanian film theory is its ability to take the theorist into account within the theory. Because it conceives the subject as a mode of resistance to ideology rather than the product of ideology—as the result of ideological interpellation's failure to produce fully an ideological identity—the new Lacanian film theory philosophically accommodates a theoretical endeavor in which a theorist works to expose the functioning of ideology. For this theory, the film theorist is the subject who pays attention to the real point at which ideology fails.

The role of the film theorist undergoes an extreme revolution in the move from early Lacanian film theory to the new version, which exhibits a different attitude concerning the relationship between theory and film. This theory takes an interest in film for what film can reveal rather than for what film hides. Early Lacanian film theory views cinematic representation chiefly as a problem that it must attack. The new Lacanian film theory, in contrast, works to accentuate and define what the cinema represents. For it, the problem with cinema is not so much that it serves to mask the functioning of ideology or the production process, but that we as spectators fail to see what the cinema has to show us. Hence, the task of the theorist becomes one of unlocking the power of the cinema rather than fighting against it. With the emergence of the new Lacanian film theory, the theorist no longer battles against the cinema but becomes cinema's ally in the struggle to reveal the gaze.

25

The Politics of the Cinema of Intersection

THE ALLIANCE BETWEEN the theorist and the cinema as such becomes most evident in the cinema of intersection. This cinema has an implicit political urgency that derives from its effort to depict the gaze directly. By depicting the gaze directly, the films of the cinema of intersection aim at encouraging subjects to recognize that they themselves, on the level of fantasy, hold the key to the secret at the heart of the Other. In clear contrast to the cinema of integration, this cinema directs subjects away from their proclivity to seek fantasmatic support in the Other.

The cinema of integration tends to produce subjects who believe in a nonlacking Other. This cinema, as we saw in the case of Steven Spielberg, is one that posits, whether explicitly or implicitly, a symbolic father filling in the absence in the Other. The filmic world of the cinema of integration fosters the belief that absence in the Other does not really exist. Each time it depicts an absence, this cinema reveals a hidden presence. According to this cinema, the Other as such never fails.

In the cinema of intersection, we encounter the absence in the Other directly. The strict separation of the worlds of desire and fantasy in this cinema allows it to depict these worlds intersecting. At these moments, we experience the absence in the Other in a privileged way. Hence, rather than producing dependence, the cinema of intersection produces an experience of freedom. The encounter with the real is the encounter with the Other's failure, and this encounter traumatizes the subject because it deprives the subject of support in the Other. The subject derives its symbolic identity from the Other, and as a result, the encounter with the Other's lack leaves the subject without any sense of identity. The subject loses the security that derives from its link to the Other. But at the same time, this loss of support in the Other frees the subject from its dependence on the Other. Freedom depends on the recognition that the Other does not exist, that the Other cannot provide the subject a substantive identity. The encounter with the gaze in the cinema of intersection permits us to experience directly the Other's insubstantial status.

In none of the cinematic structures that we have looked at thus far does the gaze appear as an object that we can encounter. Each type of cinema, in its own fashion, suggests the impossible status of the gaze, though the cinema of integration does so unwittingly, through its failure to present the gaze as either an absence in the visible field or as a distortion of that field. In this sense, these three types of cinema affirm Lacan's contention that "the real is the impossible,"[1] and they allow us to see—except in the case of the cinema of integration—the lack in the Other and the incomplete status of ideology.

Though the cinema of desire and the cinema of fantasy affirm the impossible status of the gaze and its irreducibility to the field of the visible, neither is able to show us how we can experience and accomplish the impossible. That is to say, both kinds of cinema conceive of the gaze as impossible in the strict sense of the term. However, Lacan's conception of the real as impossible does not mean that the real cannot be reached, but that it does not fit within the logic of our symbolic structure. As he explains in *Seminar XVII*, it is impossible "not on account of a simple stumbling block against which we bang our heads, but on account of what is announced as impossible by the symbolic. It is from there that the real arises."[2] Though the real marks the point of impossibility within any symbolic system, this point of impossibility is not out of reach.

The impossible status of the real stems from our inability to trace a path to it through the symbolic order. We can identify it—and we can mark it symbolically—but we can't find a way to access the real in the way that we access other empirical objects. The example of the square root of -1 indicates the problem that the real presents to us. We can, of course, think and symbolize the square root of -1. But we cannot symbolize with real numbers what results when we try to take the square root of -1 because no squared real number will be negative. The square root of -1 requires us to create an imaginary number that exists solely in order to be the solution to this operation. This imaginary number is, in a sense, more real than any real number insofar as it indicates the point at which a certain mathematical system of symbolization breaks down. This system invites us to take the square root of numbers, but it cannot accommodate this operation being performed on every number. The square root of -1 represents what the system of real numbers cannot symbolize, and when we create imaginary numbers in order to perform this operation, we do the impossible and thereby radically transform the system of symbolization itself.

To return from mathematics to ideology, one can accomplish the impossible by refusing to accept the choices that ideology offers. Ideology functions by defining the possibilities that subjects have, by creating options that remain within ideological bounds. One can choose today, for instance, between fundamentalism and capitalist democracy, but both choices remain within the ideological orbit of contemporary global capitalism. Even opting to combat capitalist democracy by choosing fundamentalism doesn't challenge the ideological landscape. Even fundamentalist terror attacks affirm rather than question capitalist ideology as they provide an opportunity for this ideology to align itself falsely with freedom. Capitalist democracy understands fundamentalism as the other that allows it to function and to define itself.[3] That is to say, ideology establishes the game so that it wins no matter which side a subject chooses. Within an ideological structure, every possibility affirms the ideology and feeds its overall logic.

The only way to break from the controlling logic of the ideology is to reject the possibilities that it presents and opt for the impossible. The impossible is impossible within a specific ideological framework, and the act of accomplishing the impossible has the effect of radically transforming the framework. The impossible thus marks the terrain of politics as such. As Slavoj Žižek points out, "Authentic politics is . . . the art of the *impossible*—it changes the very parameters of what is considered 'possible' in the existing constellation."[4] If a political act is not impossible in this sense, it is not really political because it lacks the ability to transform the contested ideological field.[5] To create authentic change demands an act that does not fit within the possibilities that ideology lays out.

Ideology prevents subjects from opting for the impossible choice precisely by making it seem impossible to do so. That is to say, we tend to believe that the impossible really is impossible because this is what ideology tells us again and again. Herein lies the great value of the cinema of intersection. Through enacting a traumatic encounter with the gaze, this cinema shows us that we can do the impossible. At the moment we encounter the gaze, we see the field of representation thrown into relief and redefined. Everything outside of the gaze loses its former significance in light of this encounter. Through this cinematic experience, we can glimpse the impossible. We see the filmic world from the perspective of the gaze rather than seeing the gaze from the perspective of the filmic world (as occurs in the cinema of integration). After this encounter, the normal functioning of the world cannot continue in the same way and undergoes a radical transformation. Though we can accomplish the impossible, we can't do so without simultaneously destroying the very ground beneath our feet.

By facilitating an encounter with the gaze, the cinema of intersection encourages the spectator to identify with this object. Though other forms of cinema push the subject in the direction of freedom, it is only the cinema of intersection that emphasizes identification with the impossible object. In doing so, this cinema allows the subject to grasp its own nothingness—to see itself in the nothingness of the object. The reduction of the subject to the nothingness of the objet petit a is the most extreme form of freedom available to the subject. It implies a rejection of the world of the Other and an affirmation of the subject's private fantasmatic response to that world. To identify with the object is to insist on one's particular way of enjoying at the expense of one's symbolic identity.

26

The Overlapping Worlds
of Andrei Tarkovsky

THE OVERRIDING AIM of the cinema of intersection is the encounter with the traumatic real. In facilitating this encounter, it allows us to grasp the nature of our relationship to the objet petit a. Through the way that it deploys desire and fantasy, the cinema of intersection renders visible the traumatic proximity of the gaze—a proximity that the blending of desire and fantasy serves to obscure. Seeing that the object-cause of our desire is tied to our subjectivity, we challenge the resentment and paranoia that almost seem to define subjectivity as such.

Ironically, the blending of the worlds of desire and fantasy that we find in the cinema of integration works to persuade us of the absolute difference between these two worlds. When fantasy inconspicuously supplements the world of desire in this cinema (and in our everyday existence), we cannot see the distinctiveness of either world, and thus we cannot compare them with each other. The more that cinema hides fantasy's distinctiveness, the more it also hides the underlying similarity of the object in fantasy and the object in the world of desire. This is the paradox that informs and drives the cinema of integration. However, the cinema of intersection breaks from this logic and delineates an alternative. By initially creating a complete divide between the worlds of desire and fantasy, the cinema of intersection has the ability to reveal their similarity through juxtaposition. It is a similarity that we can only see after experiencing their complete separation.

The stability of our symbolic identity and of the world of desire depends on the idea of fantasy's absolute difference. Though the experience of desire and fantasy blend together, we believe that the object which animates the world of desire is not the object that we fantasize about, that we don't meet our fantasy object within the social reality. We believe, to put it in other terms, that the present is not simply repeating the past, that we are not pursuing the same object that we have pursued before. Without this idea, we cannot continue to function and move forward as desiring subjects. The ability to enter full of hope into a new relationship, for instance, depends on the belief that the new partner actually represents a new love object and that "this time things will be different." Our fantasy remains the same, but desire constantly moves forward because it never actually finds the fantasy object. When we grasp that the object does not change, every new relationship becomes visible as the repetition of an earlier one. And in this way, the object of desire ceases to be an object of desire and becomes a traumatic object. This occurs, for instance, when we recognize the underlying similarity between one's parent and one's sexual partner. The objet petit a can continue to enflame the desire of the subject as long as it remains under the guise of difference—a guise perpetuated by changing objects of desire—and this guise is precisely what Tarkovsky's films strip away. In Tarkovsky's films, we see the sameness of the object in desire and in fantasy; we see that what remains constant is the objet petit a. This emphasis on the constancy of the object locates Tarkovsky within the cinema of intersection and within Hegelian ontology.

Tarkovsky is one of the most Hegelian of filmmakers insofar as his films stress identity in the experience of difference. For Hegel, the activity of the philosopher involves nothing but recognition—the recognition of the subject's involvement in the difference of the Other. Or, as Hegel himself puts it, "Everything turns on grasping and expressing the True, not only as *Substance*, but equally as *Subject*."[1] Rather than continuing to see difference in what is distinct, according to Hegel, philosophy must recognize the identity that the distinctiveness belies. This is a difficult task because it requires that the subject give up the hope for a different future that derives from its belief in difference, which is why Hegel says that the subject "wins to its truth only . . . in utter dismemberment."[2] This "utter dismemberment" accompanies the recognition that the subject has no hope of encountering radical otherness, that its game has already been played (and will be replayed many times). Recognizing that one has no future—or at least no alternative future—does not lead to nihilism or even pessimism. Instead, this recognition provides the basis for the rebirth of the subject.

Commentators on Tarkovsky's films and even Tarkovksy himself often discuss his films in terms of the spiritual renewal that they either enact or advocate.[3] In a certain sense, this is the proper way to think about this type of cinema, provided that we understand what spiritual renewal means here. It does not mean a rebirth of hope but almost precisely the opposite. The spiritual renewal that Tarkovsky's films demand is one in which we recognize the presence of the beyond in our daily lives. In these films, God no longer inhabits a transcendent beyond that we cannot know or access, but actually manifests himself fully in the human world. This conception of God spiritualizes the quotidian, which is why miracles often occur in the films of

Tarkovsky. But at the same time this idea of God invalidates the usual paths of faith. If one accepts Tarkovsky's spiritualization of the world, one must abandon all recourse to the mystery or the unknowability of God.[4] In Tarkovsky's filmic universe, God becomes a presence rather than an absence. This allows us to believe, but it doesn't allow us to hope for a future salvation or for a kingdom of heaven structured differently from earth itself. Whatever salvation or heaven there is, whatever God can provide, has already been realized in the present.[5] The fantasy ideal is already present here in the quotidian world of desire.

It is in this way that Tarkovsky is an antimodern. Modernity is predicated on a belief in the future and a belief in the human capacity for progress. Tarkovsky's films completely reject any idea of progress insofar as they reveal our inability to escape the originary impossible object. Rather than moving from object to object throughout our lives (as the modern believes), we instead continue to circulate around the same object, never moving forward, never advancing out of the path of this circular drive. Even though our object of desire obviously changes, our objet petit a—the object motivating our desire—does not. The metonymy of desire is but a mask for the monotony of the drive. Tarkovsky offers us the possibility of recognizing this through the cinema. He creates works that belong to the cinema of intersection because they facilitate an encounter with the gaze through their unique overlapping of the worlds of desire and fantasy.

Tarkovsky allows us to confront the sameness of the objet petit a by establishing a dramatic division between the worlds of desire and fantasy. In Tarkovsky's films, this division is material, occurring most obviously through the use of different film stock. Following the pattern established in *The Wizard of Oz*, Tarkovsky will sometimes shoot the world of desire using black and white stock and the world of fantasy using color, as he does in *Stalker* (1979).[6] At other times, as in *Solaris* (1972), he emphasizes the distinctiveness of the two worlds through changes in mise-en-scène: the film moves from a pastoral scene at a Russian dacha to a distant space station orbiting the planet Solaris. These extreme formal differences have echoes on the level of content as well. In the first part of *Solaris*, Kris Kelvin (Donatas Banionis) prepares for a deep space voyage at his father's dacha, and here he experiences a world structured around absence—the absence of his wife, Hari (Natalya Bondarchuk), who has killed herself, and his mother. When Kris arrives at the Solaris space station, however, his situation changes dramatically: rather than suffering from the absence of Hari, he becomes unable to rid himself of her fantasmatic overpresence. Due to the influence of the planet below, the space station fantasmatically realizes the desires of the people onboard and creates what the characters call "visitors." Hari magically appears in response to Kris's desire, and though he repeatedly kills her, she continues to reappear. The fantasmatic world on the space station produces an overpresence of the object, which contrasts with the absence of the object in the first part of the film.

Tarkovsky establishes this kind of divide between the world of desire and that of fantasy not in order to stress their difference, but to expose their identity. This becomes most apparent in *Stalker* because this film initially exaggerates the difference between the two worlds more than any other of Tarkovsky's films. Not only does the film contrast black and white film with color when depicting the difference between the normal social reality and the zone, but it also contrasts the former's barren harshness with the latter's sense of openness and possibility. Tarkovsky lights the first part of the film (which takes place outside the zone) very dimly, and the sets include very little décor, even in the house of Stalker (Aleksandr Kajdanovsky). In this world, characters rarely speak to each other and rarely communicate their inner thoughts. When the film depicts the characters in the zone, the mise-en-scène changes dramatically: most of the scenes take place outside in bright light, and the zone appears full of objects. In addition, characters reveal themselves entirely to each other when we see them in the zone. The very nature of the zone and the secret room it contains that realizes one's deepest desire underscores the fantasmatic dimension of the second part of the film. These differences combine with the obvious difference in film stock to create an unmistakable contrast.

After establishing the contrast between the experience of desire and of fantasy, *Stalker* proceeds in its denouement to reveal their identity. After Stalker leads two men into the zone and they return without having entered the wish-fulfilling room, we see him back in the black and white world of desire. But color now intrudes in this world: Tarkovsky uses a color shot to show Stalker walking home with his family. Even more importantly, the final scene of the film (in black and white) depicts Stalker's daughter (Natasha Abramova) moving objects across a table using just her thoughts. This scene shows the realization of desire—moving objects in reality just through the force of desire alone—occurring within the world of desire. This type of activity is precisely what we would expect to see in the zone rather than within the film's social reality. But in fact, this is the only realization of desire that we see during the film (since the two men that Stalker brought to the room refused to enter at the last minute). The fantasy world that promises the realization of desire never delivers on this promise, but the world of absence and lack does. In this way, Tarkovsky suggests the fundamental identity of these two worlds: fantasmatic miracles are not otherworldly; they occur within the world of desire itself, within our social reality. We fail to see them, however, because we expect them elsewhere, in the world of fantasy. *Stalker* makes clear that this world of fantasy constitutes the inner truth of the world of desire. And if we grasp fantasy in this way, we can no longer believe in another world that would rescue us from this one. Without the respite of the belief in another world, we must act within this one rather than simply waiting for what is to come. *Stalker* thus pushes us to define ourselves through action.

Despite the title, *Nostalghia* (1983) does not simply invest itself in a fantasmatic nostalgia for a lost past, though this type of fantasy represents a strong force within the film. *Nostalghia* depicts the travels of Russian Andrei Gortchakov (Oleg Yankovsky) in Italy as he researches his biography of the Russian composer Sosnovsky. The majority of the film shows Andrei's extreme dissatisfaction with contemporary Italy, which we see in color. Interspersed within the account of Andrei's journey in Italy are black and white flashbacks of Russia. These flashbacks depict a satisfying world that contrasts with the current conditions in Italy. As Vida T. Johnson and Graham Petrie note, "Throughout the film Russia represents what for Tarkovsky are the eternal values of earth, maternity, family, home, patience, and spirituality, while Italy stands for a decaying and 'sickeningly beautiful' culture whose superficial attractiveness masks a declining faith and a surrender to transient and destructive material values."[7] Johnson and Petrie are certainly right to align these sorts of value judgments with Russia and Italy in the film, but this does not mean that the film simply opts for a nostalgic embrace of the values it associates with Russia, that Tarkovsky sides against a modernity that has "brought the world to the verge of ruin."[8] No, the film refuses this fantasy, which is the fantasy of Andrei and of the madman Domenico (Erland Josephson), because it, like every fantasy, relies on a false notion of difference.

Rather than embracing the fantasy of a more authentic existence that *Nostalghia* associates with Russia, Tarkovsky actually undermines its power over us. According to the logic that the film plays out, materialist Italy and pastoral Russia—the decadent present and the authentic past—are inseparable and even identical. Or, to put it in a slightly different way, Russia only has a sense of spirituality from the perspective of the superficiality of Italy. The spirituality of Russia does not exist without the superficial materialism of Italy.[9] When we understand this, the otherness of Russia vanishes. But this does not necessarily entail a turn away from Russia. Though Tarkovsky does not embrace the fantasy of Russia, neither does he reject it. *Nostalghia* aims at allowing us to see the way in which it connects with the decadent world of desire out of which it originates. Fantasy cannot facilitate an escape from this world; the best it can do is to give us this world in another form. This becomes fully apparent in the final scene of the film.

The endings of *Solaris* and *Nostalghia* envision the intersection of the worlds of desire and fantasy in a similar fashion. In both cases, Tarkovsky begins with what seems like a return: in *Solaris*, it seems that Kris has returned to his father's dacha, where he began the film, and in *Nostalghia*, it seems that Andrei has left Italy and rediscovered the pastoral beauty of his Russian home. Both scenes begin with a narrow shot focusing on the hero inserted into a previous milieu (Kris at the dacha and Andrei in Russia), but then the camera proceeds to slowly pull back. In *Solaris*, Tarkovsky creates the effect of pulling the camera back into space in order to show that the father's dacha is no longer on earth but exists as an island on the planet Solaris. A similar shot occurs in *Nostalghia*, as Tarkovsky tracks back away from the Russian scene in order to reveal that this scene exists within the ruins of an Italian cathedral depicted earlier in the film. The backward tracking shot here is crucial because it forces us initially to view the fantasmatic scene in isolation, as a world different from Italy, but as the camera subsequently tracks away, we see the identity in difference—the essential link between the world of fantasy and that of desire. These two concluding scenes move in opposite directions: *Solaris* depicts the world of desire inserted within the fantasy world, while *Nostalghia* shows the fantasy contained in the world of desire. But despite this difference, both films work to the same purpose, which is to reveal that neither the experience of fantasy nor the experience of desire can ever provide respite for the other. In one sense, unlike films in the cinema of desire, Tarkovsky's films offer a way out of desire's antagonism. But they do so only by foregrounding the lack of difference in the fantasmatic alternative. One may escape in Tarkovsky's films, but one always escapes into precisely what one was fleeing.

Though *The Mirror* also concludes with a scene that depicts the disparate worlds of desire and fantasy intersecting, its uniqueness among Tarkovsky's works stems from his use of actors. The film distinguishes between a present of desire and a fantasmatic past. The past scenes depict the experiences of the mother of the narrator (Innokenti Smoktunovsky) when the narrator was a young boy. The present scenes focus on the narrator's estranged wife. However, past and present overlap because the same actor, Margarita Terekhova, plays both the narrator's mother, Maria, and his wife, Natalia. Through this casting choice, Tarkovsky forces us to identify mother and wife—the object in the fantasy and the object of desire. Seeing this identity involves encountering the traumatic gaze: one sees how one's fantasy has shaped the object that one seems to have found in the external world.

The films of Tarkovsky demand that we grasp the underlying identity of the objet petit a as it motivates different objects of desire. With this demand, Tarkovsky realizes the existential possibilities inherent in the cinema of intersection. Cinema has the ability to create barriers that everyday life obscures, and these barriers strip away the illusion of difference. Through its emphasis on the distinctiveness of the experiences of desire and fantasy, the cinema of intersection renders visible the role that repetition plays in the existence of the subject. The subject does not progress nor does it have a future, and yet it continually invests itself in the idea of progress. This idea of progress—hope for a different future—represents a fantasmatic seduction that the subject rarely escapes. By helping the subject to disentangle itself from this fantasy, Tarkovksy's cinema confronts the subject with the inescapability of its object, and it offers the subject the possibility of identifying with this object and thereby accepting its own mode of enjoyment rather than imagining that the ultimate enjoyment is elsewhere. This is an existential recognition that the unique structure of the cinema of intersection renders possible.

27

Alain Resnais between the Present and the Past

THE PROBLEM OF recovering the impossible object becomes especially vexed when we consider our relationship to history. The historical object—history itself—has the status of an impossible object. It has the status of the gaze and thus remains inapproachable through our typical means. We can of course recover historical objects, but we can't recover the historical object as such. That is to say, we can't access a historical object in the form that it existed in, which is why this object is an objet petit a that triggers our desire. When we approach history, we do so from a specific perspective, the perspective of our present mode of subjectivity and our present social arrangements. This perspective allows us to see what fits within it and blinds us to what doesn't. It also inevitably colors our relation to the past as such. Because of our orientation relative to history, the past appears not as existing on its own but as leading to our present. Even if we eschew a progressive narrative of history development, we cannot escape this illusion of perspective that reads history through the lens of our present.

The illusion of perspective that accompanies all historicizing gives history a seeming rationality and teleology that it doesn't necessarily have. Hegel's insistence on a teleological conception of history stems not from his naïve progressivism, but from his insight into the way that we approach history. His claim in the *Philosophy of History* that "the history of the world . . . presents us with a rational process" derives from his recognition that we always narrate our history backward, from the standpoint of the present.[1] History seems rational—it seems to be heading somewhere—insofar as we always experience it retroactively. Our present epoch provides the ground

185

from which we investigate history, and hence we find the presuppositions of this epoch when we conduct historical inquiries.

Because we always narrate history from the standpoint of the present, our historical narratives inevitably come to serve a fantasmatic function. Rather than providing access to the historical object, these narratives support the current ideological structure by offering a historical justification for this structure. When opponents of gun control, for instance, defend their position by invoking the views of the framers of the U. S. Constitution, this historical narrative has nothing to with a genuine interest in the views of the Constitution's framers. The turn to history here stems from a desire to authorize a contemporary position with the weight of the past. In this sense, historicizing is akin to fantasizing about origins: through this process, one justifies one's present symbolic position by appealing to an origin that appears to be free of any pathological stain. To return to the example of the gun control opponent, such a subject invokes the authority of the framers because they seem, within the fantasy frame shared by most U. S. citizens, to have arrived at decisions based not on shrewdly calculated political interest but on a universal conception of right.

Without this fantasized image of the framers, the appeal to their authority—as opposed to the authority of the majority of contemporary citizens—would make no sense. Though this is obviously a tendentious example, every historical narrative has some operative fantasy directing its discussion of the past. The fantasy—the belief that the past will unlock some truth about the present—provides the impetus for the very inquiry into historical phenomena. This heavy reliance on fantasy when constructing historical narratives completely colors their ontological status: rather than informing us about the real of history, historical narratives instead expose our fundamental fantasies. What results is a violation of the historical real.[2]

As we saw in the previous chapter, this process becomes the most vexed when dealing with a traumatic historical event such as the Holocaust. Though ostensibly concerned with this event as such, *Schindler's List* constructs a historical narrative that approaches it from a present perspective that values the creation of the state of Israel. This perspective completely shapes the film's historical narrative, allowing that narrative of the Holocaust to conclude in Israel itself, a turn of events that has the effect, as Paul Eisenstein puts it, of "elevating Israel's statehood to the status of redemptive sign."[3] Hence, because of its investment in the present statehood of Israel, *Schindler's List* gives the Holocaust a redemptive and teleological twist, implying that the event had at least one positive outcome. Such a narrative transforms the impossible historical object—the trauma of the Holocaust—into a tool for justifying a contemporary position. This transformation violates the specificity of the Holocaust as an event and reduces its victims to objects sacrificed for a larger end.

In order to avoid this type of effacement of the historical object and to ensure its status as impossible, some filmmakers approach history through the cinema of desire, creating films that narrate a story around the historical object without ever actually encountering it. This is the strategy of a film like Claude Lanzmann's *Shoah* (1984), which stands as a counterpoint to *Schindler's List*. Through its refusal to reenact the events of the Holocaust and its insistence on approaching these events solely through the words of the survivors, scholars, and perpetrators, *Shoah* aims to respect the historical object in its singularity. The historical object figures as the fundamental absence in Lanzmann's films, and the centrality of this absence in the experience of the spectator locates *Shoah* within the cinema of desire.[4]

Like *Shoah*, the films of Alain Resnais aim at respecting the historical object. However, Resnais takes a radically different tack from Lanzmann. Rather than sustaining the impossibility of the historical object, Resnais separates the worlds of desire and fantasy in order to allow us to encounter this object through the turn to fantasy within the film. Though Resnais is a member of the French nouvelle vague, his films depart from the prevailing logic of desire developed by his fellow filmmakers. Resnais creates a world of desire, but he also depicts fantasmatic intrusions into this world. He recognizes that the historical object is an impossible object, but he also recognizes that we can encounter this object through the turn to fantasy.

The importance of Resnais as a filmmaker stems from the way he develops the cinema of intersection. By creating a filmic separation between worlds of desire and fantasy, Resnais shows that the turn to fantasy offers a mode of access to the historical object. Because fantasy must initially produce the lost object that it purports to find, it creates an experience of the object as it is being lost—which is to say, as it is becoming the impossible objet petit a.

Resnais's film about the Holocaust, *Nuit et brouillard* (*Night and Fog*, 1955), begins much in the manner of Lanzmann's *Shoah* with contemporary images of the death camps and the surrounding area. However, it departs from the logic of *Shoah* insofar as it includes documentary footage of the activities in the camps and the allies' discovery of them. *Nuit et brouillard* shows the violent contrast between the tranquility of the present and the horror of the past, and Resnais emphasizes this contrast by shooting the present in color and then cutting to black and white footage of the past.[5] The narration of the film stresses the impossibility of knowing the truth of the camps, and yet the film attempts to depict this truth through documentary images. This paradox stems from Resnais's conception of our relationship to history: by contrasting present and past through his use of form, Resnais shows the past through the lens of fantasy. We don't see a past that lies beyond our reach, but one that exists in a fantasmatic form within our present. The traumatic power of the documentary footage in *Nuit et brouillard* stems from the contrast between this footage and the images of the present.

As the film shifts from one world to the other, we experience a traumatic encounter with the real of the gaze, seeing the very incompleteness of our look. Appearing when it does in the film, the documentary footage of the camps exists in order to highlight and embody what is absent from the present images. In this sense, the documentary footage, despite its realism, functions fantasmatically in the experience of the film insofar as it reveals the invisible and the impossible. The moment of the shift allows us to see the failure of the look represented not simply as an absence (as in the cinema of desire) but as a present object. The encounter with the historical object allows us to see our very inability to see. This inability, this failure to integrate the traumatic gaze into our field of vision, is, as the film suggests, what produces the traumatic event as such. The trauma of history is the result of our look's failure to see. In this way, the film forces us as viewers to experience our own involvement in the historical object.

We have the ability to access the historical object because this object embodies the failures of the present and not simply the events of the past. The final lines of the narration in *Nuit et brouillard* describe the falsity of the belief that the Holocaust is an event solely of the past. It indicts those of us who believe that it is not now in our midst—"nous qui feignons de croire que tout cela aille dans un seul temps, et qui ne pensons pas à regarder autour de nous, et qui n'entendons pas un cri sans fin." (We pretend it all happened only once, at a given time and place. We turn a blind eye to what surrounds us, and a deaf ear to humanity's never-ending cry.) This narration articulates explicitly the logic that informs the visual structure of *Nuit et brouillard*: the traumatic historical object is not always beyond our reach but exists within our fantasies, where we attempt to ignore it. Through this and the rest of his films, Resnais shows us the path through which we can access the historical object.

If Alain Resnais were a filmmaker like Claude Lanzmann, a filmmaker concerned with representing the failure to access the traumas of the past, his first feature, *Hiroshima, mon amour* (1959), would also be a vastly different film. It would be a film about the failure of a French woman to understand the trauma of Hiroshima and even the inappropriateness of the belief that she could. But because Resnais denies the absolute otherness of historical objects, the film recounts her capacity for grasping this trauma as such. In the opening minutes of the film, we see the naked bodies of a French woman (Emmanuelle Riva) and her Japanese lover (Eiji Okada) in close-up. The man speaks the first words of the film—"Tu n'as rien vu à Hiroshima . . . rien." (You have seen nothing in Hiroshima . . . nothing.)—and his words speak to the inaccessibility of Hiroshima as a historical object. The woman insists, however, that she has seen everything: "J'ai tout vu. Tout. Ainsi l'hôpital je l'ai vu. J'en suis sûre. L'hôpital existe à Hiroshima." (I have seen everything. Everything. Thus, I have seen the hospital. I'm sure. The hospital exists in Hiroshima.) Resnais includes both the man's insistence that the woman has seen nothing and her insistence that she has seen everything not in order to force us to choose between the two options, but to show the impossibility of the historical object and possibility of experiencing this impossibility. Because it begins with the man's statement that the woman has not seen the object, the film establishes the impossibility of the object before suggesting that the woman is able to access it. Thus, we understand that she is not simply experiencing Hiroshima as she would experience an ordinary object, but as an impossible object.

We can only access the impossible historical object insofar as we pay attention to the transition from a world of desire to a world of fantasy. The film stresses the contrast between the naked bodies of the lovers and the horrific images of Hiroshima after the devastation of the atomic bomb. Here, as in *Nuit et brouillard,* the documentary images of a historical trauma do not signify realism but fantasy. Resnais embeds documentary footage within another narrative in order to stress the aesthetic dimension of the footage. We access it through narrative—through the gaps of narrative—and not directly. If we look at documentary footage as if it represents the reality of the event, we fail to see our failure to see everything. But by using the documentary footage as a fantasmatic interlude in the film, Resnais forces us to encounter the failure of our look at the very moment that we see the historical object. This makes for a new way of relating to history—seeing the past not as a validation of the present but as a testament to its failure. The spectator who comes to this recognition ceases to see in history a justification and comes to see in it an interrogation.

As we see the images of the devastation in *Hiroshima, mon amour,* the woman admits that her experience of Hiroshima is the experience of an illusion. She compares the illusion that she has of Hiroshima to the illusion that one has in a love relationship. In both, we relate to the otherness of the other through the lens of fantasy. On the one hand, the fantasy shields us from the traumatic real of the other, but on the other hand, in the very act of shielding us from this real, the fantasy must acknowledge its existence. In this sense, we fantasize the real into existence. As we enter into the fantasy, the real that fantasy conceals becomes visible in a unique way. Films such as *Hiroshima, mon amour* reveal this real through their representation of a fantasmatic scenario in its emergence.[6]

The historical event in *L'Année dernière à Marienbad (Last Year in Marienbad,* 1961) is an encounter that may have taken place between an unnamed man and woman, known as X (Giorgio Albertazzi) and A (Delphine Seyrig). Most commentators on the film stress the uncertainty surrounding what occurred between the two and the impossibility of ever arriving at any definite knowledge concerning their relationship. For instance, Thomas Beltzer claims that "though architecturally beautiful, the world of *Marienbad* is pure nonsense, chaotic and absurd by the intentional design of its makers. Robbe-Grillet and Resnais are comfortable in the chaos of the a-historical. For them the world does not make sense, so neither should art."[7] For Beltzer and numerous other critics of the film, Resnais's concern in *L'Année dernière à Marienbad* involves sustaining the mystery of the film rather than offering spectators a way of solving this mystery. According to this view, the confusion is the point: our failure to understand the film or to pin down the events that the film depicts testifies to the recalcitrance of historical events themselves— their resistance to our way of knowing. Such a view explains the basic uncertainty of the film but leaves unexplained why the film depicts this uncertainty in the way that it does. Though we cannot solve the mystery of *L'Année dernière à Marienbad* by discovering the actual event in itself, we can solve the mystery by uncovering what its structure tells us about our relationship to the historical event.

The opening of the film offers us a hint concerning how we might figure out its mystery. The film begins with a voiceover narration that accompanies a series of shots tracking through an old and beautiful hotel. The narration fades in and out as it comments on the visuals of the hotel corridors and rooms that the tracking camera provides. The same commentary repeats several times, as if it were an automated recording. Finally, however, the camera enters a room in the hotel where actors are performing a play. In this room, the camera pans to an actor in the process of speaking the narration that we have heard throughout the film's opening. Though this suggests that the actor has been the source of everything we have hitherto heard in the film, the voice of the actor is not the voice of the narrator, and the sound of the words changes as we see the actor speaking them. Rather than locating the nondiegetic narration within the diegesis, here the film shows the correspondence that exists between these two seemingly disparate realms. The absolute barrier between the nondiegetic and the diegetic that we find in most films disappears at this point in *L'Année dernière à Marienbad*.

Initially, the narration without a clear narrator or a clear addressee in the film calls into question our ability to discover the historical object. According to Keith Cohen, "Resnais uses sound in the form of a remembering voice-over in *L'Année dernière à Marienbad* to pose questions about our ability to make propositions, with certitude, about the past."[8] Whereas the voice reaches into the past and attempts to recapture an event, the image depicts its failure to do so. Usually, cinema uses flashback images that correspond to voice-over narration in order to assure the authenticity and accuracy of that narration. Here, the disjunction between voice and image illustrates the recalcitrance of the past. But the linking of the voice and the image in the play overcomes this disjunction and suggests the attainability of the historical object. The film at once implies the impossibility of this object and our ability to attain the impossible through the turn to fantasy.

The film's mise-en-scène suggests the absence of the object and thus a near-total absence of enjoyment: it is a world in which subjects desire but must endure this desire without any fantasmatic supplement. All the ways in which fantasy vivifies our existence are absent. For instance, characters often remain motionless through entire scenes, and when they move, they do so slowly and almost mechanically. X and A speak their lines with a stiffness that suggests that they are part of the narration rather than dialogue. And the décor in the hotel is cold and replete with vast empty spaces. The mechanical and empty quality of the mise-en-scène indicates the absence of a fantasmatic supplement that would give this world a sense of depth and continuity.

The mise-en-scène further indicates a world of desire through the impossible changes that it undergoes during the course of the film. The décor in the hotel often changes between cuts that otherwise do not mark the passing of time, and the arrangement of the grounds outside the hotel shifts without any apparent motivation within the narrative. What's more, the film does not even make clear when the events that it depicts are taking place because Resnais cuts between day and night within the same scene. The film creates a fundamental instability in the mise-en-scène, and this instability places the spectator in the position of the desiring subject. The spectator searches for a way of stabilizing the events and establishing a ground for making sense of what is happening in the film, but the film consistently thwarts this effort.

The spectator is also put in the position of the desiring subject through the mystery that the film establishes in its narrative. The primary action of the film revolves around the question of what occurred between X and A a year earlier. X insists throughout the film that a romantic liaison took place, while A continually denies it. Even X, however, remains uncertain concerning precisely where and when the rendezvous took place. He suggests that it occurred in Friedrichsbad, but then he adds, "Perhaps it was elsewhere . . . at Karlstadt, at Marienbad, or Baden-Salsa, or in this very room." The uncertainty surrounding the event establishes it as a mystery that engages the spectator in the search for a solution. Other ambiguities concerning the event—such as the question of whether X raped A or not, which X himself first brings up—add to the spectator's sense of nonknowledge, which acts as the engine for desire.

Resnais emphasizes the impossibility of knowing the object even through the way that he titles the film. Though the title of the film seems to indicate that the rendezvous occurred "last year in Marienbad," Marienbad is but the third in the list of possible places that X proffers in his account of their encounter to A, which emphasizes how the signifier misses the mark relative to the historical object. Even the title of the film can't manage to pin down the city in which the event that it recounts took place. The fundamental uncertainty that pervades the film leaves the spectator trapped within a world of desire in which the object motivating this desire remains not only out of reach but also impossible to define.

The film does not refuse to offer a clear answer to the question of what happened the previous year because it aims to frustrate us as viewers and to insist on the impossibility of knowing the historical object. Instead, it refuses to be definitive in order to change our way of thinking about the historical object. As long as we think of the historical object as either readily accessible or completely inaccessible (the two common ways of thinking about this object), we miss the way in which history exists within the fabric of our present. According to the logic of *L'Année dernière à Marienbad*, the impossible historical object exists within the present in a fantasmatic form, and we constantly access this object when we fantasize.

The film represents this visually when it flashes back to the encounter of the previous year. This occurs most dramatically when X and A are standing together in the hotel bar. The scene begins with a long shot of the two standing at arm's length while leaning against the bar. We see several people walk by as the camera slowly tracks closer to them. The camera stops moving as it arrives at a medium shot with X and A at each edge of the frame. Just after the camera movement stops, we see a brief—almost momentary—shot of A in her hotel room the previous year as X describes the encounter to her. The cut between the shot of the bar and the hotel room emphasizes the contrast between the two: in the hotel room, A is dressed in a white dress, not the black dress she is wearing in the bar; the hotel room is completely white (except for a wood table) whereas dark colors predominate in the bar; and the bright lighting in the hotel room contrasts with the darkness of the scene in the bar. These contrasts produce a shock when the film moves from one milieu to the other. As X continues to describe the encounter, Resnais increases the frequency and the duration of the flashbacks, until we see a flashback in which A bursts out laughing. The film immediately cuts to an image of a different woman laughing in the bar, but despite the visual cut, there is continuity on the level of sound as the laugh of A and the laugh of the woman blend together. Shocked by this intersection between the past and present—between the world of fantasy and the world of desire—A steps back from X, bumps into someone in the bar, and drops her drink, shattering the glass. Just as we see the broken glass on the floor, the film cuts back to the hotel room where X approaches A and she moves away.

In this scene, *L'Année dernière à Marienbad* illustrates the relationship that exists between the present and the past. The characters in the present seek out the past and strive to arrive at some knowledge of it. But the past does not simply exist as an object that they integrate into their symbolic universe. When it appears, even though it takes a fantasmatic form, it disrupts the fabric of the present. The historical object disrupts the present in this fashion—causing A to drop her glass—because it belongs to the present in an extimate way. To put it in the terms of Lacan, the past represents what is in the present more than the present. One cannot access it but as a disruption of the field of the visible. Resnais films its intrusion in such a way that it not only jolts A within the film but jolts the spectator as well.

Resnais's film invites us to grasp this disruption as the correlative of the subject within the filmic image and to identify with this disruption. *L'Année dernière à Marienbad* appears mysterious insofar as we fail to see that the solution to the mystery involves seeing the intersection of present (desire) and past (fantasy). In order to access the historical object, we must accept our own involvement in the creation of this object. When Resnais employs a radical cut to the past, such a cut includes the difference of the past within the sameness of the present. In so doing, he demands that we abandon our distance from history and accept that we are responsible for history even at the point of its seemingly absolute otherness.

The temptation that the film warns us against is that of believing in the absolute otherness of the historical object. Such a belief lets us off the hook for the trauma of history and, at the same time, deprives us of our freedom. When we invest ourselves in the absolute otherness of the historical object, we implicitly authorize an Other who really knows, who did know, or who might know—a subject supposed to know. Insisting on the unknowability of the historical object posits such an Other because it imagines that the historical object can be known in a more direct fashion than we know it.[9]

We know that the big Other, the domain of language, has no direct access to the historical object. As the site of mediation, it can only provide indirect knowledge. However, we fantasize about another kind of Other, an Other of the Other, who does have direct access. The belief in the Other of the Other allows us to avoid recognizing our own role in constituting the historical object as such. It is our fantasy, not the Other of the Other, that brings the historical object into existence. When we recognize this and identify ourselves with the trauma of this historical object, we assume at once our responsibility and our freedom.

Throughout his career as a filmmaker, Resnais remains surprisingly faithful to the aesthetic that he establishes his early films such as *Hiroshima, mon amour* and *L'Année dernière à Marienbad*. *Muriel ou le temps d'un retour* (*Muriel, Or the Time of Return*, 1963) shows the power of a past that never actually existed—that existed only on the level of fantasy—over the present. In *La Guerre est finie* (*The War Is Over*, 1966), we see fantasmatic images constantly interrupting the attempt by Diego Mora (Yves Montand) to leave behind the political struggle in Spain.[10] Through his use of editing, Resnais juxtaposes two drastically different worlds—worlds of present and past, worlds of desire and fantasy—and depicts what occurs when they collide. These collisions reveal the real to us; they allow us to see our own role in constituting the historical object that appears to be a site of complete otherness. Resnais's films invite us to identify ourselves with this object rather than holding it at a distance. In envisioning this possibility, Resnais glimpses an ethical response to history that the cinema of intersection exposes for us. But it falls to Wim Wenders to develop more fully the ethical implications of this cinema.

28

Wim Wenders and the Ethics of Fantasizing

W<small>E USUALLY THINK</small> of the turn to fantasy as a way of attempting to elude the other. Subjects retreat into fantasy when they can no longer endure the dissatisfaction that the social order imposes on them. In this way, the fantasizing subject opts for private imaginary satisfaction over public dissatisfaction. As a result of this valuing of the private over the public, fantasy becomes a barrier to ethics: fantasy's sine qua non appears to be a turn away from the other, a refusal to consider the other as such. Thus, there seems to be something inherently unethical at the heart of fantasy's refusal to endure the other and the dissatisfaction that stems from this encounter.

Through a look at the films of the cinema of intersection, however, the ethical possibilities of fantasy become visible. This cinema shows us that in order to shield the subject from the other, fantasy must, at the same time, expose the subject: the shielding and exposure are correlative. Fantasy provides enjoyment for the subject by imagining a threat—the other in the real—that does not exist in the public world. In this sense, fantasy might actually pave the way for the most authentic kind of ethical encounter—an encounter in which the subject opens itself to the real dimension of the other. The cinema of intersection highlights this ethical quality of fantasy, a quality hidden in other types of cinema. Through the act of imagining the threat of the other in the real, fantasy creates the space for the part of the other that remains hidden—the other as it exists privately, when no one is looking.

In the public world, subjects rarely encounter the real dimension of the other. The stability and livability of this world depend on the readiness of all subjects to disguise the real kernel of their subjectivity and to confine this kernel to the private realm. Subjects do this by adopting the conventions of the big Other—obeying the law, acting politely, and even following the popular fashions. These conventions have the effect of producing a public world structured around a relative absence of enjoyment. And while conventions have the advantage of permitting subjects to coexist without open warfare, they also deprive subjects of the experience of the other in the real. In the public world, we experience the other playing a part, acting out a symbolic identity, but we don't experience what the other is when no one is looking. It is at this point that we can begin to recognize the radical potential of fantasy. Fantasy permits us the impossible view of the other; we fantasize the hidden other. Clearly, this view of the other is our fantasy, not the other in itself, but it nonetheless acknowledges the disruptive and threatening power of the other *for us*—the dimension of the other that doesn't fit within a prescribed symbolic identity.

If we consider the situation of the subject completely wrapped up in the experience of private fantasy, this relationship between fantasy and the real begins to come into focus. The fantasizing subject experiences its triumph over all the limitations that the other represents, but this subject also experiences its own vulnerability to the look of the other. The ultimate abasement of the subject occurs at the moment when the other interrupts the subject in the middle of its fantasizing and thereby exposes the private fantasy to the public. It is not coincidental that Jean-Paul Sartre's theorization of shame takes as its point of departure a scene in which "I have just glued my ear to the door and looked through a keyhole" when I recognize that "someone is looking at me!"[1] Here, Sartre describes a moment in which the other catches the subject in the midst of fantasizing—looking through the keyhole in order to see the private side of the other. The shame that the subject feels in this experience derives precisely from the revelation of its own hidden kernel of enjoyment—the revelation of itself in the real. Thus, in addition to envisioning the real dimension of the other, the fantasizing subject renders itself open to this other through the very retreat into fantasy. In turning its attention away from the public world, this subject becomes vulnerable to the look of the other. This openness bespeaks an ethical attitude, a readiness to allow the other to impose itself on oneself.

Fantasy's unique ability to access the real dimension of the other and to expose the real dimension of the subject allows it to play a part in the domain of ethics. This requires, however, that we shift our focus in the fantasmatic experience. Rather than seeking in fantasy a way of retreating from the trauma of the enjoying other, we can focus our attention on the moment at which the enjoying other appears within the fantasy. We can also accept, rather than try to escape, our own vulnerability as fantasizing subjects. Fantasy can provide an actual opening to the other only if we remain within its logic and accept the threat that it can pose to the stability of our symbolic identity. Such is the path that the cinema of intersection opens for us.

While the early films of Wim Wenders belong to the cinema of desire, beginning in the 1980s, his films undergo a dramatic transformation and begin to enter the terrain of the cinema of intersection. We can thus see a considerable difference between early films such as *Die Angst des Tormanns beim Elfmeter* (*The Goalie's Anxiety at the Penalty Kick*, 1971) or *Im Lauf der Zeit* (*Kings of the Road*, 1976), and later films such as *Paris, Texas* (1984) or *Der Himmel über Berlin* (*Wings of Desire*, 1987). The early films emphasize the absence of the gaze within the image, and this absence almost seems to set the films adrift narratively, as if the impossibility of accessing the object-cause of desire derails the forward movement of a narrative. Rather than moving forward, the narratives turn in a circular fashion around the impossibility of representing the gaze. In the later films, on the other hand, a fantasy scenario breaks into this circular movement and thereby propels the narrative forward.[2]

Wenders himself explains this change (which he dates in the early 1980s) by describing his loss of faith in the power of images and increasing belief in the importance of narrative.[3] The effect of the change, however, resonates far beyond additional attention to narrative. The entire structure of the film shifts: whereas the early films create a world of desire by stressing the structuring absence of an impossible object, the later films add a fantasy world that envisions a possible realization of desire. The juxtaposition of the worlds of desire and fantasy becomes a defining characteristic of Wenders's cinematic vision and locates him within the cinema of intersection. Through this juxtaposition, Wenders shows the ethical importance of fantasy—how the turn to fantasy is simultaneously a turn toward the real dimension of the other.

For the desiring subject, the real dimension of the other remains constitutively out of reach. Sustaining the position of desire demands that one respect the impossibility of this real and allow it to remain impossible. The only problem with this position is that it has the effect of insulating the subject. When the subject fantasizes, however, it immerses itself in enjoyment and becomes visible to the other because it is no longer concerned with its public appearance. This visibility—this vulnerability—represents the ethical side of fantasy, the side that Wenders explores in a film like *Paris, Texas*.

The opening images and narrative moments of *Paris, Texas* situate the film securely within the experience of desire. Wenders begins the film with a traveling helicopter shot of a desert that stops as it comes on a man wearing a dirty suit and a red baseball cap who is walking aimlessly. After he passes out in an isolated general store, he wakes up in a clinic, but he never reveals his identity or even speaks. This beginning thus establishes a sense of mystery around the identity of Travis (Harry Dean Stanton), who represents the paradigmatic subject of desire, a subject almost completely bereft of fantasmatic support for his identity. Eventually, however, Travis's brother, Walt (Dean Stockwell), comes from Los Angeles to pick him up (in Texas, where he was found) and bring him home. As he stays with Walt and his wife, Anne

(Aurore Clément), Travis's life gradually begins to normalize, and he takes an interest in his son, Hunter (Hunter Carson), whom Walt and Anne have raised. Even as the details of Travis's life become clearer and he begins to take up the role of father to his son, he remains a subject of desire insofar as he insists on keeping his distance from the other.

The film emphasizes the flaw in this position. By sustaining the position of the desiring subject and respecting the impossibility of the object, Travis does not so much protect the other as himself. He insulates himself from confronting the traumatic horror of the gaze—the point at which the other would include him. The position of desire respects the gaze and accords it a sublime status. The subject in this position experiences the gaze but does so from a distance.

Travis finally decides to venture into the world of fantasy. One day, he convinces Hunter to travel with him back to Texas in search of Jane (Nastassja Kinski), his ex-wife. After locating her by spying on her bank, Travis and Hunter follow her from the bank and discover that she works in a peep show. The peep show provides a fantasmatic arena where Travis can encounter Jane, who has hitherto occupied the position of the central impossible object in the film. When Travis enters the peep show and sees Jane, *Paris, Texas* itself enters into a radically different space—a world of fantasy—and the mise-en-scène of this space marks out its difference.

The peep show initially allows Travis to see Jane without being seen by her. The booth has a two-way mirror—a mirror on Jane's side and see-through glass on Travis's side. Travis visits Jane on two occasions in the peep show booth, though it is only on the second visit that he fully invests himself in the fantasy. On this visit, he recounts to Jane the story of their relationship without using their names. The fantasmatic setting permits Travis to articulate his narrative account because it shields his identity and places Jane in a position of the willing listener. Nonetheless, Wenders indicates that Travis feels his vulnerability as he enters into this fantasy world: even though Jane cannot see through the glass, Travis turns his chair around and faces away as he speaks. He can't endure the possibility of encountering the gaze in Jane's blank stare.

As Travis provides more and more details of the relationship, Jane eventually recognizes the story and the teller even though she can't see Travis. At the initial hint of recognition, Wenders moves the camera for the first time to Jane's side of the glass, suggesting that she is now looking at Travis. When she fully recognizes him, she utters the name "Travis" and approaches the mirror to attempt to look through it. Travis turns his chair around and adjusts the light so that he becomes visible to her. In addition, before Travis leaves, Jane demands that he listen to her story of the relationship and its aftermath. This reveals the price that the subject must pay for its fantasy. In order to create his fantasmatic encounter with the impossible object, Travis must also expose himself to the other and allow the other to impact him. Travis himself becomes visible in the form of the gaze: he sees himself being seen as the fantasy space folds back on itself and intersects with the outside world.

This is a moment where the worlds of desire and fantasy intersect because at this point Travis realizes that the experience of the peep show is not just a fantasy: it implicates him completely. At the heart of the fantasy, the desiring subject itself becomes exposed. But this dimension of fantasy is only evinced when cinema divides the experience of desire and that of fantasy to reveal that latter in its purest form. This dimension of fantasy places the cinematic spectator in the same position as Travis: when we encounter the gaze while caught up in a filmic fantasy, we find ourselves fully exposed on the screen, materialized in the form of the gaze. As *Paris, Texas* shows, this is an ethical position in which we experience our fundamental vulnerability as subjects.

In *Der Himmel über Berlin*, Wenders adopts the aesthetic strategy first developed in *The Wizard of Oz* (and repeated in *Stalker*) in order to distinguish between the worlds of desire and fantasy. He shoots the perspective of the angels in black and white, while using color stock in order to indicate the contrasting mortal perspective of human beings. This contrast establishes the world of the angels as a world of pure desire and the human world as fantasmatic. Damiel (Bruno Ganz) and Cassiel (Otto Sander), the two angels that the film centers around, experience desire, but they are constitutively unable to enjoy themselves. The immortality of Damiel and Cassiel renders them incapable of having an experience that actually matters. Whatever befalls them, they exist in an unchanged state. From the perspective of this state, the angels look at humans and long for the enjoyment that exists in even the smallest human actions—an enjoyment that derives from the human ability to risk and change, and thus to have experiences in which everything is at stake.

The angels occupy the position of pure desire insofar as they exist at the level of the signifier rather than in the gaps of signification. For the angels, everything transpires through the medium of the signifier. At the beginning of the film, we see Cassiel reading from a journal in which he has recorded the human events that he has witnessed. This activity—seemingly the primary function of the angels—indicates the restriction that governs the angels' existence. They know everything, but they know only through signification. This is why, when the film takes up the perspective of the angels, not only do we see a black and white image, but we hear the thoughts of many different characters. The angels have complete access to the other on the level of the signifier, access even to what the other says to itself. Though their knowledge of the other penetrates into areas where humans cannot, the angels suffer an inability to know the other in the real. Because they are confined to the level of the signifier, the angels cannot experience enjoyment—neither their own nor that of the other. In this way, they perpetually miss the real other, an other who is enjoying. As the film shows, enjoyment occurs in the dimension of our experience that cannot be described through the signifier. It is also at these points that the subject touches the other and the other touches the subject.

Wenders establishes this contrast between the worlds of desire and fantasy in order to depict the role that fantasy plays in exposing the subject to the other. As long as the angels remain within the world of desire, they cannot make contact with the other. The film shows this when we see Peter Falk (playing himself), a former angel himself, offer his hand to Damiel after he senses Damiel's presence near him. Falk extends his hand, and both Damiel and he go through the motion of shaking hands. However, neither Damiel nor he experiences any bodily contact. As an angel stuck in the world of pure desire, Damiel cannot touch the other in the real but can only relate to the other through the signifier. At the same time, he remains distant from the other, beyond the other's reach. Even when the other gestures in his direction and attempts to have an impact on Damiel (as Peter Falk does), the subject of pure desire is always out of reach. In this sense, the world of desire is a world of safety. Here, one respects the other, but this attitude of respect insulates one from the other's impact. This is the ethical limitation of the attitude of pure desire.

After Damiel forfeits immortality and becomes human, *Der Himmel über Berlin* offers an alternative ethical possibility, one not beset by this limitation. The way in which Wenders structures the film suggests that Damiel's decision to become human represents a move from desire into fantasy. Becoming human fantasmatically resolves Damiel's desire: he gains access to the enjoyment inhering in daily human life (found even, for instance, in drinking a hot cup of coffee), and he finds the love object, Marion (Solveig Dommartin), that he longed for as a desiring subject. But at the same time that it provides the enjoyment that he previously lacked, the fantasy also places Damiel at the mercy of Marion. Whereas in the world of desire Damiel had the security of distance and absence, here he suffers the presence of the other—an other who sees his private fantasy. It is only in the fantasy world that Damiel becomes vulnerable to the other.

When Damiel finally meets Marion in a hotel bar, Wenders emphasizes this vulnerability. Damiel encounters his love object face to face, but her voice predominates in this scene. Wenders shoots Damiel and Marion from the side as they are looking directly into each other's eyes, and we hear her discuss what Damiel represents for her. Then, in the middle of her long soliloquy, Wenders cuts to a close-up of her speaking directly into the camera. This shot, which lasts less than a minute, emphasizes the vulnerability of the subject fully invested in a fantasy—in this case, both Damiel and the spectator. In this close-up, Marion tells Damiel that it is his turn to act. However, it is the overproximity of Marion's face as she speaks that makes this shot difficult to watch.

Here, the spectator experiences along with Damiel the ethical dimension of fantasy. Marion is not just speaking to Damiel; she is also speaking to us as spectators, and we find ourselves exposed, even though we're watching from the security of a darkened theater. When one fantasizes, one exposes oneself to the other in the real; one invites the other to come too close and to see what usually remains unseen—the subject's private mode of enjoying itself. This kind of self-exposure involves directly embodying the gaze: it allows the other to both know and transform the subject at its most decisive point. Only the division of the filmic experience into separate realms makes this radical experience possible because this division facilitates the direct encounter with the gaze. In doing this, the cinema of intersection directs the subject toward taking up the ethical dimension of fantasy.

The concluding image and voiceover of *The End of Violence* (1997) encapsulates the ethical potential of fantasy. The film ends on the Santa Monica pier, where protagonist Mike Max (Bill Pullman) looks out over the ocean and thinks about China. By the conclusion of the film, Mike has given himself over fully to fantasy and abandoned his former symbolic identity as a film producer. After surviving an assassination attempt, he moved in with a Mexican American family and lived the life of a gardener. On the one hand, Mike's embrace of this working class immigrant life bespeaks his romanticization of it, but on the other, it suggests a newfound ability to render himself vulnerable (in contrast to the protected and isolated existence he was leading before the assassination attempt). As he stands on the pier, Mike's voice-over indicates both of these aspects of his fantasy. He says, "Now, when I look over the ocean, I don't expect nuclear submarines or alien attackers anymore. I can see China now, and I hope they can see us." Clearly, Mike doesn't really see China—or, he sees nothing but his fantasy of China. Nonetheless, this readiness to insert himself completely in the fantasy indicates that he accepts his own visibility and vulnerability, precisely what his former paranoid attitude denied. He is prepared to allow the real dimension of the other to impact his existence. In this way, the film ends with a glimpse of fantasy's ethical possibilities.

Like *The End of Violence*, all of Wenders's later films risk sentimentality. That is to say, they risk fostering the belief that the subject can simply open itself up and create a bond with the other. What spares the films, however, is their emphasis on the risk that the subject must run in developing this type of bond. It occurs only through the turn to fantasy and only insofar as the subject immerses itself completely within the fantasy. In the process, the subject accesses the other by exposing itself. Whereas most filmic fantasies obscure the visibility that overcomes the subject during the experience of fantasy, Wenders's films emphasize this visibility. For Wenders, the fundamental value of fantasy lies in its ability to deprive the subject of its defenses, to strip away the security of a symbolic identity. If we immerse ourselves in the turn to fantasy that Wenders offers, we as spectators can experience this vulnerability—and the enjoyment that derives from it.

When subjects fantasize, they expose the core of their subjectivity to the other. Thus, fantasy's retreat from the restraints of the big Other renders the subject vulnerable in a whole new way. This vulnerability represents an ethical position insofar as it allows the subject to take the otherness of the other into account. Without the turn to fantasy, we could not grasp the possibility of such an ethical position. But in most cases, our fantasies attempt to disguise the vulnerability that they imply for the subject. As we saw with the cinema of integration, they do this by supplementing the experience of fantasy with the experience of desire, retreating from the fantasy at the precise moment where it would render the subject vulnerable to the other. The cinema of intersection rejects this retreat. Because it so explicitly separates the experience of desire and that of fantasy, the cinema of intersection reveals what's really at stake in the fantasy structure. It shows the ethical dimension of fantasy by demanding that spectators grasp their own vulnerability within the turn to fantasy.

29

The Sexual Relationship
with David Lynch

IF THE FUNDAMENTAL ideological function of cinema consists in providing a fantasmatic image of the successful sexual relationship, cinema's ability to reveal the failure of the sexual relationship marks its most important task in challenging the structure of ideology. The illusion of the successful sexual relationship marks the fundamental ground of contemporary ideology: even subjects skeptical about everything else often invest themselves in this fantasy. Its power stems from its ability to provide the subject with a sense of completion—or with a sense of the possibility of completion. In the romantic union, the subject imagines that it will find what it lacks and thereby experiences the ultimate enjoyment. As long as subjects invest themselves in the fantasy of this union and in the idea of the ultimate enjoyment, they remain subjects of ideology.

Films that depict the failure of this relationship employ film's fantasmatic dimension in order to undermine cinema's—and contemporary ideology's—fundamental fantasy. This becomes possible in a unique way in the cinema of intersection. This cinema reaches its fullest development through films that use the separation between worlds of desire and fantasy in order to permit spectators to experience this failure as a positive event. In these films, we encounter the real that emerges out of the failure of the sexual relationship. As Lacan points out, "The Real is what is determined by the inability of the sexual relationship to write itself in any fashion."[1] Hence, when we experience this failure, we grasp the hole that exists within the symbolic order. On the one hand, this traumatizes the subject, depriving the subject of the idea of ever escaping lack, but on the other hand, it frees the subject to enjoy in the real. Rather than fantasizing about an ultimate enjoyment that can never be realized, the subject can enjoy the nothingness of the object.

This type of enjoyment in the real is possible only when one grasps the failure of the sexual relationship and gives up the fantasy of its success. The sexual relationship fails because the other can never provide what the subject lacks. The subject does not lack an empirical object, an object that might exist somewhere, but an object that embodies nothingness. In short, the subject lacks, but it lacks nothing. As a result, even the perfect sexual partner fails to satisfy the subject. A sexual partner can only provide something, not nothing, and thus must leave the subject dissatisfied.

Fantasy creates the illusion of possible satisfaction by erecting a barrier between the subject and the object. This barrier takes the form of the symbolic father or paternal metaphor. Fantasy uses the paternal metaphor as a mediating barrier that the sexual partners must surmount in order to constitute the sexual successful relationship. Without this barrier, fantasy cannot envision a scenario in which the relationship comes off successfully. This becomes apparent in the cinema of intersection. Through this cinema, we see that even in fantasy, even at the point where no obstacle should exist barring the subject from its object, the subject cannot obtain the direct satisfaction of the object.

The cinema of intersection reveals the actual structure of our fantasies, their complete elaboration of the successful sexual relationship. According to Slavoj Žižek, every fantasy focuses on this same image. He claims that "fantasy is ultimately always the fantasy of a successful sexual relationship."[2] While Žižek is right to say that fantasy constructs a successful sexual relationship, it does so only fleetingly. That is to say, fantasy never provides more than a glimpse of the perfect romantic union. The key to the cinema of integration—what allows this cinema to present the illusion of the successful sexual relationship—lies in its abridgement of the fantasy structure. The cinema of integration never depicts the full realization of the fantasy. Instead, it mediates the fantasy structure with the logic of desire at the nodal point within the fantasy. As a result, we see the image of the incipient successful romantic union (usually at the end of the film) but not the point at which this union proceeds unencumbered by any barrier. In short, this image of a successfully realized sexual relationship depends on the specific way in which these films depict fantasy. The cinema of intersection serves as a corrective. This cinema depicts the structure of fantasy in its entirety, from its emergence to its dissolution, and this allows spectators to experience the failure of the sexual relationship rather than its success. While watching these films, we encounter an object that is either not enough or too much for the subject (and for us as spectators). And in the process, we see that the object that promises to complete the subject actually derails any sense of completion in the subject.

At the moment of the seeming achievement of the successful sexual relationship, the films of David Lynch force us to encounter the real impossibility of this relationship. Rather than showing us the subject realizing its desire with an object that allows the subject to complete itself, they depict an object that doesn't fit in the subject's world. In the encounter with the objet petit a, the subject experiences the object as a jolt throwing it off balance. This encounter with the gaze also throws the spectator off balance, as it exposes the spectator's own investment in the logic of the fantasy.

At the point where the subject realizes its desire, we see that the object doesn't complete the subject but instead deprives the subject of all symbolic identity and shatters the world in which the subject exists. This occurs in an almost literal way in Lynch's first feature, *Eraserhead* (1977), when Henry Spencer (Jack Nance) finally unites with the Radiator Lady (Laurel Near), his fantasy object, at the end of the film. Here, Henry seems to achieve, through the turn to fantasy, the successful sexual relationship that he has failed to have throughout the film. But as Henry achieves a romantic union with the Radiator Lady, Lynch cuts to a shot of the entire world blowing apart, indicating the devastating ramifications of this union. As *Eraserhead* shows, finding the perfect sexual partner—finding one's soulmate—doesn't solve the riddle of the subject's identity, but explodes the very ground for that identity.

Lynch's films thus refigure our ways of thinking about romance. Here, romance doesn't stabilize the experience of the subject but instead disturbs it. In fact, when we assume that we enjoy the idea of self-completion in romance, we fail to see where our enjoyment actually derives from. The enjoyment of romantic relationships derives not from the idea of self-completion that they promise, but from their ability to throw the subject off course. The image of self-completion that we find comforting actually functions as an alibi allowing us to justify the disruption that romance brings. As the subject encounters the sexual partner, the subject enjoys the nothingness of the objet petit a. The cinema of intersection offers us the possibility of embracing this enjoyment as it exposes the ultimate failure of the sexual relationship. Though many of Lynch's films separate the realms of desire and fantasy in order to render visible this failure, it finds its ultimate expression in *Lost Highway* (1997).[3]

On the one hand, *Lost Highway* shows how the subject turns to fantasy in order to discover a successful sexual relationship, but on the other, it illustrates fantasy's inability to deliver this satisfaction. Lynch begins *Lost Highway* by constructing a world of desire, a world in which the protagonist, Fred Madison (Bill Pullman), experiences his inability to fathom the desire of his wife, Renee (Patricia Arquette). For Fred, Renee represents an inapproachable objet petit a: even when Fred has sex with Renee, he fails to uncover what she desires. Throughout the first part of the film, Fred remains completely in the dark about Renee's desire: her behavior (her secretiveness and flirtations with other men) seems to indicate some form of hidden and excessive enjoyment, but Fred has no idea what this is or how to access it. As a result, Renee triggers Fred's own desire to know.

The beginning of *Lost Highway* depicts Fred as a desiring subject and creates a world of desire around him. From the very first shot, the film establishes a lack of knowledge in the spectator that corresponds to Fred's. As Reni Celeste points out, "The first world encountered in this film is enveloped in the mood of suspicion, silence, clues that have no meaning and acts that have no agent."[4] The film begins without an establishing shot that would allow spectators to orient themselves and have a sense of knowledge about the filmic world being depicted. Instead, we are thrust into this world without any knowledge as we see a close-up of Fred. The first action that the film depicts after this close-up is Fred answering the intercom (indicating that someone is at the front door of his house). He hears a mysterious voice tell him, "Dick Laurent is dead." At this point, like Fred himself, we have no knowledge about the identity of Dick Laurent and have no way of making sense of the narrative. The first moments of the film's editing structure and narrative leave both the spectator and Fred in the position of nonknowledge consistent with the experience of desire.

The mise-en-scène in the first part of the film also helps to create a world of desire. Lynch lights the house of Fred and Renee with a minimally and leaves it sparsely decorated. This creates the appearance of vast dark and empty spaces within the house, spaces out of which Fred and Renee sometimes emerge. Lynch also uses long periods of silence in the opening part of the film. The emptiness and the silence contribute to a pervasive sense of the unknown. In addition, at no point in the depiction of Fred's world does Lynch provide the spectator with an indication of time or place. The spectator's inability to locate the events temporally or spatially helps to place the spectator in the position of the desiring subject.

After establishing a world of desire in the first part of *Lost Highway*, Lynch introduces a fantasmatic alternative. The experience of desire quickly becomes unbearable for Fred: he sees clues about Renee's desire—such as when he watches her flirting with other men at a party or when he calls home and she is unexpectedly out—but he never arrives at any certainty. In this way, Renee forces Fred to confront the impossibility of the objet petit a. Throughout the first part of the film, her desire is present only as an absence. As the representative of the object-cause of desire, she leaves Fred with a question that has no answer. As long as Fred remains within the logic of desire, he will never definitively be able to name Renee's desire because no signifier can successfully pin desire down. Faced with this failure and unable to bear his lack of knowledge about Renee's desire, Fred murders her in an attempt to put this question to rest.[5] But as the film shows, this murder fails precisely because it leaves the question of her desire unanswered. The objet petit a is itself indestructible and visions of Renee continue to haunt Fred after her death.

As he sits in jail awaiting execution for the murder, Fred has a dramatic breakdown, and the result of this breakdown is his transformation into someone entirely different: Peter Dayton (Balthazar Getty). This transformation indicates Fred's—and the film's—turn from the world of desire to the world of fantasy. The turn to fantasy effects a disturbance in the narrative and formal structure of the film. This becomes most apparent when Lynch uses two different actors, Bill Pullman and Balthazar Getty, to play the same character. Pullman plays Fred Madison within the world of desire, and Getty plays Peter Dayton, Fred's representative in the world of fantasy. The visible difference between the two actors stresses the radical distinction that the film draws between these two worlds. Perhaps more than any film within the cinema of intersection, *Lost Highway* highlights the absolute distinction between the experience of desire and that of fantasy.

After Fred's transformation into Peter Dayton, the form of *Lost Highway* undergoes a shift. When we enter into the fantasy world that surrounds Peter, the shots are well lit, and the scenes are full of bright colors. Peter's world has none of the dark, empty spaces that populate Fred's, nor does it have the disturbing silences. Here, unlike in Fred's world, there is no lack of knowledge concerning the desire of the Other. The fullness of this world indicates its fantasmatic quality. The filmic differences between the two worlds that the film presents underscore the difference between the experience of desire and that of fantasy: while the desiring subject perpetually confronts absence, the fantasizing subject exists in the midst of presence.

The transformation that the object of desire undergoes as the film moves from the world of desire to that of fantasy provides the key to understanding the relationship between these two worlds. In the first part of the film, Renee is an impossible object: no matter how hard Fred tries, he cannot solve the question of her desire. When the film turns toward Fred's fantasy and Fred becomes Peter Dayton, Renee also undergoes a transformation. She becomes Alice Wakefield (also played by Patricia Arquette). Lynch uses the same actor to play Renee and Alice in order to indicate the link between the two. The only substantive change that occurs in Renee (other than her name) is her hair color: Renee's brown hair becomes Alice's blond hair—a change that further suggests a turn to fantasy.

Alice is also different from Renee as an object. Whereas in the world of desire Renee remains an impossible object for Fred, in the fantasy Peter confronts Alice as a prohibited object. Or to put it in other terms, whereas Renee represents the objet petit a, Alice is an object of desire that holds out the promise of satisfying Peter's desire. Alice is the girlfriend of a local gangster named Mr. Eddy (Robert Loggia), who represents the barrier between Peter and Alice. In fact, Mr. Eddy even articulates his interdiction of Alice after he begins to suspect Peter's involvement with her. He tells Peter that if he found out that someone had made advances on her, he would "blow his fucking brains out." On the one hand, this warning seems to establish the fantasy world as a dangerous place, a place where access to the object is even more fraught than in the world of desire. But on other hand, it sets up a clear obstacle to the object. If the subject surmounts this obstacle, the object would seem to become available. In short, the prohibition of the object rescues the object from impossibility and renders it accessible; it creates an object of desire out of the objet petit a, the impossible object-cause of desire.

Through the fantasy scenario that the film creates around the figure of Alice, Fred is able to construct a solution to the problem of Renee's desire. Whereas Renee's desire remained unknowable, Alice's desire becomes readily decipherable for Peter (even if it is at times troubling for him). This becomes clearest when a conversation between Fred and Renee is repeated within the domain of the fantasy. After attending a party where Renee was flirting with Andy (who turns out to be a henchman of Mr. Eddy), Fred asks Renee how she met him. Renee responds ambiguously that Andy once told her about a job, but she can't remember any details. Here again, Renee's desire is completely unknown: the nature of the job and the nature of Renee's relation to Andy remain mysterious. Fred believes that an illicit association exists between Renee and Andy—he kills her soon after this conversation—but he has no idea what it is.

Unlike Fred, Peter learns the details about Alice's involvement with Andy. In the fantasy world of the film, the conversation concerning Andy occurs again, though this time between Peter and Alice. Whereas Renee can't remember anything substantive about the job, Alice describes it in detail. Peter asks Alice how she became involved with Mr. Eddy and Andy, and Alice repeats, word for word, Renee's account of meeting Andy and learning about a job from him. However, Alice also remembers the job and describes it to Peter. At the point where Renee answers enigmatically, Alice provides an intricate account. As the film shows us visually, the job consisted of one of Mr. Eddy's henchman placing a gun to her head while she disrobed in front of Mr. Eddy. This description both horrifies and arouses Peter, but most importantly, it allows him to imagine a way of enjoying his object of desire: this object becomes accessible under the look of Mr. Eddy, the figure of the symbolic father within the fantasy scenario. Fantasy relieves the torments of desire by transforming the impossible object—even if this transformation involves the construction of a barrier.

By creating a fantasy structure in which Fred (as Peter) can access the impossible object, *Lost Highway* is able to reveal what occurs at the moment when the object becomes fully available. As the narrative within the fantasy world develops, Peter moves closer and closer to accessing the object directly, without the intervention of the symbolic father. Alice convinces Peter that he will have this untrammeled access if he agrees to rob and kill Andy, an act that would allow Alice and Peter to run away together. After Peter kills Andy and he drives with Alice to the desert to sell the jewels they've stolen from Andy, the film depicts what happens at the point when the fantasy would realize the successful sexual relationship. The consistency of the fantasmatic world depends on the barrier that exists between the subject and the object of desire. Fantasy envisions access to the object as a circumventing of the barrier that the symbolic father establishes. When this barrier disappears, when the subject finds itself able to access the object directly, the consistency of the fantasmatic world breaks down and the nothingness of the objet petit a, hidden within the seemingly accessible object of desire, becomes evident. This is what occurs with Alice and Peter in the desert.

While they wait for a rendezvous with their buyer, Alice and Peter begin to have sex in the middle of the desert with the light from their car's headlights streaming over them during the act. The shot of them together, naked in the wide open space of the desert night, suggests an ultimate moment of enjoyment. This is the point at which Peter seems on the verge of realizing the sexual successful relationship—a bliss without constraint providing him with a sense of completion. And as occurs in *Eraserhead* at the moment when Henry Spencer fantasmatically accesses his impossible object, an overwhelming bright light encompasses the screen, a light so bright that the spectator can barely continue to look directly at the filmic image. This light (from the car headlights) indicates the proximity of the ultimate enjoyment present in the successful romantic union. But the film quickly reveals that even at the level of fantasy this relationship fails. During the sex act, Peter tells Alice, "I want you, I want you." After a few moments, Alice says to Peter, "You'll never have me," and she simply walks away. When Alice enters a nearby cabin, the film returns to the world of desire, and Peter again becomes Fred Madison. Just as Peter is on the verge of realizing his desire and achieving the successful sexual relationship, he loses the object of desire altogether. Even within fantasy, as *Lost Highway* shows, the subject cannot sustain a direct relation with its object. When the subject accesses the object, the fantasy reveals it as the embodiment of nothing, as nothing but the subject's own lack.

The shot of the blinding car headlights allows the spectators a direct experience of the gaze. Lynch shoots them so that the spectator must look away, an act which has the effect of rendering the spectator visible. Here, one experiences on both a physical and psychic level one's involvement in the events on the screen. The disturbance in film form registers the disruptiveness of the sexual relationship and the impossibility of successfully realizing it. *Lost Highway* reveals the moment of its apparent success to be a failure, and this failure reaches out to us as spectators.

Though fantasy constructs a world of fullness and presence, it cannot transform an object of desire into a present object without at the same time destroying its desirability. When this object actually appears within the fantasy, it becomes an objet petit a that tears apart the very fabric of the fantasmatic world. The radical opposition between the fantasy and the objet petit a causes the latter to stick out. At this point, the cinema of intersection offers us the opportunity to identify with the nothingness of the object and with the point at which the sexual relationship fails. In doing so, we break the spell that the image of the successful sexual relationship has over us.

The nothingness of the object is at once our own nothingness as well. The gaze is nothing but our presence in what we are looking at, but we are nothing but this gaze. We are, that is to say, a distortion in Being. The direct encounter with the gaze exposes us as this distortion and uproots every other form of identity to which we cling. It marks a genuine existential turn in the cinema, made possible by films that present us with a divided cinematic experience. These films accomplish the impossible and demand that we follow them in doing so.

For many who go to Hollywood and for many who flock to Hollywood's films, the cinema's ability to offer us the impossible constitutes its lasting charm. We experience in a movie theater what we could not otherwise experience. But the problem with most Hollywood films—the problem with what I have called the cinema of integration—lies not with their proclivity for giving us the impossible, but with their failure to do so. When we genuinely experience the impossible—as in *Lost Highway* or Lynch's later film *Mulholland Drive* (2001)—we do enjoy, but this is an enjoyment that completely transforms us as subjects. The only genuine enjoyment we can experience is necessarily traumatic. In the experience of cinema this enjoyment occurs most radically in the direct encounter with the gaze. We go to the movies to enjoy the trauma of the gaze. And in the trauma of the gaze lies the freedom of the subject.

Notes

Preface

1. Janet Staiger, *Perverse Spectators: The Practices of Film Reception* (New York: New York University Press, 2000), 1.

2. For a discussion of this secular conception of the miracle, see Eric Santner, "Miracles Happen: Benjamin, Rosenzweig, Freud and the Matter of the Neighbor," in Slavoj Žižek, Eric L. Santner, and Kenneth Reinhard, *The Neighbor: Three Inquiries in Political Theology* (Chicago: University of Chicago Press, 2005), 76–133.

Introduction

1. See Jacques Lacan, "The Mirror Stage as Formative of the *I* Function as Revealed in Psychoanalytic Experience," in *Écrits: The First Complete Edition in English*, trans. Bruce Fink (New York: Norton, 2006), 75–81.

2. See Louis Althusser, "Ideology and Ideological State Apparatus (Notes Toward an Investigation)," in *Lenin and Philosophy and Other Essays*, trans. Ben Brewster (New York: Monthly Review Press, 1971), 127–186.

3. Though I group these theorists and others under the rubric "traditional Lacanian film theorists," many would not have identified themselves in this way. But they nonetheless share the idea, an idea associated with a certain reading of Lacan, that typical film spectatorship involves an illusion linked to that of the mirror stage.

4. There have been numerous summaries of this movement within film theory, but Henry Krips provides the definitive (critical) account. See Henry Krips, *Fetish: An Erotics of Culture* (Ithaca, NY: Cornell University Press, 1999), 97–117.

5. Lacan notes that "the total form of his body, by which the subject anticipates the maturation of his power in a mirage, is given him only as a gestalt, that is, in an exteriority in which, to be sure, this form is more consti-tutive than constituted" (Lacan, "The Mirror Stage," 76).

6. Christian Metz, *The Imaginary Signifier: Psychoanalysis and Cinema*, trans. Celia Britton, et al. (Bloomington: Indiana University Press, 1982), 54.

7. Jean-Louis Baudry, "Basic Effects of the Cinematographic Appara-tus," in *Movies and Methods*, vol. 2, ed. Bill Nichols (Berkeley: University of California Press, 1985), 539.

8. Metz, *Imaginary Signifier*, 3.

9. See Laura Mulvey, "Visual Pleasure and Narrative Cinema," in Nichols, *Movies and Methods*, vol. 2, 303–315.

10. The many books and essays written in the wake of Mulvey's essay nearly constitute a minor industry within film studies. They range in tone from polite disagreement to fierce critique and include works such as Mary Ann Doane's *The Desire to Desire: The Woman's Film of the 1940s* (Bloom-ington: Indiana University Press, 1987); Kaja Silverman's *The Acoustic Mirror: The Female Voice in Psychoanalysis and Cinema* (Bloomington: In-diana University Press, 1988); and Carol Clover's *Men, Women, and Chain-saws: Gender in the Modern Horror Film* (Princeton, NJ: Princeton University Press, 1992), to name but a few.

11. In *Reel to Real: Race, Sex, and Class at the Movies*, bell hooks exem-plifies this mode of criticism. She writes, "Mainstream feminist film criticism in no way acknowledges black female spectatorship. It does not even con-sider the possibility that women can construct an oppositional gaze via an un-derstanding and awareness of the politics of race and racism" (bell hooks, *Reel to Real: Race, Sex, and Class at the Movies* [New York: Routledge, 1996], 205). What hooks here calls "mainstream feminist film criticism" is the Lacanian version created by Mulvey and her followers.

12. David Bordwell and Noël Carroll, introduction to *Post-Theory: Re-constructing Film Studies*, ed. David Bordwell and Noël Carroll (Madison: University of Wisconsin Press, 1996), 1.

13. Noël Carroll, "Prospects for Film Theory: A Personal Assessment," in Bordwell and Carroll, *Post-Theory*, 45.

14. Stephen Prince, "Psychoanalytic Film Theory and the Problem of the Missing Spectator," in Bordwell and Carroll, *Post-Theory*, 83. Prince's critique here occurs in response to a genuine problem with traditional Lacan-ian film theory: its conception of the spectator does indeed miss the mark. However, Prince quickly moves from a justifiable dissatisfaction with the pre-vailing conception of spectatorship to an attempt to eliminate all conceptu-alization in the study of spectatorship. He argues that though there are areas in which film theory can be properly speculative, spectatorship is not one of

them. As he says most emphatically, "Spectatorship is an area for empirical inquiry" (83). This call for empiricism in the analysis of spectatorship fails to see that empiricism in no way avoids the pitfalls of abstraction. The problem with empiricism, as Herbert Marcuse once said, is that it is never empirical enough; it always smuggles concepts into its analysis. When film theorists follow Prince's program and analyze "actual spectators," they will not, as he believes, approach these spectators without conceptualizing them in any way. Instead, these "empirical theorists" will inevitably approach them with at least some minimum amount of conceptualization simply because the very project of studying film spectators is conceptual in its nature. In fact, even the elementary operation of positing causality in the relationship between a film and a spectator involves a conceptualization that goes beyond mere empiricism. The call for an empirical approach to spectatorship is thus in effect a call for an approach to spectatorship that blinds itself to its conceptualizing effects. As Hegel points out, "Empiricism . . . labours under a delusion, if it supposes that, while analysing the objects, it leaves them as they were: it really transforms the concrete into an abstract" (G. W. F. Hegel, *[Lesser] Logic*, trans. William Wallace [Oxford: Clarendon Press, 1975], 63). With its call for an empirical account of spectatorship, *Post-Theory* reveals itself as pre-Kantian.

15. Though the contributors to *Post-Theory* lament the privileged status of psychoanalysis within film theory, their attack comes about twenty years after the height of its popularity. Given the current position of psychoanalysis with film theory, *Post-Theory* is flogging a dead horse. In fact, it is psychoanalytic theory's very lack of popularity—its weakened, degraded state—that has occasioned this attack. One attacks an authority not for its strength but for its weakness.

16. This idea of the gaze as an object that one encounters rather than as the look of the subject has its philosophical antecedent in Jean-Paul Sartre's discussion of "the existence of others" in *Being and Nothingness*. See Jean-Paul Sartre, *Being and Nothingness*, trans. Hazel E. Barnes (New York: Washington Square Press, 1956).

17. Jacques Lacan, *The Four Fundamental Concepts of Psycho-Analysis*, trans. Alan Sheridan (New York: Norton, 1978), 105. In a later seminar, Lacan further explains the role of the gaze in aesthetics: "The objet a in the scopophilic field, if we try to translate it to the level of aesthetics, is exactly this blank, or this black, as you wish, this something that lacks behind the image" (Jacques Lacan, *Le Séminaire, livre XVI: D'un Autre à l'autre, 1968–1969*, ed. Jacques-Alain Miller [Paris: Seuil, 2006], 289–290, my translation).

18. Lacan adds the scopic and invocatory drives to those that Freud discovers in the *Three Essays on the Theory of Sexuality*.

19. With the publication of *The Sublime Object of Ideology* in 1989, Slavoj Žižek introduced a new understanding of Lacan, focused on the

importance of the real, to the English-speaking world. As a result of this book and the many that followed in its wake, he is, of course, the pioneer in the dissemination of this "real" Lacan—a grasp of Lacan that captures the latter's radicality as a (political) thinker in ways that no one prior to Žižek ever imagined. Žižek even brings his version of Lacanian theory to bear on film. But because Žižek's numerous discussions of film often focus on filmic content rather than form or spectatorship (at least prior to the publication of *The Fright of Real Tears* in 2001), some critics have dismissed his forays into film theory. As Stephen Heath puts it, "It is indicative that Žižek has, in fact, little to say about 'institution,' 'apparatus,' and so on, all the concerns of the immediately preceding attempts to think cinema and psychoanalysis (films and novels will thus mostly be referred to without any particular distinction between them as forms)" (Stephen Heath, "Cinema and Psychoanalysis: Parallel Histories," in *Endless Night: Cinema and Psychoanalysis, Parallel Histories*, ed. Janet Bergstrom [Berkeley: University of California Press, 1999], 44). This objection centers around Žižek's very way of talking about film. Instead of engaging Lacanian theory to facilitate a new way of approaching film, film seems to be, for Žižek, nothing but a source for fecund examples that demonstrate the truths of Lacanian theory. But if Žižek has not fully elucidated the importance of the emphasis on the real for film theory as such, it is nonetheless implicit throughout his work. In the case of Joan Copjec, however, the same cannot be said. Copjec has made the link between an emphasis on the real and film theory explicit in her work, and yet film theory has largely remained deaf to the ramifications of Copjec's argument. See Joan Copjec, *Read My Desire: Lacan Against the Historicists* (Cambridge: MIT Press, 1994) and Joan Copjec, *Imagine There's No Woman: Ethics and Sublimation* (Cambridge: MIT Press, 2002). This project is indebted in its very origins to the theoretical innovations of both Copjec and Žižek.

20. In his essay entitled "Returns in the Real," Michael Walsh notes the neglect of the real in favor of the symbolic and imaginary among Lacanian film theorists. However, his attempt to reclaim the real for film theory does not focus on the gaze. For Walsh, taking the real into account is important because it will allow us to grasp more fully the psychotic or hallucinatory dimension of the filmic experience, a dimension that film theory has ignored. He claims that "studies of cinema influenced by psychoanalysis remain more or less comfortably identified with the neurotic, and have been less willing to engage in the more difficult (in some sense, impossible) project of identifying with the psychotic" (Michael Walsh, "Returns in the Real: Lacan and the Future of Psychoanalysis in Film Studies," *Post Script* 14, nos. 1 and 2 [1994–1995]: 23).

21. As Jean Wyatt notes, "Because the gaze cannot ever be apprehended, because it is missing, it can stand in for the subject's fundamental lack" (Jean Wyatt, *Risking Difference: Identification, Race, and Community in Contemporary Fiction and Feminism* [Albany: State University of New York Press, 2004],

132). There is, however, a certain sense of mastery involved in recognizing the gaze. One can find pleasure in the mastery one achieves in finally seeing the skull hidden in *The Ambassadors*, even if the skull indicates the ultimate failure of mastery. But here the pleasure of mastery acts as a lure inducing the subject toward an encounter with what will undermine mastery. (I am indebted to Quentin Martin for pointing this out to me.)

22. Copjec, *Read My Desire*, 19. My discussion of traditional Lacanian film theory's misunderstanding of the gaze here is indebted to Copjec's extraordinary work.

23. As Nietzsche puts it in *Beyond Good and Evil*, "Life itself is *essentially* appropriation, injury, overpowering of what is alien and weaker; suppression, hardness, imposition of one's own forms, incorporation and at least, at its mildest, exploitation" (Friedrich Nietzsche, *Beyond Good and Evil: Prelude to a Philosophy of the Future*, trans. Walter Kaufmann [New York: Vintage, 1966], 203). What differentiates Nietzsche from those who take up his conception of desire—namely, Foucault and traditional Lacanian film theory—is that rather than attempt to counter the desire for mastery in some way, the entire effort of his philosophy consists in conceiving its ethical dimension. The predominance of the Nietzschean conception of desire (desire figured purely as desire for mastery) enters into French thought through the existentialism of Jean-Paul Sartre. Throughout *Being and Nothingness*, the subject's relation to the Other always revolves around the attempt to master the Other in its otherness (as a subject for-itself rather than as an object in-itself). In contrast to both Nietzsche and Foucault, Sartre sees this project as necessarily doomed to failure, which actually places him in proximity to Lacan.

24. According to Foucault, of course, this conception of the gaze—a hidden subject and an exposed object—reaches its apotheosis in Bentham's conception of the panopticon. The panopticon functions precisely like the cinematic apparatus insofar as it allows the viewer to see without being seen. And seeing without being seen is, for both Foucault and a traditional Lacanian film theorist like Laura Mulvey, the ultimate form of power.

25. Mulvey, "Visual Pleasure," 309.

26. As Studlar puts it, "Many of the assumptions adopted by film theorists from Freudian metapsychology or Lacan seem inadequate in accounting for cinematic pleasure" (Gaylyn Studlar, "Masochism and the Perverse Pleasures of the Cinema," in Nichols, *Movies and Methods*, vol. 2, 616).

27. Jacques Lacan, *Le Séminaire, livre V: Les Formations de l'inconscient, 1957–1958*, ed. Jacques-Alain Miller (Paris: Seuil, 1998), 313, my translation. Lacan sustained this position concerning the absolute centrality of masochism throughout his career, even after he turned away from discussions of desire. In *Seminar XXIII*, for instance, he links masochism to enjoyment in the real, claiming that "masochism is the main enjoyment that the real gives" (Jacques Lacan, *Le Séminaire, livre XXIII: Le Sinthome, 1975–1976*, ed. Jacques-Alain Miller [Paris: Seuil, 2005], 78, my translation).

28. Lacan, *Four Fundamental Concepts*, 182.

29. As Renata Salecl says, "That which arouses the subject's desire . . . is the very specific mode of the Other's *jouissance* embodied in the object *a*" (Renata Salecl, *(Per)versions of Love and Hate* [New York: Verso, 1998], 64).

30. Many Lacanian thinkers reject completely the idea of translating the term "jouissance" at all, but especially as "enjoyment." For instance, Roberto Harari argues that "its meaning is lost by translating it as 'enjoyment'" (Roberto Harari, *Lacan's Seminar on "Anxiety": An Introduction*, trans. Jane C. Lamb-Ruiz [New York: Other Press, 2001], lxxi). Throughout this book, I will use the terms interchangeably because, thanks to the proliferation of Lacanian analyses in English, much of the sense of "jouissance" has now become attached to the word "enjoyment." "Enjoyment," as I use the word in what follows, is always a disturbing enjoyment that one suffers—pleasure in pain, as opposed to pure pleasure.

31. Alenka Zupančič, *Ethics of the Real: Kant, Lacan* (New York: Verso, 2000), 225.

32. In "Desire and Jouissance in the Teachings of Lacan," Néstor Braunstein provides a clear account of the distinction between desire and jouissance: "Desire points toward a lost and absent object; it is a lack in being, and a craving for fulfillment in the encounter with the lost object. Its concrete expression is the phantasy. Jouissance, on the other hand, does not point to anything, nor does it serve any purpose whatsoever; it is an unpredictable experience, beyond the pleasure principle, different from any (mythical) encounter" (Néstor Braunstein, "Desire and Jouissance in the Teachings of Lacan," in *The Cambridge Companion to Lacan*, ed. Jean-Michel Rabaté [Cambridge: Cambridge University Press, 2003], 106–107).

33. Sigmund Freud, "Hysterical Phantasies and Their Relation to Bisexuality," in *The Standard Edition of the Complete Psychological Works of Sigmund Freud*, vol. 9, trans. and ed. James Strachey (London: Hogarth Press, 1955), 155–166.

34. Jacques Lacan, *Le Séminaire, livre X: L'Angoisse, 1962–1963*, ed. Jacques-Alain Miller (Paris: Seuil, 2004), 294, my translation. As Elizabeth Cowie explains, "The gaze is the inverse of the omnipotent look, which is the imperial function of the eye" (Elizabeth Cowie, *Representing the Woman: Cinema and Psychoanalysis* [Minneapolis: University of Minnesota Press, 1997], 288).

35. Metz makes this connection in *The Imaginary Signifier*: "The filmic state as induced by traditional fiction films . . . is marked by a general tendency to lower wakefulness, to take a step in the direction of sleep and dreaming. When one has not had enough sleep, dozing off is usually more a danger during the projection of a film than before or even afterwards" (Metz, *Imaginary Signifier*, 106–107). Despite recognizing their similarity, Metz claims that there remain substantive differences between the film and the dream because the film is alien to us in a way that the

dream is not. The problem with this claim is the extent to which it fails to recognize the agency responsible for the form of our dreams. Because the subject of the unconscious "directs" the dream, the conscious subject experiences the dream as alien and untrue in the same way that the subject experiences the cinema.

36. Lacan, *Four Fundamental Concepts*, 75.

37. Sigmund Freud, *The Interpretation of Dreams* (Second Part), in Strachey, *Standard Edition*, vol. 5 (1953), 488.

38. Given the similarities in the subject's experience in the cinema and in the psychoanalytic session, the fact that psychoanalysis and film were in some sense born in the same year—the Lumière brothers screened their first film in 1895, the year that Breuer and Freud's *Studies on Hysteria* was published—suggests that the cinematic experience proper and the psychoanalytic experience are linked.

39. Jean-Louis Comolli, "Notes on the New Spectator," trans. Diana Matias, in *Cahiers du Cinema: The 1960s—New Wave, New Cinema, Revaluating Hollywood*, ed. Jim Hillier (Cambridge: Harvard University Press, 1992), 214.

40. Lacan, *Four Fundamental Concepts*, 75. The limitation of phenomenology as a mode of analyzing experience stems from its failure to grasp how an object—specifically the gaze—might show itself without being already accounted for by consciousness. To put it in Husserl's terms, the gaze is an object for which consciousness has no noemata, no way of accounting for its appearance, because it marks the point at which experience exceeds what the subject constitutes in it.

41. Perhaps it doesn't need mentioning, but this conception of freedom from the constraints of the big Other has nothing to do with freedom in the neoliberal sense of the term. The freedom that U.S. foreign policy attempts to safeguard is an economic freedom that one finds only through submission to the big Other, not through the rejection of it. In embracing this notion of freedom, one finds one's sense of who one is in neoliberal ideology rather than in confronting the ultimate groundlessness of one's subjectivity, which is the conception of freedom toward which psychoanalysis leads the subject.

42. Paul Eisenstein, *Traumatic Encounters: Holocaust Representation and the Hegelian Subject* (Albany: State University of New York Press, 2003), 71.

43. Theodor W. Adorno, *Minima Moralia: Reflections from Damaged Life*, trans. E. F. N. Jephcott (New York: Verso, 1978), 206.

44. While on the one hand the account of the different deployments of the gaze is unabashedly auteurist, on the other hand, the conception of the auteur in what follows is not tied to an idea of the conscious control of the director. The auteur is, for me, nothing but a placeholder for a way of constructing a specific kind of filmic relationship to the gaze.

1. Fantasy and Showing Too Much

1. Lacan's most extensive discussion of fantasy occurs in the as yet unpublished *Seminar XIV*, which is titled "The Logic of Fantasy."

2. See Giorgio Agamben, *State of Exception*, trans. Kevin Attell (Chicago: University of Chicago Press), 2005.

3. Of course, disruptions to the world in which everything seems to fit do occur. Empty spaces in our social reality do occasionally become visible, and these are always potentially revolutionary times. The perpetuation of an ideological edifice depends on its ability to obscure its points of emptiness, and the successful obscuring of them constitutes our everydayness.

4. Joel Black, *The Reality Effect: Film Culture and the Graphic Imperative* (New York: Routledge, 2002), 61.

5. Barthes claims, "Obtuse meaning, a new practice—rare and asserted against a prevailing one, that of the signification—inevitably appears as a luxury, an expenditure without exchange" (Roland Barthes, "The Third Meaning: Notes on Some of Eisenstein's Stills," trans. Richard Howard, *Artforum* 11, no. 5 [1973]: 49).

6. Because excess cannot be reduced to the level of signification, Kristin Thompson notes that Barthes's use of the term "obtuse meaning" is unfortunate. As she puts it, "The choice of the term 'meaning' is a misleading one, since these elements of the work are precisely those that do not participate in the creation of narrative or symbolic meaning" (Kristin Thompson, *Eisenstein's* Ivan the Terrible: *A Neoformalist Analysis* [Princeton: Princeton University Press, 1981], 288).

7. Ibid., 292, 291.

8. Ibid., 293.

9. This is the essence of Hegel's critique of Kant: if we are able to understand that an idea transcends our understanding, as Kant shows in the *Critique of Pure Reason*, we have in some sense already understood it in its very incomprehensibility. Hence, this "beyond" actually exists within our understanding, not outside of it (as Kant claims). Or, in Hegel's terms, "The very fact that something is determined as a limitation implies that the limitation is already transcended. For a determinateness, a limit, is determined as a limitation only in opposition to its other in general, that is, in opposition to that which is *free from the limitation*; the other of a limitation is precisely the *being beyond* it" (G. W. F. Hegel, *The Science of Logic*, trans. A. V. Miller [Atlantic Highlands, NJ: Humanities Press International, 1969], 134).

10. The reduction of all excess to normal signification represents the opposite danger of the one that befalls Barthes, Heath, and Thompson. Such a position refuses to accept that any cinematic element lacks a signified. According to this view, everything in a film contributes on some plane to the narrative structure. This rejection of the possibility of excess is a fundamentally cynical position because it defines narrative (and by extension, ideology)

through its ability to include everything. This position thus renders the disruption of narrative (or ideology) unthinkable.

11. See Linda Williams, *Hardcore: Power, Pleasure, and the "Frenzy of the Visible"* (Berkeley: University of California Press, 1999).

12. Brett Farmer, *Spectacular Passions: Cinema, Fantasy, Gay Male Spectatorships* (Durham: Duke University Press, 2000), 81.

13. Patricia White makes a related point about lesbian spectators. See Patricia White, *Uninvited: Classical Hollywood Cinema and Lesbian Representability* (Bloomington: Indiana University Press, 1999).

2. Theoretical Fantasizing

1. Hugo Münsterberg, *Hugo Münsterberg on Film: The Photoplay: A Psychological Study and Other Writings*, ed. Allan Langdale (New York: Routledge, 2002), 91.

2. Sergei Eisenstein, *Film Form: Essays in Film Theory*, trans. Jay Leyda (San Diego: Harcourt Brace, 1949), 130.

3. Rudolf Arnheim, *Film As Art* (Berkeley: University of California Press), 109–110.

3. The Politics of Cinematic Fantasy

1. One of Kant's chief aims in writing the *Critique of Pure Reason* is to convince us to accept the limitations of reason and abandon our speculative, philosophical fantasies concerning the impossible questions that reason cannot answer. See Immanuel Kant, *Critique of Pure Reason*, trans. Paul Guyer and Allen W. Wood (New York: Cambridge University Press, 1998).

2. In "Critique of Violence," Walter Benjamin stresses the irreducibility of violence in every legal institution and arrangement. He notes, "The origin of every contract . . . points toward violence. It need not be directly present in it as lawmaking violence, but is represented in it insofar as the power that guarantees a legal contract is, in turn, of violent origin even if violence is not introduced into the contract itself" (Walter Benjamin, "Critique of Violence," trans. Edmund Jephcott, in *Selected Writings Volume I: 1913–1926* [Cambridge: Harvard University Press, 1996], 243–244).

3. According to Jean Laplanche and Jean-Bertrand Pontalis, fantasies "intend to provide a representation and a 'solution' to what, for the child, present themselves as major enigmas; they dramatize as moments of emergence, as the origin of a history, what appears to the subject as a reality of a nature such that it requires an explanation, a 'theory'" (Jean Laplanche and Jean-Bertrand Pontalis, *Fantasme Originaire, Fantasmes des Origines, Origines du Fantasme* [Paris: Hachette Littératures, 1985], 67–68, my translation).

4. Slavoj Žižek, *Welcome to the Desert of the Real: Five Essays on September 11 and Related Dates* (New York: Verso, 2002), 18.

4. Early Explorations of Fantasy

1. David Bordwell, *The Cinema of Eisenstein* (Cambridge: Harvard University Press, 1993), 72.

2. Béla Balázs, *Theory of the Film: Character and Growth of a New Art*, trans. Edith Bone (New York: Dover, 1970), 285.

5. The Coldness of Kubrick

1. Robert Phillip Kolker, *A Cinema of Loneliness: Penn, Kubrick, Scorcese, Spielberg, and Altman*, 2nd ed. (Oxford: Oxford University Press, 1988), 89.

2. Ibid., 157.

3. Jacques Lacan, *The Seminar of Jacques Lacan, Book VII: The Ethics of Psychoanalysis, 1959–1960*, trans. Dennis Porter (New York: Norton, 1992), 103.

4. Joseph Gelmis, "Interview with Stanley Kubrick," in *Perspectives on Stanley Kubrick*, ed. Mario Falsetto (New York: G. K. Hall, 1996), 32.

5. Most commentators who discuss *Eyes Wide Shut* respond very dismissively to the orgy scene and stress its lack of eroticism. It is my feeling that these attacks on the scene stem from a misconception concerning what produces eroticism. The complaint that the orgy is not "sexy" because it is cold and mechanical completely misunderstands the relationship between coldness and eroticism. Coldness is in fact erotic because it marks the separation of eroticism from all tenderness. In most romantic interactions, tender and erotic feelings run together, and this has the effect of diluting our sexual desire. The more our tender feelings obtrude upon our erotic feelings, the less we can give ourselves over to our erotic feelings. But in the completely cold and mechanical orgy that Kubrick creates, there is no tenderness, which gives free reign to the erotic feelings. (I am indebted to Mike Ashooh for this point.)

6. Michel Chion, *Eyes Wide Shut*, trans. Trista Selous (London: BFI Publishing, 2002), 21. It is significant that this scene represents one of the few radical changes that Kubrick made to Arthur Schnitzler's novel in adapting it into a film. Victor's explanation to Bill has no equivalent in the novel.

7. Michael Bérubé points out that HAL's malfunction is the direct result of his position as the leader of the mission. Unlike the rest of the crew, HAL knows the truth about the mission, and he must conceal this truth from the crew. In a sense, his position as a symbolic authority forces him to lie, thereby paving the way for the other sins that follow. This indicates that the contradictions that inhere in the position of symbolic authority produce the perversity that symbolic authority figures constantly display in Kubrick's films. See Michael Bérubé, *Public Access: Literary Theory and American Cultural Politics* (New York: Verso, 1994).

6. Spike Lee's Fantasmatic Explosions

1. Desson Howe, "*25th Hour*: Overly Spiked Punch," *Washington Post*, January 10, 2003.

2. Ibid. This criticism of Lee also exists in the scholarly response to his films. For instance, bell hooks takes Lee to task for his use of formal excesses in the film *Crooklyn* (1994), especially the use of an anamorphic lens to depict the Southern relatives whom Brooklyn native Troy (Zelda Harris) visits. According to hooks, "The switch to an anamorphic lens confuses. No doubt that is why signs were placed at ticket booths telling viewers that this change did not indicate a problem with the projector. Fancy attempts at cover-up aside, in these scenes Lee mockingly caricatures in an uninteresting fashion the southern black middle class" (hooks, *Reel to Real*, 39).

3. In fact, in many of Lee's films, the narrative barely moves forward at all. Instead, his films depict a series of events that reveal the hidden jouissance implicit in daily life. See, for instance, *She's Gotta Have It* (1986), *Mo' Better Blues* (1990), *Crooklyn*, and *25th Hour*.

4. Lacan, *Ethics of Psychoanalysis*, 80.

5. Douglas Kellner, "Aesthetics, Ethics and Politics in the Films of Spike Lee," in *Spike Lee's* Do the Right Thing, ed. Mark A. Reid (New York: Cambridge University Press, 1997), 82.

6. This dynamic of contemporary racism explains the failure of Paul Haggis's *Crash* (2005), despite its effort to reveal the thoroughgoing racism of contemporary American society. The film fails on a formal level to come to grips with the way that racism manifests itself today. *Crash* realistically shows characters articulating their racist fantasies, which has the effect of placing these fantasies on the level of the social reality itself, where they do not in fact appear. As a result, the spectator who harbors racist fantasies can leave the film assured that she/he bears no resemblance at all to characters such as the vile Jean (Sandra Bullock). In a Spike Lee film, by contrast, one experiences the indictment on the precise level of one's own racism, which is why Lee's films cannot earn the widespread acclaim that accompanied the release of *Crash*.

7. As the film shows, white subjects derive much of their own enjoyment from such fantasies, fantasies that involve black enjoyment. Fantasmatically, everyone wants to be black in order to access this excessive enjoyment, which is why blackface becomes so popular in the film. White subjects put on blackface in order to approach the jouissance they posit in black subjectivity.

7. Michael Mann and the Ethics of Excess

1. Walter Goodman, review of *Manhunter*, *New York Times*, August 15, 1986.

2. For this reason, it is not at all surprising that Lee has publicly expressed criticism for Mann's work, especially *Ali*. Because Mann focuses on the ethical rather than the ideological aspect of excess, his films must, we might imagine, strike Lee as overly optimistic, even romantic.

3. Immanuel Kant, *Critique of Practical Reason*, in *Practical Philosophy*, trans. and ed. Mary J. Gregor (New York: Cambridge University Press, 1996), 163–164. In the second *Critique*, Kant locates the moral law at precisely the point of fantasmatic excess. In this sense, Kantian ethics marks a fundamental break from the implicit, antifantasmatic ethic of the first *Critique*. For Kant, our very ability to give laws to ourselves sticks out excessively from the phenomenal world of representation.

4. Immanuel Kant, *Groundwork of the Metaphysic of Morals*, in Gregor, *Practical Philosophy*, 45.

5. Ibid., 77.

6. Nick James, *Heat* (London: BFI Publishing, 2002), 51.

7. Because all of Mann's heroes are men and often they leave women behind in their devotion to duty, it is tempting to write Mann off as a fundamentally sexist filmmaker and to dismiss his conception of ethical duty. While it is true that Mann's focus is solely on men and their duty, he is in no way an antifeminist. The women whom the men leave behind are never characterized in a negative way. Instead, the need to leave women behind becomes visible as the inherent limitation of the male ethos that Mann depicts. Men— or so Mann shows—can only perform their duty by constituting themselves as an exception because of the very structure of male subjectivity (its constitution relative to the phallus as the exceptional signifier).

8. Slavoj Žižek, *Tarrying with the Negative: Kant, Hegel, and the Critique of Ideology* (Durham: Duke University Press, 1993), 42.

9. Kant, *Groundwork*, 95.

8. The Bankruptcy of Fantasy in Fellini

1. As Peter Bondanella points out, "His name has become synonymous with fantasy and exuberant creativity" (Peter Bondanella, *The Cinema of Federico Fellini* [Princeton: Princeton University Press, 1992], 19).

2. William Van Watson, "Fellini and Lacan: The Hollow Phallus, the Male Womb, and the Retying of the Umbilical," in *Federico Fellini: Contemporary Perspectives*, eds. Frank Burke and Marguerite R. Waller (Toronto: University of Toronto Press, 2002), 73.

9. Desire and Not Showing Enough

1. The difference between desire and the drive is evident in the attitude that the subject takes toward the path that desire follows. When the subject experiences the path of desire as an end in itself rather than as a way of seeking something beyond that path, the subject moves into the drive.

2. Christian Metz, *Film Language: A Semiotics of the Cinema*, trans. Michael Taylor (Chicago: University of Chicago Press, 1974), 116.

3. Ibid., 69.

4. We might think of the opposition between the cinema of fantasy and the cinema of desire in parallel with the relationship between Georges Bataille and Maurice Blanchot. Their thought is at once linked together and completely opposed, and the opposition between them almost exactly duplicates the opposition between the cinema of fantasy and that of desire. As Eleanor Kaufman puts it, "While Bataille is the thinker of excess, eroticism, and transgression, Blanchot is the thinker of restraint, the neuter, and thought from the outside" (Eleanor Kaufman, *The Delirium of Praise: Bataille, Blanchot, Deleuze, Foucault, Klossowski* [Baltimore: Johns Hopkins University Press, 2001], 18).

5. Cinema is in fact hospitable to desire because of its relationship to narrative movement. Unlike literature, cinema always depicts events happening. As Roland Barthes notes, "In contrast to the literature of 'nothing happens' (the prototype of which would be *Sentimental Education*), the cinema, even the kind which doesn't seem at the outset to be commercial, is a discourse in which the story, the anecdote, the plot (with its major consequence, *suspense*) are never absent; even 'fantasy,' which is the emphatic, caricatural category of the anecdotal, is not incompatible with very good cinema. At the movies, 'something is happening'" (Roland Barthes, *The Grain of the Voice: Interviews 1962–1980*, trans. Linda Coverdale [Berkeley: University of California Press, 1991], 17).

6. Peter Brooks, *Reading for the Plot: Design and Intention in Narrative* (Cambridge: Harvard University Press, 1984), 37. In order to support this conception of desire (that desire is the desire for an end), Brooks misreads Freud, excluding the compulsion to repeat from Freud's understanding of desire. Even when Brooks does specifically address repetition, he conceives it as an aspect of the desire for an end.

7. Of course, nonnarrative film also operates by prompting spectator desire concerning what will happen next. This is part of the reason why Metz suggests that all cinema is in some sense narrative cinema.

8. As Edward Branigan points out, "Narration comes into being when knowledge is unevenly distributed—when there is a disturbance or disruption in the field of knowledge" (Edward Branigan, *Narrative Comprehension and Film* [New York: Routledge, 1992], 66).

9. Neither Bordwell nor Metz explicitly spends much time discussing the role of desire in the cinema. And in fact, because psychoanalytic film theory focused so exclusively on the problem of identification, there has been little attempt to think about the role of desire in the cinematic experience in a theoretical way. For a notable exception, see Jacqueline Rose, *Sexuality in the Field of Vision* (New York: Verso, 1986). Rose directly takes Metz to task for stressing identification at the expense of desire.

10. David Bordwell, *Narration in the Fiction Film* (Madison: University of Wisconsin Press, 1985), 52.

11. Branigan, *Narrative Comprehension and Film*, 82.

12. Lacan, *Les Formations de l'inconscient*, 320, my translation.

10. Theoretical Desiring

1. André Bazin, "The Cybernetics of André Cayatte," in *Bazin at Work: Major Essays and Reviews from the Forties and Fifties*, trans. Alain Piette and Bert Cardullo, ed. Bert Cardullo (New York: Routledge, 1997), 99.

2. André Bazin, "Marginal Notes on *Eroticism in the Cinema*," in *What Is Cinema?* vol. 2, trans. Hugh Gray (Berkeley: University of California Press, 1971), 170.

3. As Alan Williams points out, the identification of Bazin with "realism" causes us to miss the nuances in Bazin's conception of realism, the way in which, for him, cinematic realism has the effect of making everyday reality strange for the spectator. According to Williams, "Modern film theory tries to purge itself of Bazinian idealism, and in so doing it rejects what was most original and productive in the critic's thinking, the inextricable mingling of idealist and realist impulses. The notion of cinematic realism was the major point of departure for all of his thinking, but he did not assume it as a neutral, scientific fact. For Bazin, the photographic image did not merely reproduce reality but transformed it, radically altering its nature for the spectator by the very fact of reproducing it as literally as possible. The result was surprisingly close to the Russian Formalist critical ideal of *ostraneniye*, or 'making strange'" (Alan Williams, *Republic of Images: A History of French Filmmaking* [Cambridge: Harvard University Press, 1992], 310).

4. Siegfried Kracauer, *Theory of Film: The Redemption of Physical Reality* (Princeton, NJ: Princeton University Press, 1960), 71.

5. Kracauer contends that film's inability to represent depth is the source of the genius of the medium, but he also recognizes that this accounts for the paucity of philosophical films. He says, "Films cling to the surface of things. They seem to be the more cinematic, the less they focus directly on inward life, ideology, and spiritual concerns. This explains why many people with strong cultural leanings scorn the cinema" (Kracauer, *Theory of Film*, l–li).

6. Though Bazin and Kracauer tend to praise the kind of films that we could locate within the cinema of desire, my interest here is more theoretical than practical. Which is to say that though some of the films that I discuss in this chapter may be among the favorites of Bazin and Kracauer, there is no one-to-one correspondence between the films that I see operating within the cinema of desire and those that they esteem.

11. The Politics of Cinematic Desire

1. Even though many commentators on Lacan attribute his conception of desire to the influence of Hegel (and Alexandre Kojève), here we can see a key difference. Unlike Lacan, Hegel does conceive of desire in terms of the desire for recognition. It is an indication of Hegel's prepsychoanalytic status that he could not yet think the impossible object despite understanding that the desire for recognition always and necessarily ends in failure.

2. Lacan, *Ethics of Psychoanalysis*, 321.

3. Put in this way, it is easy to see the affinity between Lacan's ethic of psychoanalysis and Sartrean existentialism, two positions rarely associated with each other. For Lacan, psychoanalysis existentializes the subject, forcing the subject to embrace its actual existential situation without the illusory guarantees of the big Other. If Lacan is critical of Sartre, his critique lies in the direction of Sartre's failure to recognize the power of the big Other over the subject (which is of a piece with Sartre's rejection of an unconscious for the for-itself). But in his conception of what constitutes the subject's ethical path, Lacan follows Sartre very closely, much more so than other French thinkers after Sartre.

4. As Richard Boothby puts it, "The object is ceded not in order to preserve an already formed desire but, in the most radical sense, desire originates precisely in such ceding. The object is thrust away so that it can be desired, it is lost so that it can be found for the first time. Desire paradoxically comes into being in and through its limitation, the upsurge of desire is thus coincident with its inhibition" (Richard Boothby, *Freud as Philosopher: Metapsychology After Lacan* [New York: Routledge, 2001], 247).

12. The Impossible Object of the *Nouvelle Vague*

1. According to Anne Gillian, the beginning and ending reveal the film's investment in the fantasy of fusion with the maternal body. She writes, "The wish for fusion with a maternal figure is expressed, in the introduction and conclusion of the film, by images of a mythic nature. The credits appear in a series of shots that evoke the quest of an impatient camera to be reunited with the Eiffel Tower. In a similar way, at the end of the film, a long tracking shot accompanies the child up to the exact place on the beach where the waves touch the sand. The poets have said for a long time that the shore is a maternal body where the child comes into the world" (Anne Gillian, *François Truffaut: Le Secret perdu* [Paris: Hatier, 1991], 37, my translation). The problem with this interpretation of the beginning and ending of the film is that it misses the film's emphasis on the failure of any "fusion" with the object. Gillian claims that "*Les 400 Coups* would not have been the success that it was if it was only a simple story of failure and despair" (36, my translation). But the success of the film—its ability to generate desire—in fact

depends on the centrality of failure in the film. It is on the basis of failure and impossibility that the subject desires.

2. If *Les quatre cents coups* shows us how the perpetual disjunction between the subject and the social order sustains desire, Jean-Luc Godard's early films all reveal the impossibility of one subject's desire ever coinciding with that of another. These films insist that an antagonism haunts every couple. This is evident in *À Bout de souffle* (*Breathless*, 1960), *Une Femme est une femme* (*A Woman Is a Woman*, 1961), *Le Mépris* (*Contempt*, 1963), *Bande à part* (*Band of Outsiders*, 1964), *Alphaville* (1965), and *Pierrot le fou* (1965), among others. These films are politically important because contemporary ideology is first and foremost an ideology of romance: the image of the romantic partner promises to fill in the subject's lack in a way the society itself cannot. Even if we doubt social authorities today, we continue to have faith in our fantasy of the soul mate. Godard's films represent a response to the predominance of this fantasy.

3. Lacan, *Four Fundamental Concepts*, 103.

4. Sandy Flitterman-Lewis, *To Desire Differently: Feminism and the French Cinema*, expanded ed. (New York: Columbia University Press, 1996), 269.

5. Flitterman-Lewis, *To Desire Differently*, 283.

6. Even the title of the film—*Cléo de 5 à 7*—indicates the impossibility around which desire is structured. Whereas the title seems to promise that the film will follow Cléo for two hours, the film itself follows her until only six thirty, not seven o'clock. By leaving out the final thirty minutes suggested by the title, Varda makes clear that no fantasy can ever finally resolve the subject's desire. But there is also another reason for the title: "5 à 7" is French slang for an afternoon sexual encounter. This sense of the title further confirms the film's fidelity to the logic of desire in the face of fantasmatic inducements. The title suggests that the film is going to deliver the fantasy of an afternoon fling, and one watches throughout expecting this, but the film never shows any sexual encounter whatsoever, forcing the spectator to remain in the position of the desiring subject.

13. The Banality of Orson Welles

1. The films of Michelangelo Antonioni represent, in a sense, the opposite danger. While the films of the nouvelle vague may allow the spectator to fantasize a future resolution of desire, Antonioni's films often treat the impossible object nostalgically, suggesting that that this object was once possible in the past. That is, though Antonioni's films conclude by affirming that the objet petit a is a lost and impossible object, they often depict the object as having been lost in the course of the film. In *Blowup* (1968), for instance, though the body of a murder victim disappears and becomes impossible to locate, the camera of Thomas (David Hemmings) is able to capture its presence at one

point. Through his insistence on the objet petit a as a lost object that we once had, Antonioni opens up the possibility of the nostalgic fantasy—allowing us to believe that it is only the passing of time that bars our access to the object.

2. G. W. F. Hegel, *Science of Logic*, trans. A. V. Miller (Atlantic Highlands, NJ: Humanities Press International, 1969), 706.

3. Even *Citizen Kane*, of course, almost never received a public screening. The famous offer of one million dollars that RKO received to burn the negative of the film might have consigned the film to a fate worse that Welles's other mutilated and underfinanced projects. RKO head George Schaefer's refusal of this offer represents the only act of courage that any executive in Hollywood displayed in relation to Welles's films.

4. Lacan, *Ethics of Psychoanalysis*, 14.

5. The irony of *Citizen Kane* is that Welles uses deep-focus photography not in order to reveal some reality that film usually hides, but to reveal a hitherto missing absence. The focus of the film is on what we can't see, what the plenitude of the filmic image cannot deliver.

6. Laura Mulvey, *Fetishism and Curiosity* (Bloomington: Indiana University Press, 1996), 99.

7. In his insightful book on Welles, Johan-Frédérik Hel-Guedj links the inaccessibility of the object to the failure to complete the construction of Xanadu (which would be the signifier adequate to the object). He writes, "It is because [Kane's] past is nowhere to be found that Xanadu remains unfinished" (Johan-Frédérik Hel-Guedj, *Orson Welles: La Règle du faux* [Paris: Éditions Michalon, 1997], 66–67, my translation).

8. Rodowick notes, "'Rosebud' will never explain the narrative of Kane's life. The sled consumed by fire in the closing images of the film is the sign of the impossibility of a stable identity or a totalizing life-narrative. It is called up out of the virtual space of memory only to disappear immediately, unrecognized by any character. It confirms no recollection; rather it undermines any hope of a full or exact recollection" (D. N. Rodowick, *Gilles Deleuze's Time Machine* [Durham: Duke University Press, 1997], 94).

9. In this sense, Christopher Nolan's *Memento* (2000) represents a contemporary retelling of *Citizen Kane*. *Memento* utilizes a reverse chronology—each scene takes place earlier than the previous one and ends with the moment that begins the previous scene—in order to create the expectation that the film will conclude by revealing the originary trauma: the truth of the rape and murder of the wife of the hero, Leonard Shelby (Guy Pearce). The film concludes not by keeping the origin unknown in the manner of the nouvelle vague, but by revealing the origin itself to be a lie: we see Leonard decide to knowingly lie to himself in order to inaugurate the mystery that he have just seen played out. By depicting a lie at the origin, *Memento*, like *Citizen Kane*, illustrates the ordinariness of the impossible object. The truth of Leonard's investigation is nothing other than his own lie, just as the truth of the investigation into Kane is nothing but a sled.

10. Orson Welles and Peter Bogdanovich, *This is Orson Welles*, ed. Jonathan Rosenbaum (New York: HarperCollins, 1992), 114.

11. In Welles's original, lost version of the film, George was an even more detestable character. The studio decision to cut some of his more odious moments represents a clear act of censorship, an attempt to limit the film's disruptiveness, given that the film asks us to identify with George's desire.

12. If we contrast George's comeuppance with that received by the typical Hollywood villain, the radicality of Welles's film becomes apparent. When, for instance, Hans Gruber (Alan Rickman) falls to his death in *Die Hard* (John McTiernan, 1989), we feel nothing but satisfaction in seeing Hans receive precisely the punishment that he deserves.

13. This allows us to gain insight into Welles's lifelong love for the character of Falstaff, the love that resulted in the film *Chimes at Midnight* (1965). Falstaff's very raison d'être consists in exposing the banality or emptiness of the privileged object, and this is precisely what Welles emphasizes in his film version of Falstaff's adventures. In contrast to Shakespeare, Welles's film emphasizes that Falstaff reveals the emptiness of even the noble Prince Hal. In the film, Falstaff articulates what could be his tag line: "Give me the spare men, and spare me the great ones."

14. Claire Denis and the Other's Failure to Enjoy

1. Slavoj Žižek, *The Plague of Fantasies* (New York: Verso, 1997), 32.

2. *Vendredi soir (Friday Night, 2002)* seems to be the exception among Denis's films since it focuses on a scene of actual enjoyment: a one-night sexual affair between Laure (Valérie Lemercier) and Jean (Vincent Lindon), a man who hitches a ride with Laure. However, the way that Denis shoots their affair indicates the partiality of the enjoyment it provides. Their sexual encounter occurs almost entirely in close-ups. Rather than medium or long shots that would allow us to see what Laure and Jean look like together, we see only close-ups of their hands, their feet, their faces, and so on. At times, it becomes difficult to discern what body parts we see. By shooting the scene in this way, Denis deprives the spectator of the image of a complete jouissance that we expect from cinematic sexual encounters, which is perhaps why so many reviews found the film's depiction of sex unerotic.

3. I am indebted to Hilary Neroni for much of this analysis of *Chocolat*. See Hilary Neroni, "Lost in Fields of Interracial Desire: Claire Denis' *Chocolat*" (1988) *Kinoeye* 3, no. 7 (June 9, 2003), *www.kinoeye.org/03/07/neroni07.php*.

4. The final scene of the film depicts airport workers loading African artifacts into the plane that France (the character) is taking on her return to France (the country). The scene implies French pillaging of Cameroon, which has its basis in the fantasy of an exotic Africa. By concluding with this image, Denis stresses the larger political implications of this fantasy.

5. As Joan Copjec notes, "In place of the All, the original Plenum, we have these little objects, which are . . . partial incarnations of a lost . . . One" (Copjec, *Imagine There's No Woman*, 55).

15. Political Desire in Italian Neorealism

1. James Carville and Mary Matalin represent the apogee of this attitude. Despite their loudly articulated political claims, the fact that their desire for each other transcends their politics testifies to the unimportance of whatever claims they make and the unimportance of politics as such.

2. As Christopher Wagstaff notes, "The neo-realists developed a *new* narrative," and they were able to do this because their films "are all rather like road movies; they have plots that involve repetition and circularity; they end with no concrete resolution" (Christopher Wagstaff, "Rossellini and Neo-realism," in *Roberto Rossellini: Magician of the Real*, ed. David Forgacs, Sarah Lutton, and Geoffrey Nowell-Smith [London: BFI Publishing, 2000], 40, 41).

3. Almost every Hollywood film that overtly tackles politics relies on a fantasmatic resolution for desire. Think of *Mississippi Burning* (Alan Parker, 1988), *The American President* (Rob Reiner, 1995), and *The Life of David Gale* (Alan Parker, 2003), just to name a few. In each case, the film initiates a politicized desire in the spectator only to depict a clear way of resolving that desire.

4. Peter Bondanella, *The Films of Roberto Rossellini* (Cambridge: Cambridge University Press, 1993), 55.

5. This scene evinces Vincent Rocchio's claim that "the temporary although frequent subordination of narrative progression to social exposition becomes the preeminent stylistic norm in *Bicycle Thieves*" (Vincent F. Rocchio, *Cinema of Anxiety: A Psychoanalysis of Neorealism* [Austin: University of Texas Press, 1999], 54). Despite recognizing the way that *Ladri di biciclette* breaks up narrative movement with social exposition, Rocchio finds the film invested in Antonio's individualist fantasy and criticizes the film for this. However, this reading leaves unanswered the question of why the film demonstrates the abject failure—rather than the success—of this fantasy.

6. Capitalism thrives on fantasmatic promises of the ultimate enjoyment, but it is constitutively incapable of tolerating any actual enjoyment. This is because subjects who are really enjoying themselves are not good consumers. The good consumer must believe in the fantasy of the possible object, whereas the subject who accepts the impossible status of the object no longer seeks this object in the form of the latest commodity.

7. This is one of the fundamental antagonisms of capitalist ideology. This ideology proclaims the importance of individual difference and exceptionalism, while at the same time the power of reification constantly creates equivalence of difference. Within capitalism, because everything must stand out, nothing can.

8. Lacan, *Les Formations de l'inconscient*, 338, my translation.

16. The Intermixing of Desire and Fantasy

1. Jacques Lacan, *The Seminar of Jacques Lacan, Book XX: Encore 1972–1973*, trans. Bruce Fink (New York: Norton, 1998), 32. Bruce Fink points out that "the only *truth* of psychoanalysis . . . is that there is no such thing as a sexual relationship, the problem being to bring the subject to the point of encountering that truth" (Bruce Fink, *The Lacanian Subject: Between Language and Jouissance* [Princeton, NJ: Princeton University Press, 1995], 121).

2. For more on the ideological function of the fantasy of a successful sexual relationship, see Hilary Neroni, *The Violent Woman: Femininity, Narrative, and Violence in Contemporary American Cinema* (Albany: State Universtiy of New York Press, 2005), 83–112.

3. Probably the greatest example of this in the history of cinema is the conclusion of Taylor Hackford's *An Officer and a Gentleman* (1982). This film initially lays out the failure of the sexual relationship in very traditional terms. It depicts the relationship between fledgling navy pilot Zack Mayo (Richard Gere) and Paula Pokrikfi (Debra Winger), a relationship that fails because Zack's desires and Paula's desires are at odds. Whereas Zack says that he simply wants to enjoy himself during his training program, Paula has long-term hopes for the relationship. When Zack nears the end of his training, the antagonism between the two produces a break-up, as Zack stops calling Paula. This break-up is, however, nothing but a preamble to their eventual reconciliation in the fantasy of the successful sexual relationship.

The final scene of the film reveals how this fantasy allows us to experience the gaze as a reassuring rather than traumatic object. The scene involves Zack entering the paper factory where Paula works and taking her away for a life with him. Throughout the scene, an instrumental version of Joe Cocker and Jennifer Warnes's love song "Up Where We Belong" plays in the background. The music starts as Zack enters the factory, and its uplifting melody serves to transform the factory into a romantic setting for the union that the film will depict.

Here, Zack functions as the gaze, and as the scene unfolds, we can see the status of the gaze undergo a transformation. Wearing his bright white naval uniform, Zack does not fit within the factory setting, where everything is drab and dirty. When he enters the factory, Zack is the impossible object. As such, he should disrupt the visual field or else remain an absence within it. And in fact, at first Zack is a present absence in the scene. The initial shot shows him walking behind a large machine that obscures all but brief flashes of his white uniform. The first four shots of the scene alternate between Zack barely visible walking behind this machine, and people looking up from their work to notice him. When the film finally allows us to see Zack, he appears only briefly in a long shot from the side. He becomes fully visible as he walks past Paula's mother, who is working on a machine, and touches her hand. As he approaches Paula herself, we can see Zack transition from embodying the impossible gaze—the desire of the Other—to embodying a desire that fits securely within our fantasy structure.

The film shows Paula working on her machine, oblivious to Zack's entrance into the factory. Zack then appears as a white, blurry figure in the background of the shot. As this blurry figure, he remains in the position of the gaze, but this quickly changes. As he approaches Paula, he becomes clearer until he comes up behind her and kisses her neck. At this moment, the romantic music grows louder. Zack then picks up Paula and begins to carry her out of the factory. This gesture erases all doubts about Zack's desire: he simply wants Paula. In the final shot of the film, the camera pans to follow Zack walking out of the factory while holding Paula in his arms, and as she takes his officer's hat from his head and places it on her own, the film culminates in a freeze frame, suggesting the immortality of this moment of the perfect romantic union. After the freeze frame, the vocals to "Up Where We Belong" begin, and they describe the ability of the perfect romantic union to lift us above all antagonism in "the world below."

By concluding *An Officer and a Gentleman* in this way, director Taylor Hackford allows us to experience the ultimate power of the fantasy of the successful sexual relationship. As this fantasy unfurls, all the antagonisms that the film presents disappear. This fantasy solves the antagonism that exists between Zack and Paula, and it eliminates the gaze as an impossible object. Zack's desire, which has remained indecipherable even to himself throughout the film, becomes in this final scene completely clear. Zack now fits successfully in his world.

4. According to Raymond Bellour, "After a certain situation posed at the start as a problem or as an enigma, the film gradually leads to a final solution which allows the more or less conflicting terms posed at the beginning to be resolved, and which in the majority of cases takes the form of marriage" (Janet Bergstrom, "Alternation, Segmentation, Hypnosis: Interview with Raymond Bellour," in *Feminism and Film Theory*, ed. Constance Penley [New York: Routledge, 1988], 187).

5. The other problem with compromise is that it never really works. Compromise actually sustains all problems rather than allowing us to escape them. This is why Freud rejects it entirely in psychoanalytic practice. As Lacan notes, "Since [Freud] constantly points out that compromise is behind all the miseries his analysis assuages, we can say that resorting to compromise, whether explicit or implicit, disorients all psychoanalytic action and plunges it into darkness" (Jacques Lacan, "The Instance of the Letter in the Unconscious or Reason Since Freud," in *Écrits*, 435).

6. Joseph Breuer and Sigmund Freud, *Studies on Hysteria*, in Strachey, *Standard Edition*, vol. 2 (1955), 305.

7. Sigmund, Freud, "Negation," in Strachey, *Standard Edition*, vol. 19 (1961), 237.

8. If we understand psychoanalysis as normalizing in precisely this sense, we can see the extent to which the leftist attacks leveled at Freud miss their mark. Freud does not envision psychoanalysis as a contribution to greater conformity, despite its many misuses in that direction (especially in the United States). The normal subject that Freud aims at is a subject with the ability to transgress and to change the world in actuality rather than in the realm of fantasy.

17. The Theoretical Opposition

1. As I noted in the introduction, the problem with the attack made by traditional Lacanian film theory involves its absolute hostility to the fantasmatic dimension of the cinema. We can call into question what I call the cinema of integration for its particular deployment of fantasy without dismissing the cinematic deployment of fantasy altogether.

2. Jean-Louis Baudry, "Basic Effects of the Cinematographic Apparatus," 540.

3. Laura Mulvey, "Visual Pleasure and Narrative Cinema," 308.

4. Jean Baudry, "The Apparatus: Metapsychological Approaches to the Impression of Reality in the Cinema," trans. Jean Andrews and Bernard Augst, in *Narrative, Apparatus, Ideology*, ed. Philip Rosen (New York: Columbia University Press, 1986), 313.

5. As Daniel Dayan points out in his discussion of classical Hollywood cinema's use of suture, "The film-discourse presents itself as a product without a producer, a discourse without an origin. It speaks. Who speaks? Things speak for themselves and, of course, they tell the truth. Classical cinema establishes itself as the ventriloquist of ideology" (Daniel Dayan, "The Tutor-Code of Classical Cinema," in *Movies and Methods*, ed. Bill Nichols, vol. 1 [Berkeley: University of California Press, 1976], 451). Traditional Lacanian film theory spent so much time with the concept of suture because of the role that it plays in producing fantasy. The suturing effect of shot/reverse shot works to eliminate the spectator's grasp of the productive apparatus. Prior to a suturing reverse shot, the spectator is able to perceive the productive apparatus at work in its framing of the shot. According to Jean-Pierre Oudart's classic essay, after an initial experience of the jouissance of the image, the spectator "has discovered the framing. Suddenly, he senses the space he cannot see, hidden by the camera, and wonders, in retrospect, why such a framing was used" (Jean-Pierre Oudart, "Cinema and Suture," *Screen* 18, no. 4 [1977–1978]: 41). For a moment, the spectator becomes aware of the productive process, but through the effect of suture, this awareness almost instantly dissolves into a fantasmatic pleasure in the sense of closure that the reverse shot provides.

18. The Politics of the Cinema of Integration

1. Neither desire nor fantasy has an intrinsic ideological valence, though Lacanian cultural theorists tend to associate fantasy with ideological manipulation and desire with an ethical resistance to this manipulation. But fantasy can just as easily provide the terrain on which a subject might contest ideology. It is thus not a matter of choosing between desire and fantasy, but of paying attention to their interaction.

19. The Ordinary Cinema of Ron Howard

1. Friedrich Nietzsche, *Human, All Too Human*, trans. R. J. Hollingdale (New York: Cambridge University Press, 1986), 45.

2. Even Marx, who usually resists utopianism, moves in this direction when he proclaims that communist society represents "the *genuine* resolution of the conflict between man and nature and between man and man" (Karl Marx, *Economic and Philosophic Manuscripts of 1844*, trans. Martin Milligan [New York: International Publishers, 1964], 135). This image of a future society reconciled with itself attests to the power of this fantasy insofar as it appears in the work of a thinker dedicated to uncovering social antagonism at precisely those points where fantasy obscures it.

3. In a certain sense, there is a formal similarity between Howard's aesthetic and that of Orson Welles. Both filmmakers materialize the impossible object after initially suggesting its resistance to the visual field. So why doesn't Welles belong, with Howard, in the cinema of integration? The difference resides in how each filmmaker treats the impossible object. When this object materializes in Welles's films (when we see, for instance, the sled at the end of *Citizen Kane*), it represents the failure rather than the success of signification. When the impossible occurs in Howard's films, it has the effect of providing meaning within the filmic world and completing the signifying structure that the film establishes. After the impossible is accomplished, the filmic world makes sense. For Welles, in contrast, the impossible object always acts as a stumbling block to sense.

4. The contrast between *A Beautiful Mind* and *Fight Club* is instructive given this similarity in their structures. Whereas *A Beautiful Mind* allows John to coexist harmoniously with his delusions once he masters them, *Fight Club* reveals the impossibility of any such peaceful coexistence. The hero (Edward Norton) has to shoot himself in order to escape his delusion. In *Fight Club*, the stain of the delusion is traumatic in a way that it is not in *A Beautiful Mind*.

5. The fact that this is a true story, that John Nash did actually overcome his delusions through the use of reason, in no way obviates the ideological

work that the film is doing here. Even though the source material for the film is an actual event, Howard nonetheless chooses how to depict that event. That is to say, in actuality Nash's solution to his problem was merely the solution to a problem, not the resolution of an impossible antagonism (as it became in the film).

20. Steven Spielberg's Search for the Father

1. Jacques Lacan, *Les Formations de l'inconscient*, 146, my translation.

2. Breuer and Freud's statement about "common human misery" being the best that subjects can hope for stems from their recognition that the symbolic father is nothing but a dead letter. The idea of happiness requires the living father's presence in order to protect the subject from the gaze.

3. *Duel* focuses on a paternal figure, David Mann (Dennis Weaver), who must confront a gaze that continually frustrates him throughout the film. The film depicts Mann driving from Los Angeles to northern California on a business trip. Along the way, he encounters a mysterious truck driver who torments him and eventually tries to kill him. Throughout this ordeal, the identity and the desire of the truck driver remain completely obscure. Mann incessantly asks himself the fundamental question of desire, "What does he want from me?" But because the gaze is a blind spot in the field of his vision, he cannot answer this question; he cannot attain a sense of mastery over this recalcitrant object gaze. The film contains multiple shots of Mann trying to see the face of the truck driver (either directly or through the rearview mirror), but the truck driver's face remains always obscured in shadow, hidden behind the truck's seemingly opaque windshield. Mann never meets the truck driver, and he never identifies him. Even more importantly, he never figures out why the truck driver wants to kill him. In this way, Spielberg uses the filmic image itself to reveal the workings of desire—how desire emerges in response to the indecipherable gaze.

The film emphasizes that in order to defeat the trucker and survive the trauma of the gaze, Mann must cede all his emblems of masculinity and phallic power. By shedding his attachment to paternal authority, Mann is able to confront the gaze as an absent object rather than trying to avoid it. As the truck approaches Mann for the final showdown, Spielberg uses a series of jump cuts of him in his car waiting for the battle. The jump cuts here indicate the disruption of the filmic field by the encounter with the gaze, but they also suggest Mann's abandonment of his paternal symbolic identity. The stability that paternal authority provides makes its absence felt here even in the film form itself. At this point, Mann places his briefcase on the gas pedal in order to power the car as he runs alongside it and steers it in the direction of the oncoming truck. When Mann puts the briefcase on the gas pedal, Spielberg includes a close-up on the case's nameplate, which identifies Mann as the owner. This close-up indicates to us what Mann is sacrificing at this moment in order to endure the gaze: not just his car and his briefcase, but his entire symbolic—and paternal—identity. He gives up the identity that the signifier "David Mann" provides for him, and in doing so, he defeats the trucker. But he does not defeat the gaze itself. The death of the trucker in no way answers the question of the Other's desire, which is why Spielberg does not include an image of the trucker's face even after his death. The film leaves us with nothing but the fundamental deadlock of desire as it exposes paternal authority's complete failure to resolve that deadlock and protect us from the gaze.

4. *Munich* (2005) marks a return to the cinema of desire that Spielberg first developed in *Duel* and *Sugarland Express*. It depicts the absence of the father figure who would allow Avner (Eric Bana), an Israeli secret agent who heads a secret assassination team targeting suspected Palestinian terrorists, to reconcile his duty to Israel and a personal sense of ethics. We hear about Avner's heroic father throughout the film, but he is conspicuous only in his absence. The film ends by highlighting the antagonism that exists between Avner and the man who sent him on his mission. This conclusion succeeds in not providing the spectator a way out of the impasse that haunts the struggle against terrorism.

5. Antonia Quirke, *Jaws* (London: BFI Publishing, 2002), 24–25.

6. Jonathan Lemkin notes that Amity is a mythologized American ideal. He writes, "The landscape in the film is an environment that never really existed, except in the collective consciousness of the vast majority of Americans. The setting is the archetypal American coastal town—absolutely the earliest American image, the settlements of the pilgrims on the coast of New England. It is the predecessor of the American rural ideal, and in that sense, the truest America. It is also a creation of nostalgia, a *pure* American community which is nothing less than mythic" (Jonathan Lemkin, "Archetypal Landscapes and *Jaws*," in *The Films of Steven Spielberg: Critical Essays*, ed. Charles L. P. Silet [Lanham, MD: Scarecrow Press, 2002], 4). Spielberg constructs this type of ideal in order to make clear the power of the gaze: it can reach us even at the point where we feel the most protected and secure.

7. The construction of the penultimate scene in *Minority Report* (2002) indicates Spielberg's specific concern for the redemption of the father. The failure of the father lies in the background of the entire film: while swimming at a public pool with his son, John Anderton (Tom Cruise) lost him to an unknown abductor, and despite working as a police investigator, John has never been able to find his son nor to solve the crime. This failure precipitates the break-up of John's marriage and the emergence of a drug habit. Out of this abject paternal failure, the film depicts John's redemption. By rescuing Agatha (Samantha Morton), a Precog used to predict future crimes, and solving the murder of Agatha's mother, John reveals himself as a capable father despite his earlier lapse. Spielberg emphasizes John's status as father when we see him reunited with his wife at the end of the film. He shows the two embracing in their house, and in this shot, her

appearance suggests that she is pregnant. However, the film is not content with simply hinting at this pregnancy and at John's status as a father. Spielberg adds a gesture by John—he places his hand on his wife's midsection—in order to leave no doubt about the existence of the coming child. This redundancy testifies to the extent of Spielberg's investment in redeeming the father. Rather than leaving any ambiguity concerning John's status, Spielberg adds this clearly paternal gesture.

8. In terms of how each film understands the trauma of the Holocaust, there is a fundamental similarity between *Schindler's List* and Claude Lanzmann's *Shoah* (1984), the film most often opposed to Spielberg's. Like *Schindler's List*, *Shoah* depicts the Nazi gaze as the impossible object that no amount of historical research can access. The difference between the films becomes apparent, however, in the trajectory that the gaze follows after beginning as an impossible object.

9. Paul Eisenstein, *Traumatic Encounters*, 93.

10. Omer Bartov, "Spielberg's Oskar: Hollywood Tries Evil," in *Spielberg's Holocaust: Critical Perspectives on* Schindler's List, ed. Yosefa Loshitzky (Bloomington: Indiana University Press, 1997), 44–45.

11. Bryan Cheyette, "The Uncertain Certainty of *Schindler's List*," in Loshitzky, *Spielberg's Holocaust*, 237.

21. D. W. Griffith's Suspense

1. Qtd. in François Truffaut, *Hitchcock: The Definitive Study of Alfred Hitchcock by François Truffaut*, rev. ed. (New York: Simon and Schuster, 1985), 73.

2. Noël Carroll, *Theorizing the Moving Image* (Cambridge: Cambridge University Press, 1996), 101.

3. Jacques Aumont insists that Griffith is actually a filmmaker of excess rather than continuity and would locate him (to use our terms) in the cinema of fantasy. He sees this excessiveness in Griffith's use of the close-up. Aumont writes, "The close-up in Griffith's work, as elsewhere, is that which functions precisely as *extra-* (extra-scenic, for example) and as such, is a sign of the discontinuity of the discourse, at once already perforated to facilitate the fetishistic cutting up of the body of the text, and an index, in the narrative fabric itself, of the principle of discontinuity enshrined in editing" (Jacques Aumont, "Griffith: The Frame, the Figure," in *Early Cinema: Space, Frame, Narrative*, ed. Thomas Elsaesser [London: BFI Publishing, 1990], 356). Because of this conception of Griffith's editing style, Aumont sees him as the precursor of filmmakers such as Jean-Luc Godard and Luis Buñuel.

4. As Gerald Butters points out, *Birth of a Nation* marks a dramatic political shift in Griffith as a filmmaker. He writes, "Griffith, the southern Conservative, became Griffith, the Radical racist, with the production of *The*

Birth of a Nation" (Gerald R. Butters, Jr., *Black Masculinity on the Silent Screen* (Lawrence: University Press of Kansas, 2002).

5. Jean-Paul Sartre, "What is Literature?" trans. Bernard Frechtman, in "*What is Literature?*" *and Other Essays* (Cambridge: Harvard University Press, 1988), 68.

6. Béla Balázs, *Theory of the Film*, 50.

7. Sergei Eisenstein, *Film Form*, 234.

8. Miriam Hansen notices Griffith's investment in fantasy in the content of many of his parallel editing sequences. She claims that "Griffith's favorite narrative paradigm [is] the last-minute rescue of victimized womanhood" and that this paradigm mirrors the "rescue fantasy" that Freud describes (Miriam Hansen, "The Hieroglyph and the Whore: D. W. Griffith's *Intolerance*," in *Classical Hollywood Narrative: The Paradigm Wars*, ed. Jane Gaines [Durham: Duke University Press, 1992], 188). The rescue fantasy, according to Freud, allows the son to identify himself with paternal authority and thereby have the forbidden object.

9. The fantasy of possibility does not necessarily inhere in suspense as such, which is to say that there is a form of suspense that runs counter to Griffith. We see this is the case of Alfred Hitchcock, a filmmaker who properly belongs in part 4. Though Tom Gunning claims that Hitchcock's brand of suspense marks him as "one of Griffith's most important heirs in the realm of filmic discourse," their modes of creating suspense differ dramatically in the relationship that they adopt toward fantasy (Tom Gunning, *D. W. Griffith and the Origins of American Narrative Film* [Urbana: University of Illinois Press, 1991], 296). Both filmmakers use suspense to stimulate spectator desire, to prompt spectators to question what will happen next. However, Hitchcock's suspense consistently rejects the easy resolution of desire. It accomplishes this by revealing the disruptiveness of the turn toward fantasy. Like Griffith, Hitchcock employs both desire and fantasy in his suspense— he creates desire by showing characters in peril and also hints at potential fantasmatic resolutions of these perils—but unlike Griffith, he shows how the fantasy actually throws the world of desire out of balance at the very moment it would resolve the problem of desire: though we can envision different possible resolutions, no one seems perfectly satisfying.

In the typical suspense film, suspense derives from our fear that the villain will vanquish the hero or an innocent victim, and we feel relief at the moment of the hero's triumph over the villain. This is the type of suspense that Griffith enacts through parallel editing. Hitchcock's suspense differs insofar as it refuses to resolve our desire in this way. The moment of the hero's triumph, for Hitchcock, is also the moment of the villain's defeat. While this seems, at first glance, commonsensical, most films manage to depict the hero's triumph without paying attention to the villain's experience of defeat. In Hitchcock's films, this defeat contains the gaze and thereby stains the filmic image.

The conclusions of *Murder!* (1930), *Sabotage* (1936), *Saboteur* (1942), and *Notorious* (1946) bring the underlying fantasy of the villain's demise to light in a way that disrupts the world of desire established in these films. In the first two films, the villain effectively punishes himself by accomplishing a suicidal act: Fane (Esme Percy) hangs himself after his trapeze performance in *Murder!*, and Verloc (Oskar Homolka) doesn't act to prevent his wife (Sylvia Sidney) from stabbing him (and in fact seems almost to help her to do so). In the second two films, Hitchcock's depiction of the demise of the villain creates sympathy for him: in *Saboteur*, Frank Fry (Norman Lloyd) literally hangs by a thread from the Statue of Liberty about to fall to his death, and in *Notorious*, Alexander Sebastian (Claude Rains) awaits death at the hands of his Nazi colleagues.

In each of these cases, the film's turn toward fantasy does not result in stabilizing the world of desire but in disrupting it. The denouement of Hitchcockian suspense is fantasy, but Hitchcock overwhelms us with too much fantasy. As a result, we must bear the burden of experiencing the impossible object and confronting our own involvement in what we see. Rather than smoothly resolving desire in the manner of Griffith's suspense, the Hitchcockian version forces us to confront the ramifications of such a resolution—the collapse of our position within the world of desire.

The point is not simply that Hitchcock concludes the suspense sequence differently than Griffith (though he does). It is rather that the very structure of the suspense itself differs because it is not organized around the fantasmatic resolution of desire. Hitchcockian suspense does not structure desire around a single focus, but rather divides our desire between two different antagonistic possibilities. We desire to see the villain punished, but we also experience sympathy for the villain's predicament. In this sense, Hitchcockian suspense unleashes desire in an almost pure form—without pointing toward its fantasmatic resolution. Because our desire is divided between two (or more) possibilities that cannot coexist, the perfect fantasmatic resolution becomes inconceivable. To put it in Carroll's terms, Hitchcock creates suspense around "two logically opposed outcomes" that each have a claim to a certain moral correctness. In other words, in Hitchcockian suspense we do not just experience the desire of the hero and the victim but also the desire of the villain, and this renders a single morally correct outcome—a successful fantasmatic resolution—unthinkable. Hitchcock's emphasis on the desire of the villain reveals the antagonistic nature of desire itself: desire is divided between two logically opposed possibilities. Hence, fantasy's attempt to resolve desire necessarily involves a traumatic encounter insofar as it implies a choice between the two possibilities.

10. The extreme racism of *Birth of a Nation* actually had the effect of eliminating the black villain from Hollywood cinema. As Donald Bogle explains, "One thing was certain after *The Birth of a Nation*: never again could the Negro be depicted in the guise of an out-and-out villain. This treatment was too touchy and too controversial. Griffith's film had succeeded because of

its director's artistry and technical virtuousity, but no studio dared risk it again" (Donald Bogle, *Toms, Coons, Mulattoes, Mammies, and Bucks: An Interpretive History of Blacks in American Films*, 4th ed. [New York: Continuum, 2001], 16). Though Hollywood would retreat from the content of Griffith's film, it would wholly embrace the form and thus take up his racism in this way. Most Hollywood films create suspense following the fantasmatic method of Griffith. They depict a villain with a clear desire to steal our enjoyment and a hero who can, in the end, control this desire. Even when the villain is a white male (as is most often the case in contemporary films), films work to evoke the paranoid fantasies that inform a racist mindset. If a subject believes that the other is out to steal its enjoyment, this subject is prepared to slip into racism, even if the paranoia in the film centers around a white villain.

22. Films That Separate

1. This is undoubtedly why David Lynch has such affection for *The Wizard of Oz*. Even though it finally retreats from the radicality it suggests, the film does manage to inaugurate a filmic technique—the division into separate worlds of desire and fantasy—that would revolutionize cinema's capacity for presenting the gaze and would become an integral part of Lynch's own filmmaking.

2. Despite signaling the transition between the filmic worlds with the violence of a tornado, *The Wizard of Oz* doesn't take this violence far enough. The tornado that transports Dorothy to Oz occurs within her dream (after the real tornado has knocked her unconscious), and it never actually threatens her. Though this tornado seems to lift Dorothy and her house hundreds of feet off the ground, she never feels any fear and simply looks out the window as if she's watching a film. This rendering of the divide between the world of desire and the world of fantasy dramatically understates the difference between the two worlds.

3. Linda Rohrer Paige, "Wearing Red Shoes: Dorothy and the Power of Female Imagination in *The Wizard of Oz*," *Journal of Popular Film and Television* 23, no. 4 (1996): 152.

4. According to Steven Hamelman, the film's depiction of Oz actually reveals the failure of fantasy to reconcile us with the world of desire. He claims, "What the movie really tells us is that to find Oz is as impossible as to go home again" (Steven Hamelman, "The Deconstructive Search for Oz," *Literature/Film Quarterly* 28, no. 4 [2000]: 316). The fantasy fails because language in Oz is constantly deconstructing itself and leading in circles. While Hamelman is undoubtedly correct to see Oz as the land of deconstruction run amok, this is no way disrupts its fantasmatic power. The essence of fantasy lies in its ability to transcend the laws of the signifier, including the law of noncontradiction. The more that language is "weirdly ineffective" in the fantasy, the more the fantasy illustrates the unimportance of the limits that accompany signification.

5. The disguising of the gaze caused by the blending of desire and fantasy becomes apparent when the film depicts Marty kissing his mother, Lorraine (Lea Thompson), in the fantasy world. Attracted to Marty and unaware that he is actually her son, Lorraine kisses him passionately while they are sitting in a parked car outside a school dance. This kiss represents a potential encounter with the gaze—a point at which we see Marty interact with an impossible object. Rather than show this as a traumatic moment, however, the film navigates the trauma through Lorraine's reaction. After kissing Marty, Lorraine pulls back with a look of disgust on her face, and she says, "It's all wrong. I don't know what it is, but when I kiss you, it's like I'm kissing my brother." There is no justification for Lorraine's recoil from the kiss within the fantasy world; to her, Marty is an attractive guy, not her son. Her recoil thus testifies to the film's blending of desire and fantasy and shows how this blending eliminates the potential trauma of the gaze, which we as spectators would experience if Lorraine actually enjoyed the kiss.

23. The Separation of Desire and Fantasy

1. If we liken the film to the dream, the cinema of intersection offers us the experience of a dream within a dream. For Freud, this type of dream has a very particular function: it depicts the desire that we wish we didn't have—the desire that we are attempting to renounce.

2. The incompleteness of fantasy becomes evident in the Kantian antinomies (which are nothing but the fantasies of reason). The antinomies result from the attempt to think the world as a completed totality—for instance, the absolute beginning of the world—and they reveal our inability to conceive the world in these terms. The attempt to think the absolute beginning of the world leaves us, according to Kant, with two opposed possibilities, both of which are false: the world neither has a beginning in time and space, nor is it infinite temporally and spatially. Reason's attempt to think an absolute beginning allows us to see that our fantasmatic image of the world must remain constitutively incomplete. Any attempt to complete it reveals its illusory, fantasmatic status.

3. Jacques Lacan, *Le Séminaire, livre XVII: L'Envers de la psychanalyse*, ed. Jacques-Alain Miller (Paris: Seuil, 1991), 64, my translation.

4. Jacques Lacan, *Le Séminaire IX: L'Identification, 1961–1962*, unpublished manuscript, session of May 30, 1962, my translation.

5. On one level, neurosis is a radical position because it refuses to be satisfied with the sacrifice of enjoyment that the social law demands. However, the neurotic wants to access this enjoyment without paying the price, without experiencing the trauma that necessarily accompanies it. The neurotic wants to short-circuit the path to the gaze.

6. Lacan, *L'Identification*, session of March 14, 1962, my translation.

24. Theorizing the Real

1. Walter Davis, *Deracination: Historicity, Hiroshima, and the Tragic Imperative* (Albany: State University of New York Press, 2001), 6.

2. Though this makes it seem as if all traditional Lacanian film theorists were vulgar Marxists, none would have actually put their idea of the filmic medium this way. However, most of these theorists had a tendency to adopt this position de facto, through their assumptions concerning the relationship between film and ideology.

3. To put it in the plainest terms: according to the thought of Louis Althusser, Louis Althusser cannot exist, which is perhaps why he was preoccupied with the act of self-criticism.

4. This is precisely, according to Hegel, the problem with Spinoza's philosophical system. Spinoza can explain everything through his system except his own ability to discover the system, which is why Hegel's correction of Spinoza involves simply adding the subject—which is to say, the space for the theorist.

25. The Politics of the Cinema of Intersection

1. Lacan, *L'Envers de la psychanalyse*, 143, my translation.

2. Ibid., 143, my translation.

3. In fact, it is probably more accurate to say that capitalist democracy and fundamentalism represent precisely the same choice insofar as they share the same underlying logic. The appearance of the fundamentalist "alternative" is thus nothing other than the making explicit of the hidden truth of capitalist democracy itself.

4. Slavoj Žižek, *The Ticklish Subject: The Absent Centre of Political Ontology* (New York: Verso, 1999), 199.

5. This is the chief problem with the popular idea—articulated most famously by Judith Butler—of conceiving agency as the act of "resignifying." According to this idea, one has agency through performing one's (ideologically given) identity in a new way, with a new variation, thereby resignifying it. However, this form of agency fails to break from the ideological structure that supplies the identity in the first place. The resignifying takes place within the structure and never challenges the structure as such. That is to say, resignifying reshuffles the cards that one has been dealt, but it never attempts to change the very nature of the game itself.

26. The Overlapping Worlds of Andrei Tarkovsky

1. G. W. F. Hegel, *The Phenomenology of Spirit*, trans. A. V. Miller (Oxford: Oxford University Press, 1977), 10.

2. Ibid., 19. At the basis of Hegel's entire philosophical enterprise is an attempt to think without hope. This gives Hegel, I would contend, a political

radicality unmatched by any other philosopher, inclusive of Marx. Most often it is the hope of escaping our miserable situation that keeps us entrenched in our misery.

3. For instance, Vida T. Johnson and Graham Petri claim that "*Stalker*, *Nostalghia*, and *The Sacrifice* draw most of Tarkovsky's basic ideas together in attributing the self-destructive elements in modern civilization to materialism, blind reliance on technology, loss of respect for nature, loss of faith, and an abandonment of spiritual values that has infected modern art and literature as well as daily life" (Vida T. Johnson and Graham Petri, *The Films of Andrei Tarkovsky: A Visual Fugue* [Bloomington: Indiana University Press, 1994], 235).

4. This is why Herbert Marcuse claims that Hegel's conception of God as actually fully manifesting himself in the world represents the definitive statement of atheism.

5. This is how also how Nietzsche reads the teachings of Christ, which he opposes to the Christianity that developed out of this teaching. According to Nietzsche, Christ taught that "the Kingdom of God does not 'come' chronologically-historically, on a certain day in the calendar, something that might be here one day but not the day before: it is an 'inward change in the individual,' something that comes at every moment and at every moment has not yet arrived" (Friedrich Nietzsche, *The Will to Power*, trans. Walter Kaufmann and R. J. Hollingdale [New York: Random House, 1968], 161).

6. *Nostalghia* (1983) reverses the dynamic in *Stalker*, presenting the world of desire in color and the fantasy in black and white. *The Mirror* (1975) uses both black and white and color stock in the depiction of each realm, which prevents us from distinguishing them in this way.

7. Vida T. Johnson and Graham Petrie, "Tarkovsky," in *Five Filmmakers: Tarkovsky, Forman, Polanski, Szabó, Makavejev*, ed. Daniel J. Goulding (Bloomington: Indiana University Press, 1994), 35.

8. Ibid., 35.

9. This is precisely what conservatives who champion a return to traditional values fail to recognize (and why Tarkovsky, despite appearances, is in no way a conservative filmmaker). The attractiveness of traditional values derives from the fallen position from which we see them, not from the values themselves. When we include ourselves and our position in the equation as Tarkovsky does, this conservative nostalgia becomes unsustainable. The authentic conservative should champion the crass superficiality of contemporary culture because this very superficiality gives value to the old traditional values insofar as it provides a perspective from which they look attractive.

27. Alain Resnais between the Present and the Past

1. G. W. F. Hegel, *The Philosophy of History*, trans. J. Sibree (New York: Dover, 1956), 9.

2. It is for this reason that Walter Benjamin insists that the historical materialist, in contrast to the typical historian, "regards it as his task to brush history against the grain" (Walter Benjamin, "On the Concept of History," trans. Harry Zohn, in *Selected Writings Volume 4: 1938–1940* [Cambridge: Harvard University Press, 2003], 392).

3. Paul Eisenstein, *Traumatic Encounters*, 93.

4. The constitutive role of desire in the film leads Lanzmann to avoid shooting in the gas chambers—even forty years after the event. For Lanzmann, documentary evidence or footage could never capture the truth of the event. In fact, he famously claimed that if he had found actual footage of what happened in the gas chambers, he would have destroyed it.

5. Even the opposition within the title of the film suggests the division into a world of desire and a world of fantasy.

6. For Resnais, we remain caught between the need to remember and the inability to do so adequately. This is why we must resort to fantasy. As Gaston Bounoure points out in his discussion of Resnais, "Bad memory, at Hiroshima as at Auschwitz, renders fragile, suspect, every restitution of the past. And yet, at Auschwitz as at Hiroshima, memory is . . . an act constitutive of being" (Gaston Bounoure, *Alain Resnais* [Paris: Éditions Seghers, 1974], 44, my translation).

7. Thomas Beltzer, "*Last Year at Marienbad:* An Intertextual Mediation," *Senses of Cinema* 10 (November 2000), www.sensesofcinema.com/contents/00/10/marienbad.html. This apparent lack of a definitive sense to the film prompts Jean-Louis Leutrat to adopt a relativist position and to claim, "Each person can and must interpret the film in his/her own way" (Jean-Louis Leutrat, *L'Année Dernière à Marienbad*, trans. Paul Hammond [London: BFI Publishing, 2000], 31).

8. Keith Cohen, "Pleasures of Voicing: Oral Intermittences in Two Films by Alain Resnais," *L'Esprit Createur* 30, no. 2 (1990): 60.

9. Several characters in the film evince their believe in the Other who really knows relative to the game introduced by M (Sacha Pitoëff), the seeming husband (or lover) of A. Throughout the film, M plays a version of the game Nim (which involves players removing markers from a series of rows and ends when the loser removes the last marker) with different guests at the hotel. M tells the others that he always wins the game, though he can lose. After several victories, we hear the different guests proffer various theories concerning the game, suggesting that the first player always wins, that the solution is a logarithmic series, and so on. These theories testify to the guests' collective belief in the special knowledge of M—their belief in the Other of the Other. In advancing the different theories about the secret of the game, the guests fail to recognize their own involvement in the very introduction of the game. M addresses the game to the look of the guests, a look that never asks why M proposes the game in the first place. He introduces the game precisely in order to establish his mastery as a subject supposed to know. This

mastery depends on the paranoia of the other guests and their collective refusal to see lack in the Other. By including the game and the guests' responses to it, Resnais demonstrates how and why one fails to encounter the
historical object.

10. *La Guerre est finie* marks a slight change in Resnais's pattern,
though his predominant concern remains the same. The fantasmatic intrusions in this film depict possible futures, not possible pasts. Nonetheless, fantasy continues to be the terrain on which the subject addresses its existence
as an historical being.

28. Wim Wenders and the Ethics of Fantasizing

1. Jean-Paul Sartre, *Being and Nothingness*, 347, 349. I am tempted to
claim that one feels shame *only* when one's fantasy becomes exposed. No experience of shame occurs unless the subject makes an effort to conceal what
is revealed, and this effort to hide indicates the existence of a fantasmatic attachment. For instance, the obsessional feels shame with the revelation of
bathroom activity because this activity has a libidinal charge. For other subjects, the exposure of such activity would occasion no shame whatsoever.
Shame does not derive from the exposure of what has been hidden, but the
exposure of the attempt to hide itself. Without this attempt to hide—which is
the fundamental gesture of fantasizing—one feels no shame.

2. This dramatic transformation in Wenders's filmmaking occurred
during the making of *Der Stand der Dinge* (*The State of Things*, 1983). Consequently, this film bears the marks of the change within it: it begins in the
style of Wenders's earlier films (stressing the absence of the impossible
object) and concludes like his later ones (juxtaposing the experience of the
object's absence with that of its overpresence).

3. In explaining this change in his filmmaking, Wenders himself says, "I
no longer trust the narrative power of images, because the landscape around
them has been undermined. The narrative force of images has disappeared
to the same degree that their commercial force has increased. Today, images
have to sell, not tell. Therefore we can no longer indulge in the narrative
power of images as naively and innocently as we used to" ("Excerpts from Interviews with Wenders," in *The Cinema of Wim Wenders: Image, Narrative,
and the Postmodern Condition*, eds. Roger F. Cook and Gerd Gemünden
[Detroit: Wayne State University Press, 1997], 86.

29. The Sexual Relationship with David Lynch

1. Jacques Lacan, *Le Séminaire XXI: Les Non-dupes errant, 1973–1974*,
unpublished manuscript, session of Februrary 12, 1974, my translation.
2. Slavoj Žižek, *Tarrying with the Negative*, 117.

3. For a more thorough discussion of Lynch's films, see Todd McGowan, *The Impossible David Lynch* (New York: Columbia University Press, 2007).

4. Reni Celeste, *"Lost Highway*: Unveiling Cinema's Yellow Brick Road," *Cineaction* 43 (Summer 1997): 34.

5. The film shows Fred driven to this murder by the pressure of his superego, which creates in him a sense of guilt for his failure to enjoy Renee while someone else seems to be enjoying her. Lynch embodies Fred's superego in the figure of the Mystery Man (Robert Blake). Lynch externalizes the superego in this way in order to illustrate the distance that exists between the subject and its own superego. The superego is an incomprehensible voice for the subject, even though the subject itself gives birth to this voice.

Index

9686318R0

Made in the USA
Lexington, KY
19 May 2011